Chinese Theories of Literature

James J. Y. Liu

Chinese Theories of Literature

The University of Chicago Press
Chicago and London

JAMES J. Y. LIU is professor of Chinese and chairman of the Department of Asian Languages at Stanford University. His many publications include *The Art of Chinese Poetry*, *The Chinese Knight Errant*, and *The Poetry of Li Shang-yin* (all published by the University of Chicago Press).

THE UNIVERSITY OF CHICAGO PRESS, CHICAGO 60637
THE UNIVERSITY OF CHICAGO PRESS, LTD., LONDON

Printed in the United States of America

Library of Congress Cataloging in Publication Data

Liu, James J Y
Chinese theories of literature.

Bibliography: p.
Includes index.
1. Criticism—China. 2. Literature—Philosophy.
I. Title.
PN99.C5L58 801 74-11631
ISBN 0-226-48692-3

Contents

Contents

Preface

THE study embodied in this book began in the spring of 1971, when a grant from the Committee on East Asian Studies at Stanford University enabled me to engage as my research assistant Louisa McDonald Read, a Ph.D. candidate in Oriental Art, who helped me compile indexes of critical terms to a number of Chinese critical texts. The study itself was carried out for the most part during my sabbatical year, 1971–72, when I held successively a Guggenheim Fellowship and a grant from the American Council of Learned Societies. Final completion of the book was made possible during the summer of 1973 by a grant from the Humanistic Studies Support Fund at Stanford. To all the organizations concerned I wish to express my gratitude.

I am indebted to Professor Kurt Mueller-Vollmer of the Department of German Studies, Stanford, for having read the first two chapters of the manuscript and made valuable comments. My indebtedness to other colleagues and friends, as well as to previous writers, on particular points is acknowledged in individual notes.

Part of the Introduction has appeared in *Literature East and West* 16, no. 3 (1972).

The Glossary-Index has been prepared by my student Stuart Sargent, whose services were made possible by another grant from the Committee on East Asian Studies.

Since this book is not intended exclusively for students of Chinese literature, I have tried to avoid technical discussions in the main text so that it may remain comprehensible to those who do not know Chinese, while relegating such discussions as well as bibliographical references to notes, which, together with the bibliography and the glossary-index, should enable the specialist in Chinese literature to identify my sources and consult other works on the subjects discussed.

All quotations from Chinese works are translated by me, not because I consider my translations superior to all existing ones, but because my understanding of a text often differs from previous translators' in places, and further because they may have had aims different from mine, which is to bring out the underlying concepts. My translations therefore aim at accuracy of meaning and intelligibility rather than elegance of style, although I have made some efforts to reflect the style and tone of the original. To enable the reader to compare my translations with others or to read, in toto, works from which I have quoted excerpts, I have given references to some existing translations. When many versions of the same work exist, only the best or most widely used ones are mentioned. When there is no English translation, but a French or German one, this is noted, since most readers presumably can read either or both of these languages. The same cannot be presumed about Japanese, and Japanese translations of Chinese works are too numerous to mention in any case. When quoting from works in Western languages other than English, I have generally used existing translations, except for a few works in French that have no English translations, in which case I have translated the passages quoted myself. (The English translation of Mikel Dufrenne's *Phénoménologie de l'expérience esthétique* appeared too late for me to use, but readers may wish to consult it, and so I have added it to the bibliography.)

Furthermore, the following guidelines have been observed:

1. Chinese words and names are romanized according to the Wade-Giles system, as found in *Mathews' Chinese-English Dictionary*, with these minor modifications: the circumflex above the *e* is omitted in all cases, as is the breve above the *u* in *ssu*, *tzu*, and *tz'u*; the *i*, when occurring alone, is replaced by *yi*.

2. Chinese characters are given in the notes, the bibliography, and the glossary-index, except when it is essential to have them in the main text.

3. Apart from casual references, at the first mention of a Chinese work a brief description is given, either in the text or in a note. Dates of persons and works are given at first mention and repeated in the bibliography and the glossary-index; dates of historical periods are repeated in each chapter so that readers not familiar with Crinese history will have no doubt as to the period to which a work under discussion belongs.

Table of Chinese Dynasties

Dynasty	Dates
Shang Yin	1751 – 1112 B.C.
Chou	1111 – 256 B.C.
Ch'un-ch'iu (Spring and Autumn) period	722 – 481 B.C.
Chan-kuo (Warring States) period	403 – 221 B.C.
Ch'in	221 – 207 B.C.
Han	206 B.C. – A.D. 220
Three Kingdoms	
Wei	A.D. 220 – 265
Shu Han	221 – 264
*Wu	222 – 280
Chin	265 – 419
Western Chin	265 – 316
*Eastern Chin	316 – 419
Southern and Northern Dynasties	
Southern	
*Sung	420 – 478
*Ch'i	479 – 501
*Liang	502 – 556
*Ch'en	557 – 589
Northern	
Northern Wei	386 – 534
Northern Ch'i	550 – 557
Northern Chou	557 – 580
Sui	589 – 618
T'ang	618 – 907
Five Dynasties	907 – 959
Sung	960 – 1279

Table of Chinese Dynasties

Yüan (Mongol)	1280 – 1368
Ming	1368 – 1644
Ch'ing (Manchu)	1644 – 1911

* Known as Six Dynasties

1

Introduction

IN order to define clearly the subject, nature, and scope of this book, I shall first propose to draw certain distinctions among various kinds of literary studies. It appears generally agreed that the study of literature may be divided into two main branches—literary history and literary criticism—although sometimes a tripartite division is followed: literary theory, criticism, and history.[1] The latter classification, in which "literary criticism" in fact refers to practical criticism, has not been universally adopted, and many writers continue to use the term "literary criticism" to include both theoretical discussions and practical criticism.[2] I propose to maintain the distinction between these, regarding both as subdivisions of literary criticism, and to make a further distinction between theories of literature and literary theories,[3] the former being concerned with the basic nature and functions of literature, the latter with aspects of literature, such as form, genre, style, and technique. These two kinds of theories, which deal with literature at two different levels, the one at the ontological and the other at the phenomenological or the methodological, are of course interrelated. For instance, one's conception of style will be influenced by one's conception of literature, while on the other hand one can formulate a theory of literature in terms of style. Nevertheless, if we do make this distinction, it will clarify critical issues and views. As for practical criticism, this consists, I believe, mainly of interpretation (including description and analysis) and evaluation. When we turn to the study of literary criticism, we may draw the same distinctions as in the study of literature itself. The distinctions proposed above may be tabulated as follows:

- I. Study of Literature
    - A. Literary history
    - B. Literary criticism
        - 1. Theoretical criticism
            - a. Theories of literature
            - b. Literary theories
        - 2. Practical criticism
            - a. Interpretation
            - b. Evaluation

- II. Study of Literary Criticism
  - A. History of criticism
  - B. Criticism of criticism
    - 1. Theoretical criticism of criticism
      - a. Theories of criticism
      - b. Critical theories
    - 2. Practical criticism of criticism
      - a. Interpretation
      - b. Evaluation

The subject of this book is traditional Chinese theories of literature, and its nature is primarily analytical and hermeneutical, and secondarily historical, although, since I am discussing the nature of criticism, there is an element of theory of criticism as well. On the whole I shall refrain from overt evaluation of the theories to be discussed, apart from pointing out inconsistencies and illogicalities, so that the reader may form his own judgment, though it would not be difficult to see where my affinities and predilections lie.

In writing this book I have three purposes in mind. The first and ultimate one is to contribute to an eventual universal theory of literature by presenting the various theories of literature that can be derived from the long and, in the main, independent tradition of Chinese critical thought, thus making it possible to compare these with theories from other traditions. I believe that comparative studies of historically unrelated critical traditions, such as the Chinese and the Western, will be more fruitful if conducted on the theoretical rather than practical level, since criticism of particular writers and works will have little meaning to those who cannot read them in the original language, and critical standards derived from one literature may not be applicable to another, whereas comparisons of what writers and critics belonging to different cultural traditions have thought about literature may reveal what critical concepts are universal, what concepts are confined to certain cultural traditions, and what concepts are unique to a particular tradition. This in turn may help us discover (since critical concepts are often based on actual literary works) what features are common to all literature, what features are confined to literature written in certain languages or produced in certain cultures, and what features are unique to a particular literature. Thus a comparative study of theories of literature may lead to a better understanding of all literature.

The mention of a "universal theory of literature" will perhaps elicit an amused smile from a sophisticated or pragmatic-minded reader. Actually, I am not so naïve as to believe that we shall ever arrive at a universally accepted definition of literature, any more than that we shall ever arrive at a universally accepted definition of the meaning of life; but just as the awareness that we cannot hope to find a universally accepted definition of the meaning of life need not lead us to abandon all attempts at finding some meaning in life, so a similar awareness with regard to literature need not prevent us from trying to formulate, heuristically, theories of literature more adequate and more widely applicable than existing ones. The inherently paradoxical nature of attempts at theorizing about literature, indeed of all literary criticism, has been recognized by various critics. T. S. Eliot, after remarking, "I assume that criticism is that department of thought which either seeks to find out what poetry is, what its use is, what desires it satisfies, why it is written and why read, or recited; or which, making some conscious or unconscious assumption that we do know these things, assesses actual poetry," goes on to say that "criticism, of course, never does find out what poetry is, in the sense of an adequate definition; but I do not know of what use such a definition would be if it were ever found."[4] In a somewhat similar vein, Allen Tate concludes his essay "Is Literary Criticism Possible?" with the words, "Literary criticism, like the Kingdom of God on earth, is perpetually necessary and, in the very nature of its middle position between imagination and philosophy, perpetually impossible. . . . It is of the nature of man and of criticism to occupy the intolerable position. Like man's, the intolerable position of criticism has its own glory. It is the only position that it is ever likely to have."[5]

To pursue the paradox further, I would say that just as all literature and art are attempts to express the inexpressible, so all theories of literature and art are attempts to explain the inexplicable. If we are willing to accept this paradox and to continue working towards that remote and admittedly unattainable goal of a universal theory of literature, then we should consider theories from as many different literary traditions as possible. It is my hope that Western comparativists and literary theorists will take into account the Chinese theories to be presented in this book, and will no longer formulate general theories of literature based on the Western experience alone. I am encouraged in this hope by signs of growing awareness among Western comparativists of the need to study non-Western literature and criticism. René Etiemble, in particular, has strongly advocated the study of non-Western literature and argued that "littérature comparée" will inevitably lead to a "poétique comparée;"[6] René Wellek, who has always regarded the comparative study of historically unrelated literatures as a legitimate part of comparative literature, has accepted Etiemble's position in principle, even though he is skeptical about its practicability.[7] And Haskell Block has also expressed the view that comparative literature should no longer be concerned merely with "rapports de fait" but with "rapports de valeur."[8] I am furtrer encouraged by the efforts of two scholars, Makoto Ueda and Earl Miner, to compare Japanese theories of literature with Western ones, efforts that sometimes involve comparisons with Chinese theories as well.[9] In the present work I have made some modest attempts at comparisons between certain Chinese and Western theories of literature, but comprehensive and thorough comparisons are beyond its scope.

My second and more immediate purpose is to elucidate Chinese theories of literature for students of Chinese literature and criticism, for although there exist (in Chinese and Japanese) a dozen or so general histories of Chinese literary criticism, some of which are little more than quotations strung together with factual narrative, as well as numerous articles and monographs (including some in English) on particular topics or works, many important critical concepts and terms remain obscure, and the main Chinese theories of literature have not been adequately delineated. (The discussion of Chinese views of poetry contained in my earlier work, *The Art of Chinese Poetry*, is too sketchy and needs elaboration and modification.) This is not surprising, because Chinese theories of literature are seldom systematically expounded or explicitly described but often briefly adumbrated or implicitly suggested in scattered writings. The earliest extant Chinese work devoted to a discussion of literature is the essay entitled "A Discourse on Literature" (*Lun-wen*) by Ts'ao P'i (187–226), known posthumously as Emperor Wen of Wei. This, apart from a preface, is the only surviving part of his book *Classical Discourses* (*Tien-lun*), which, brief though it is, does contain theoretical discussions of literature. In much earlier works not primarily concerned with literature, such as the writings or recorded sayings of Confucius (552–479 B.C.) and other early philosophers and even pre-Confucian works, there are occasional remarks on literature, especially poetry, as well as remarks on other topics, which later critics applied to literature. Though not intended as theories of literature or literary criticism, these remarks have to be taken into consideration, because many theories of literature originated from them. Since Ts'ao P'i's essay there have been a few comprehensive theoretical works on literature, as well as innumerable essays, epistles, prefaces, postfaces, collected remarks on poetry (*shih-hua*), commentaries, notes, marginalia, and what not, containing nuggets of theories which one can sift from the thick sands of technical discussions, practical criticism, quotations, and anecdotes. Much of the relevant material from such diverse sources has been collected and given some orderly treatment by modern scholars, notably Kuo Shao-yü and Lo Ken-tse, but we need more systematic and thorough analyses to bring out the theories of literature that are latent in the writings of Chinese critics. (I shall continue to use the word "critic" to refer to a "theorist of literature" or "literary theorist," since in fact one person often combined all three roles. What is more, in traditional Chinese society there were no professional critics, and most critics were also poets or prose writers.) In the ensuing pages I shall endeavor to carry out such analyses, following a scheme to be described below, and to present various Chinese theories of literature, tracing their origins and sketching the highlights of their subsequent developments down to the late nineteenth or early twentieth century. I shall not deal with twentieth-century Chinese theories, except those held by purely traditionalist critics, since these have been dominated by one sort of Western influence or another, be it Romanticist, Symbolist, or Marxist, and do not possess the same kind of value and interest as do traditional Chinese theories, which constitute a largely independent source of critical ideas.[10] In any case, twentieth-century Chinese theories of literature have already received some scholarly attention in the West.[11]

My third purpose is to pave the way for a more adequate synthesis than yet exists of Chinese and Western critical views so as to provide a sound basis for the practical criticism of Chinese literature. It should be self-evident that any serious criticism of Chinese literature must take into account what Chinese critics have said about their own literature, and that one should not apply, wholesale, to Chinese literature critical standards derived solely from Western literature; yet a modern critic, of whatever nationality, studying Chinese literature in a cosmopolitan context may not find it satisfactory to accept any traditional Chinese theory of literature as the necessary or sufficient basis of criticism. Hence, a need exists for a synthesis of Chinese and Western critical concepts, methods, and standards. Although some efforts have been made in this direction,[12] more are required, and a prerequisite for such efforts is a better understanding of traditional Chinese theories of literature.

At this point a question might be raised: is it desirable to analyze traditional Chinese criticism, since much traditional Chinese thinking is not analytical but intuitive? Part of my answer to this question is already implied in the statement of my third purpose, and it should be obvious that I am not making analysis for the sake of analysis but as a preparation for possible future synthesis. After all, synthesis must be preceded by analysis: without first analyzing natural rubber one would not know how to make synthetic rubber. Furthermore, whereas it may be possible to understand traditional Chinese critical writings without going through a process of analysis if one is reading them in the original, the same is not true if one is reading them in the vicarious form of translations. To present translations of Chinese critical writings without any analysis could lead to serious misunderstandings.

Difficulties in the Study of Chinese Criticism

The study embodied in this volume has involved manifold difficulties. To begin with, in Chinese critical writings the same term, even when used by the same writer, often denotes different concepts, while different terms may in fact denote the same concept. This, of course, is not a uniquely Chinese phenomenon: just think of such words as "style" and "form" in English! To give an example from Chinese: the word *ch'i*, which literally means "vapor," "air," or "breath," is used by Ts'ao P'i to signify three interrelated concepts—individual genius based on temperament, personal style as an expression of this genius, and regional style or manifestation of *genius loci*, as well as in the literal sense of "breath."[13] On the other hand, what Ts'ao calls *ch'i* in any of its senses may be called something else by another critic. The problem of ambiguity is serious enough with regard to monosyllabic Chinese words, but becomes further complicated when it comes to disyllables, since the two syllables often stand in a syntactically ambiguous relation to each other; indeed, sometimes we are not even sure whether the relation between them is a syntactic one or a morphological one, or, in other words, whether the two syllables denote two concepts or only one, and if the former, what their relation to each other is. For example, the word *shen* by itself could mean "god," "spirit," "spiritual," "divine," "inspired," "mysterious," or "miraculous"; the word *yün* could mean "resonance," "consonance," "rhyme," "rhythm," "tone," or "personal airs." Together, *shen-yün* could theoretically be interpreted in a bewildering variety of ways, some of which would make sense and others nonsense.[14] Yet another difficulty arises from the practice on the part of some Chinese critics of using highly poetic language to express not so much intellectual concepts as intuitive percepts, which by their very nature defy clear definition.

All these difficulties, which are inherent in any study of Chinese literary criticism, loom even larger when one is discussing Chinese theories of literature in English; for whereas a writer in Chinese or Japanese can resort to definition by synonyms or pleonasms or by quoting original passages without comment or interpretation, one who is writing in a Western language can hardly do so but rather has to face the problem of translation. It is often impossible to draw an equation between a Chinese word and an English one with not only the same referent but precisely the same implications and associations,[15] even on the level of everyday discourse, let alone in sophisticated discussions of literature. In fact, in Chinese there is no word that is the exact equivalent, in conception and scope, of "literature," as the word is commonly used in English today,[16] but there are several Chinese terms that correspond more or less to it. Since this is a matter of crucial importance to us, we need to pause and examine these terms.

VARIOUS MEANINGS OF *Wen*

In classical Chinese, the nearest counterpart to "literature" is *wen*. The earliest known occurrences of this word, now written 文, are found among the inscriptions on animal bones and tortoise shells used for divination purposes, as well as on some bronze vessels, of the later part of the Shang or Yin dynasty (ca. 1300–1100 B.C.), where it appears in various forms including 文, 文, and 文,[17] and is used as part of the title of a deceased king.[18] The original meaning of the word is not known for certain. The theory held by some modern scholars that the graph originally represented a tatooed human figure impersonating the dead king and receiving sacrificial offerings is not supported by adequate evidence[19] and does not fit all the variant forms, only some of the more elaborate ones. The traditional interpretation, as given in the first Chinese etymological dictionary, Hsü Shen's *Explanations of Simple and Compound Characters* (*Shuo-wen chieh-tzu*, ca. A.D. 100), seems more plausible: "*Wen* [consists of] intersecting strokes, representing a criss-cross pattern."[20] This interpretation is corroborated by various ancient texts. For example, in a section of the *Book of Documents* (*Shu-ching*, the earliest historical work in Chinese) generally accepted as authentic and probably belonging to the eleventh century B.C., there is mention of *wen-pei* or "striped cowrie,"[21] and a poem which has been dated 778 B.C. in the *Book of Poetry* (*Shih-ching*, the first anthology of Chinese poetry) contains the phrase *wen-yin* or "patterned mat," explained by commentators as a mat made of tiger skin.[22] In some texts ranging in date from the fifth century to the first century B.C., *wen* is used to refer to various kinds of physical markings or patterns, such as birth marks on the palm of the hand,[23] patterns on colored woven silk,[24] and painted designs on carriages.[25] However, from very early times the word was already used in figurative and abstract senses too. Apart from the title of the Yin king already referred to, the actual founder of the Chou dynasty—one of the standard sage-kings in the Confucian tradition—was called

King Wen (reigned 1171–1122 B.C.), the "Civil King" or "Civilized King" or "Civilizing King," one who excelled in civil virtues and the arts of peace and who exerted civilizing influence on his subjects,[26] in contrast to his son King Wu, the "Martial King," who conquered the Yin and officially proclaimed the new dynasty. In the *Analects* (*Lun-yü*) of Confucius, *wen* is used in several senses. Sometimes it means "culture" or "civilization";[27] at other times it means "cultural refinement" or "outward embellishment" in contrast to *chih*, which means "natural quality" or "inner substance";[28] at still other times it means "scholarship" or "learning."[29] In some texts belonging to the fourth century B.C., we find *wen* used to signify written words or writings in general.[30] It was only from the second century B.C. that *wen* came to mean something like what we now call "literature."

During the Han dynasty (206 B.C.–A.D. 220), the word *wen* was often used to refer to writings that were characterized by certain embellishments, especially parallelism and rhyme, and that had a predominantly aesthetic rather than pragmatic purpose.[31] Sometimes, instead of the monosyllabic *wen*, writers would use the disyllable *wen-chang* (literary compositions), which had earlier meant "cultural refinement," like the monosyllabic word itself.[32] At the same time, another disyllable, *wen-hsüeh* (literary learning), which had meant learning in general, largely retained its earlier meaning.[33] During the Six Dynasties period (222–589), *wen-hsüeh* and *wen-chang* became synonymous with each other,[34] and both with *wen* sometimes. Meanwhile, in the fifth century, "literature" (*wen-hsüeh*) was officially separated from "scriptural scholarship" (*ching-hsüeh*, the study of the Confucian Scriptures or Canon), "philosophy" (*hsüan-hsüeh*), and "history" (*shih-hsüeh*).[35] A further development in terminology took place when *wen* was distinguished from *pi*, which literally means "writing brush." According to some scholars, both ancient and modern, the distinction was based on a formal criterion: writings that used rhyme were called *wen*, those without rhyme were called *pi*. According to others, the distinction was based on difference in purpose: works that had the primary purpose of expressing emotion were called *wen*; those which had more utilitarian purposes were called *pi*. Perhaps both considerations were involved.[36] In this narrower sense, *wen* corresponds to "belles lettres," and *pi* may be translated as "plain writing." This distinction has gradually disappeared since the T'ang period (618–907), when *wen* was used sometimes to mean "prose,"[37] in contradistinction to *shih* (poetry or verse), although the broader meaning of *wen* as "literature" including both prose and verse has continued to exist, as indeed have most of its other meanings.

In modern Chinese, the commonest expression for "literature" is *wen-hsüeh*. Next comes *wen-yi* (literary art), which seems to imply a conception of literature as an art rather than a kind of learning. The monosyllabic *wen* is now rarely used on its own, but occurs often in such common compounds as *wen-jen* (literary man) and *wen-t'an* (the literary world) in addition to *wen-hsüeh* and *wen-yi*.

It will be seen that some of the meanings of *wen*, especially the earlier ones, fall outside the scope of "literature" as the term is generally understood. We shall therefore not concern ourselves with them per se, but they may still be relevant to some concepts of literature. Without going into a detailed discussion of the varying conceptions of literature denoted by the terms *wen*, *wen-chang*, and *wen-hsüeh*, we may state that although the scope of literature changed both in actual content and in conception from time to time in China, the bulk of what has been designated by these terms since the second century B.C. corresponds roughly to what is generally called "literature" in English.

ANALYTICAL SCHEME AND RELATED QUESTIONS

After this brief excursion into philology, let us return to our consideration of the difficulties involved in our study. In order to overcome the difficulties arising from ambiguity in terminology and in order to provide a conceptual framework for the analysis of Chinese critical writings so as to bring out the theories of literature they may contain, I have devised an analytical scheme, as well as a set of questions to be asked about any critical statement. This scheme is based on the same four elements as in that devised by M. H. Abrams in *The Mirror and the Lamp*, but they are arranged in a different pattern. In Abrams's scheme, the four elements involved in the total situation of a work of art—namely, the work, the artist, the universe (which may consist of "people and actions, ideas and feelings, material things and events, and super-sensible essences"[38]), and the audience—are arranged in a triangular pattern:

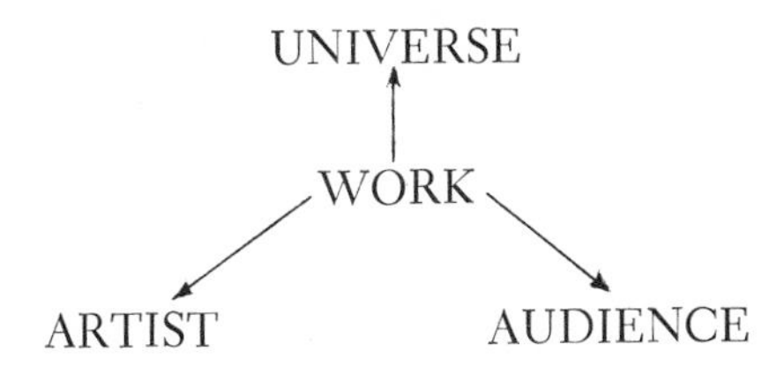

Applying this scheme, he found that all Western theories of art exhibit a discernible orientation toward one of the four elements and consequently fall into four classes, three of which attempt to explain a work of art by relating it to the universe, the audience, or the artist, and the fourth by considering it in isolation. These four classes of theories he named, respectively, mimetic, pragmatic, expressive, and objective.[39] Abrams's admirable scheme has been applied to the analysis of Chinese literary criticism by several scholars,[40] but my own study shows that while some Chinese theories are remarkably similar to Western ones and may be classified in the same way, [41] others do not fall easily into any of Abrams's four classes. I have therefore rearranged the four elements as follows:

UNIVERSE

READER WRITER

WORK

Since I am concerned with theories of literature only, I have substituted "writer" for "artist" and "reader" for "audience," although the scheme would apply to other forms of art as well as to literature. This arrangement demonstrates how the interrelations among the four elements can be viewed as the four phases that constitute the whole artistic process, by which I mean not only the writer's creative process and the reader's aesthetic experience but also what precedes the former and what follows the latter. In the first phase, the universe affects the writer, who responds to it. Out of this response he creates a work: this is the second phase. When the work reaches the reader, it affects him immediately: this is the third phase. In the final phase, the reader's response to the universe is modified by his experience of the work. Thus the whole process completes a full cycle. At the same time, since the reader's response to the work is influenced by the way the universe has affected him, and since by responding to the work he comes into contact with the writer's mind and recaptures the latter's response to the universe, the cycle operates in reverse as well. Hence the arrows point in both directions in the diagram. No arrow is drawn between "universe" and "work" because no work can come into being without a writer and no work can reveal the reality of the universe without the writer's having perceived it first. Similarly, no arrow is drawn between "writer" and "reader" because they can only communicate with each other through the work. Of course, this necessarily simplistic diagram is only a device to facilitate analysis and not an adequate pictorial representation of the actual artistic process.

One might think that this scheme leaves no room for any "objective" theory, which sees the work as an object by itself. In fact, however, without necessarily denying the objective existence of a literary work apart from the writer's experience of creating it and the reader's of re-creating it,[42] or going into the difficult problem of the ontological status or "mode of existence" of a work of art,[43] we may nevertheless assert that no one, not even an "objective" critic, can discuss literature without adopting either the writer's point of view or the reader's. For example, when Aristotle or a neo-Aristotelian discusses the "plot" of a tragedy, he does so from the dramatist's point of view; when a New Critic or a structuralist analyzes the linguistic structure of a poem, he generally does so from the reader's point of view (for, after all, one must *read* a poem to perceive its linguistic features and poetic effects). Thus, apparently objective discussions of literature, if conducted from the writer's point of view, will be seen to pertain to phase 2 of the cycle, but if conducted from the reader's, will be seen to pertain to phase 3.

It may also be pointed out that this scheme enables us to draw a distinction between the *immediate* artistic effects of a literary work and the possible *aftereffects* or long-term practical consequences. Some critics are concerned with the aesthetic effects of literature, which pertain to phase 3; others with the moral, social, or political effects of literature, which pertain to phase 4. It seems desirable to distinguish the aesthetic concern from the pragmatic.

In connection with the analytical scheme described above, we may ask a series of questions when analyzing any critical statement (though we need not ask all of them each time):

1. On what level is the critic theorizing about literature: do his remarks amount to a theory of literature or a literary theory?

2. On which of the four phases of the artistic process is his attention primarily focused?

3. Is he discussing literature from the writer's point of view or the reader's? As we have seen, this is relevant to the preceding question. Of course, a critic may adopt both points of view, but hardly in the same remark. It is our task to identify a critic's point of view in each remark, if necessary.

4. Is his manner of discourse descriptive or prescriptive? This question is closely related to the preceding one. If a critic adopts the writer's point of view, he will tend to be prescriptive, advising would-be

writers on how to write; if he adopts the reader's, he will tend to be descriptive, for only by describing his own experience and perceptions can he advise others on how to read. However, the two manners of discourse and two points of view do not always coincide. It is possible, for instance, to describe a writer's creative experience without postulating this is how one should write.

5. What is his conception of the artistic "universe": is it to be identified with the material world, or human society, or some "higher reality," or something else? It is necessary to raise this question, since without identifying the "universe" we may fail to distinguish basically different theories that are all focused on phase 1.

6. What is his conception of the nature of the relation between the two elements involved in that phase on which his attention is focused? This is also of great importance, for two theorists both focusing attention on the same phase may have different conceptions of the nature of the relation between the two elements involved in that phase. For instance, if both are focusing attention on phase 1 and both identify "universe" with human society, one of them may see the writer as *consciously* describing contemporary social reality while the other may see the writer as *unconsciously* reflecting it. The theories that result will be very different from each other and need to be distinguished.

The answers to some or all of these questions can clarify critical concepts and help resolve difficulties due to ambiguous terminology. Take, for example, the word *ch'i* again. Ts'ao P'i, in his "Discourse on Literature," remarks,

> In literature, the main thing is *ch'i*. The purity [or lightness, *ch'ing*] or impurity [or heaviness, *cho*] of this *ch'i* has substance, and cannot be achieved by strenuous efforts. To draw an analogy with music: though the tune may be the same and the rhythm regulated the same way, when it comes to the drawing of breath [*ch'i*], which will be different [from person to person], or the skillfulness or clumsiness, which depends on natural endowment, even a father cannot pass it on to his son, or an older brother to a younger brother.[44]

These remarks can be regarded as a theory of literature in embryonic form, and the word *ch'i* as the expression of a concept of individual genius or talent based on each writer's temperament. But when in the same essay he says of a contemporary, Hsü Kan, that he "often has the *ch'i* of Ch'i [a region where the people were said to be slow]," and when in a letter he says of another contemporary, Liu Chen, that he has an "untrammeled *ch'i*,"[45] the term denotes two different concepts of "style": style as a reflection of the spirit of a region in the one case, and as the manifestation of the writer's individual genius in the other —concepts that belong to the level of literary theory. At the same time, the concept of *ch'i* as individual genius pertains to phase 2, while that of *ch'i* as a perceptible quality in someone's writings pertains to phase 3. Furthermore, when he says that *ch'i* can be pure or impure and that it cannot be achieved by strenuous efforts, he is speaking from the writer's point of view and in a prescriptive manner, advising writers not to go against their grains; but when he speaks of the "*ch'i* of Ch'i" or an "untrammeled *ch'i*," he is describing what he has perceived from the reader's point of view. These are only a few of the many meanings of *ch'i* as used by critics,[46] but they are enough to demonstrate, I hope, how our analytical scheme and the related questions can help clarify ambiguities in terminology and reveal the underlying concepts by directing us toward the general area of meaning where more precise meanings are to be sought.

THE TRANSLATION OF CRITICAL TERMS

Turning to the problem of translation, once we realize that a Chinese critical term cannot be expected to yield a single, clearly defined concept but several interrelated and overlapping ones, we shall naturally no longer aim at a consistent translation of the same term in all contexts. Instead, we shall translate a term according to what predominant concept it appears to denote in a given context and what subsidiary concepts it may also connote, using different English words each time if necessary, and offering alternative versions, while indicating what the original term is. Conversely, when we find essentially the same concept denoted by different Chinese terms, we shall not hesitate to translate them by the same English word, again taking care to point out the original term. In attempting to discern the concept or concepts underlying each term, not only do we have to ask, about the immediate context, some or all of the questions raised above, but we also have to take into consideration the critic's general intellectual orientation, the examples he gives (if any), and earlier and contemporary usages of the same term, in literary criticism as well as in other kinds of writings. In this connection, etymology may be helpful, but cannot be relied on as an infallible guide, for obviously what a word originally meant need not throw any light on its subsequent meanings: to know that the English word "poetry" is derived from the Greek *poesis*, which means "making," will not tell us much about, say, Coleridge's conception of poetry. As for intuitive percepts, since we are engaged in rational discourse and not intuitive communication, we cannot follow the happy example of the Ch'an master who continued to answer a disciple's questions by hitting him on the head with a big stick until the latter achieved sudden enlightenment, but can only "translate" these into intellectual concepts. To do so may rob them of their poetry but not, I hope, of their essential meaning.

The Classification of Chinese Theories of Literature

Applying the analytical scheme described above and bearing in mind the relevant questions, I have discerned in traditional Chinese criticism six kinds of theories of literature, which I have decided to designate metaphysical, deterministic, expressive, technical, aesthetic, and pragmatic respectively. These categories are not established a priori but rather are discovered inductively. The characteristics of each kind, the similarities and differences among these kinds, as well as their resemblances to and differences from some Western theories, will be the main concern of the following chapters. For the present, I wish to point out that these theories are not necessarily incompatible with each other but are often interrelated, since different theories can be derived from common sources, and one theory can give rise to or be merged with another, as a shift of focus or a change of point of view occurs. On the other hand, they can naturally cause contradictions. In the final chapter I shall discuss some cases of contradictions, real or apparent, between different critics; self-contradictions and inconsistencies within the writings of the same critic; and attempts, whether successful or not, at reconciling apparently contradictory theories. I further wish to make clear that in distinguishing six kinds of theories I do not imply the existence of six distinct schools of critics. In fact, Chinese critics are generally eclectic or syncretic, and it is common to find a critic who combines, say, an expressive theory with a pragmatic one. Because of this, the opinions of one critic may be scattered in different parts of the book. Unfortunate as it may be, this is unavoidable. The alternatives would have been either to deal with all the critics in chronological order, thus producing a mere chronicle or collection of translated excerpts of critical texts linked by factual narrative and running commentary, or to indulge in obscurantism and mumbo-jumbo by means of Zen-ny (if not zany) sayings calculated to perpetuate the myths of the "mysterious Orient" and the "inscrutable Chinese." If some readers should still object to my analysis of Chinese critics and wish that I had presented their works as organic entities, I could only reply that, in the first place, I am not concerned with individual critics or works but with critical concepts and theories, and, secondly, similar objections could be leveled at all analytical treatments of literature and criticism, from Aristotle's *Poetics* to Northrop Frye's *Anatomy of Criticism*. After all, one cannot make an omelette without breaking eggs, and in any case the scattered remarks made by Chinese critics, often over a number of years, can hardly be considered organic entities. If we were to insist on treating each critic's views as an organic entity, we would have to refrain from analyzing, say, Coleridge's critical ideas and instead would have to read the whole of *Biographia Literaria* as an entity. However, when we come to discuss attempts at reconciling different theories, we shall be able to see at least a few examples of how various strands of thought are brought together by an individual critic. Furthermore, even though the various kinds of theories are often found together, we may still identify them, just as we may identify the presence of carbohydrates, protein, and other compounds in food even when they are found together.

SELECTION OF MATERIAL

In choosing works for discussion, I have concentrated attention on those which introduce new ideas or significantly modify traditional concepts of literature, rather than those which merely reiterate age-old ideas, or those which contain excellent practical criticism or interesting theories about style, genre, and the like but contribute little to general theories of literature.

From what has been said above it should be plain that this book is intended neither to supercede existing histories of Chinese literary criticism nor merely to repeat in English what has been written in Chinese on the subject. Nor is it primarily intended to be a glossary of Chinese critical terms, although the glossary-index at the end of the book may incidentally serve such a purpose to some extent.

One feature of the book that may seem strange to a Western reader unfamiliar with Chinese literary history and criticism is the scarcity of references to drama and fiction. This is the inevitable result of the historical facts that drama and fiction, as full-fledged literary genres, emerged relatively late in China and were generally not considered serious literature until modern times, and that, consequently, traditional Chinese criticism is primarily concerned with poetry and secondarily with prose but seldom with drama or fiction. Such dramatic criticism as there is usually deals with technical details of prosody or theatrical music, or treats dramatic verse simply as a subgenre of poetry. Critics of fiction too are usually content with commenting on particular works, instead of attempting to formulate general theories. Thus, except when a general concept of literature emerges from the criticism of drama or fiction, I have not dealt with such criticism.

2

Metaphysical Theories

The Metaphysical Concept of Literature Defined

Under the rubric "metaphysical" may be subsumed theories that are based on the concept of literature as a manifestation of the principle of the universe. These theories were not the most influential or the most ancient among Chinese theories of literature, but I have chosen to begin our discussions with them and to devote the most space to them because, first, they are primarily focused on what I have called phase 1 of the artistic process, and secondly, presenting as they do the most interesting points for comparison with Western theories, these are the theories from which distinctively Chinese contributions to an eventual universal theory of literature are most likely to be derived.

In metaphysical theories, the principle of the universe is generally referred to as the Tao (literally, "way"), a word that has various meanings in Chinese philosophy and literary criticism.[1] As used by most metaphysical critics, Tao may be briefly described as the unitary principle of all things and the totality of all being.[2] This concept of Tao was shared to some extent by the early Taoists and the Confucian authors of the *Commentaries* (*chuan*) on the *Book of Changes* (*Yi-ching* or *I Ching*), an ancient manual for divination to which were later added a number of commentaries of metaphysical and psychological import and which became one of the works in the Confucian Canon (*ching*).[3] Moreover, although the Confucians thought of the Tao principally in moral and social terms, as a way of life, or rather The Way of Life, they regarded this Way as being in accordance with the Way of Nature. There was therefore no irreconcilable contradiction between the Taoist and Confucian conceptions of Tao, but only a difference in emphasis: the Taoists emphasized the importance for the individual, in his relation to Nature, of apprehending the Tao and living in harmony with it; the Confucians emphasized the importance for the individual, in his relations with others, of following the moral Way which the sages had established in accordance with the Way of Nature. In any case, since Chinese critics were as eclectic or syncretic in their philosophical orientations as in their critical thinking, they had no great difficulty in accepting a Taoistic concept of Tao as part of a concept of literature without necessarily abandoning all their Confucian tenets.

The metaphysical concept of literature raises two questions: how the writer apprehends the Tao, and how he manifests it in his writings. Since a critic's answer to the former question amounts to a description of his conception of the nature of the relation between the universe and the writer, it forms an important part of that critic's theory of literature. We shall discuss such answers later, after having first traced the origins and early developments of the metaphysical concept of literature itself. The latter question does not often feature prominently in metaphysical theories, and when it does, the discussion easily becomes concerned with "how to write" instead of "what literature is," thus shifting from the level of theory of literature to that of literary theory. We shall therefore not pursue this question in detail but only touch on it when necessary, especially when comparing Chinese metaphysical theories with Western theories later in this chapter.

ORIGINS OF THE METAPHYSICAL CONCEPT

The origin of the concept that literature manifests the Tao of Nature can be traced to the *Commentaries* on the *Book of Changes.* Traditionally, the invention of the sixty-four hexagrams that formed the basis of divination, each consisting of two trigrams (each of which in turn consists of three lines, either whole or broken: ☰ ☱ ☲ ☳ ☴ ☵ ☶ ☷), was attributed to the mythical sage-king Fu-hsi (also called Pao-hsi); the brief explanations of the hexagrams to King Wen of Chou; the explanations of the individual lines to himself or his son, the Duke of Chou; and the *Commentaries,* also known as the *Ten Wings* (*Shih-yi*), to Confucius.[4] These attributions have been questioned by modern Chinese scholars, who differ in their opinions about the date and authorship of the *Book of Changes.* However, the prevailing view is that the text or "canon," comprising the hexagrams and the explanations of these and of the lines, was a product of late Yin or early Chou times (ca. 12th century B.C.), and the commentaries were by various Confucian scholars of the late Warring States period (ca. 3d century B.C.).[5] Several passages from different commentaries on the *Book of Changes* contain ideas that germinated the metaphysical concept of literature.

The "Commentary on the Decision" (*T'uan-chuan*) under the twenty-second hexagram, Pi, contains the following:

> Contemplate the configurations [*wen*] of heaven to observe

> the changes of seasons; contemplate the configurations of man to accomplish the [cultural] transformation of the world.[6]

In the original, the subject is not identified. Translators have supplied "we" as the subject, but since not everyone is in a position to "accomplish the cultural transformation of the world," perhaps the implied subject is the sage-king. Be that as it may, for our present purpose it is sufficient to note that this passage draws an analogy between the "configurations of heaven" (*t'ien-wen*) and the "configurations of man" (*jen-wen*), which refer respectively to the heavenly bodies and human institutions,[7] and that this analogy was later applied to natural phenomena and literature as parallel manifestations of the Tao.

Another example of the analogy between the natural world and the human world is seen in the "Commentary on the Images" (*Hsiang-chuan*) under Ko, the forty-ninth hexagram:

> The great man changes as the tiger: his [or its, or their] patterns [*wen*] are bright. . . . The superior man changes as the leopard: his patterns are profuse.[8]

In the "Appended Words" (*Hsi-tz'u*, also called *Ta-chuan* or "Great Commentary"), the *Book of Changes* itself is said to reveal the Tao of the universe:

> The *Book of Changes* is co-equal with heaven and earth, and therefore it can encompass and enwrap the Tao of heaven and earth. With it [the sage] contemplates the configurations [*wen*] of heaven above and the orderly arrangements [*li*] of the earth below, thereby understanding the causes of darkness and light.[9]

In another part of the "Appended Words" we read a legendary account of the invention of the Eight Trigrams, which later writers regarded as the prototype of the Chinese script:

> In ancient times, when Pao-hsi ruled over the world, he lifted his head and contemplated the signs in heaven; he bent down and contemplated the orders on earth. He contemplated the patterns [*wen*] on birds and beasts, and the suitabilities of the earth. He drew [ideas] from his own person, and from objects afar. Thereupon he first invented the Eight Trigrams.[10]

This passage has been interpreted by Lo Ken-tse as an expression of the idea that writing (and hence literature) imitates Nature,[11] but since the Eight Trigrams are obviously abstract symbols and not pictograms imitating natural objects, it would be truer to say that the passage suggests that writing symbolizes the underlying principles of Nature.

None of the passages quoted above is concerned with literature as we now understand the term, but all contain references to *wen*. Since this word, as we have seen, covers a whole spectrum of meanings (marking—pattern—embellishment—culture—learning—writing—literature), a writer can, by shifting the focus from one sector of the spectrum to another, turn a remark about culture or embellishment or writing into one about literature, as we shall see.

Another possible source of the metaphysical concept is the "Record of Music" (*Yüeh-chi*), which forms a chapter of the *Book of Rites* (*Li-chi*), a book on ancient ritual compiled in the first century B.C., and another work in the Confucian Canon.[12] After repeatedly stating that "music is the harmony of heaven and earth,"[13] the "Record" explains why:

> The vital breath [*ch'i*] of earth reaches upwards, and that of heaven descends downwards. The forces of *yin* and *yang* rub against each other; heaven and earth stir each other. When [this interaction] is roused by thunder, stimulated by wind and rain, moved by the four seasons, and warmed by the sun and moon, then all kinds of changes arise. That is why music is the harmony of heaven and earth.[14]

In view of the fact that in ancient China music and poetry were closely associated, this theory that music reflects cosmic harmony could easily have influenced concepts of poetry.

The same analogical mode of thinking is prominent in a group of books (ca. 1st century B.C.–1st century A.D.) known as the *Apocrypha* (*Wei-shu*), books purporting to interpret the Confucian Canon but actually expounding cosmological theories which involve complex correspondences between the macrocosm and the microcosm, interactions between *yin* and *yang* and among the Five Agents (*wu-hsing*, also translated as the Five Elements), and astrological omens. *The Apocryphal Commentary on the Book of Poetry* (*Shih-wei*) contains the statement, "Poetry is the mind [*hsin*, which also means 'heart'] of heaven and earth."[15] Whether we take *hsin* to mean "mind" or "heart," the statement expresses a metaphysical concept of poetry.

Continuing the analogical tradition, Juan Yü (d. 212), one of the "Seven Masters of the Chien-an Period" of the Han dynasty, in an essay on *wen* [cultural refinement/outward embellishment] and *chih* [natural quality/inner substance], wrote:

> I have heard: the sun and moon adhere to the sky[16]—they can be viewed from a distance but are hard to approach; the multitudes of things are located on earth—they can be seen and are

> easy to control. Now, what is far and cannot be known is the contemplation of *wen;* what is near and can be observed is the use of *chih.*[17]

He therefore concluded that *chih,* natural quality or inner substance, was more important than *wen,* cultural refinement or outward embellishment. Apparently to refute this essay, Ying Yang (d. 217), another of the "Seven Masters," wrote an essay with the same title, in which he argued in favor of *wen.* He too resorted to the cosmological analogy:

> The sun and moon move their lights, the arrayed constellations brighten their configurations [*wen*], all kinds of grains adhere to the earth,[18] fragrant blossoms flourish in the spring. Therefore, the sages, whose virtue [or power, *te*] joins that of heaven and earth, whose innate vital force [*ch'i*] was pure and spiritual, lifted their heads to contemplate the signs in the dark beyond [i.e., the heavens], and bent down to observe the shapes among the multitudes of objects.[19]

Ying's essay has sometimes been referred to as a discussion of literature,[20] but in fact, like Juan's, it is concerned with *wen* in the broad sense indicated above. The debate about the relative importance of *wen* and *chih* was an old one which had been going on since the time of Confucius,[21] but it is interesting to see it being conducted in a cosmological framework.

Early Expressions of the Metaphysical Concept

From such discussions it was an easy step to proceed to discuss *wen* in the narrower sense of "literature" in the same fashion. Chih Yü (d. ca. 312) of the Chin dynasty, of whose *Records of and Discourses on the Ramifications of Literature* (*Wen-chang liu-pieh chih-lun*) only a few fragments remain, appears to be taking this step when he writes:

> Literature [*wen-chang*] is that by which we manifest the signs above and below [i.e., in heaven and on earth], clarify the order of human relationships, exhaust principles, and fully understand human nature, in order to investigate the suitabilities of all things.[22]

In spite of its didactic tone, this statement, at least in part, unmistakably expresses the metaphysical concept of literature.

Indications of the metaphysical concept of literature are also perceptible in Lu Chi's (261–303) *Exposition on Literature* (*Wen-fu;* the *fu,* also known in English as "rhymeprose" or "poetic essay," being a mixed genre of prose and verse, generally dealing with premeditated subjects), which combines various theories of literature. We shall consider later Lu Chi's views on the writer's relation to Nature and on the creative process; for the present we shall merely note that at the end of the *Exposition*, when he enumerates the functions of literature, he declares:

> As for the functions of literature:
> It is the means by which all principles are known;
> It expands over ten thousand ages so that no obstacles remain,
> And spans over a million years to form a bridge.[23]

Although he goes on to mention more practical functions, he seems to regard the manifestation of the principles of the universe as the most important function of literature.

Full Development of the Metaphysical Concept

The metaphysical concept of literature found its most eloquent expression in *The Literary Mind: Elaborations* (*Wen-hsin tiao-lung*,[24] completed before A.D. 502) by Liu Hsieh (d. ca. 523), the most comprehensive work on literature in Chinese. Written in Parallel Prose (*p'ien-wen*, a kind of euphuistic prose marked by parallelism, ornate diction, and allusiveness), the book consists of fifty chapters, and contains theories of literature and literary theories, as well as literary history and practical criticism. As far as his theories are concerned, Liu Hsieh is a great syncretist,[25] combining elements of various theories, and changing his emphasis from one theory to another as he shifts the focus of his attention from one phase of the artistic process to another. However, the theory that predominates in his first chapter, in which his basic conception of literature emerges, is a metaphysical one, as I shall demonstrate. It is only fair to add that this is not the only possible interpretation; on the contrary, this chapter, together with some other chapters, has been a subject of much controversy. But since the present work is not devoted to a study of *The Literary Mind*, I cannot refer to all the different and often conflicting interpretations, but can only offer my own interpretation. Nor shall I repeat all the annotations, some of which merely quote Liu Hsieh's alleged sources, whether relevant or not, without throwing any light on the text. Instead, I shall add notes only when they seem needed for a full understanding of the text, or when my translation calls for an explanation.

The opening chapter of *The Literary Mind* bears the heading "Yüan-tao," which has been used by writers before and after Liu Hsieh to mean "tracing the origin of the Tao,"[26] but here it means, elliptically, "literature originates from the Tao," or "tracing the origin of literature to the Tao." Throughout the chapter Liu skillfully plays on the polysemy of *wen* so as to emphasize the analogy between literature and other forms of configuration or embellishment. This makes it almost impossible to translate the word by any single English word, so I shall transliterate it and then indicate in brackets the various concepts denoted or connoted by the word, in what appears to be their order of importance in each case. Liu begins:

> The power of *wen* [configurations/culture/literature] is great indeed! It was born together with heaven and earth. How so? [At first] the dark [i.e., heaven] and the brown [i.e., earth][27] interspersed their colors; [then] the square [i.e., earth] and the round [i.e., heaven] separated their bodies; the sun and moon, twin jade discs, suspended their signs attached to heaven;[28] the mountains and rivers, shining like fine silk, spread their orderly arrangements over the earth—these are really the *wen* [configurations/embellishments] of the Tao. Looking up, one might contemplate that which emitted lights, and bending down, observe that which contained compositions [*chang*] within. When the high [i.e., heaven] and the low [i.e., earth] each had its position fixed, then the Two Forms [*Liang-yi*][29] were born. Man alone made a third, being the concentration of natural spiritual powers [*hsing-ling*]. These are called the Trinity. [Man] is the finest essence of the Five Agents, and truly the mind of heaven and earth. When mind was born, then language was established; when language was established, then *wen* [literature/patterns] shone forth. This is a natural principle [*tao*].[30]

By linking literature (*wen*) with the configurations (*wen*) of natural phenomena, Liu is able to trace the origin of literature to the beginning of the universe, and to elevate literature to a status of cosmic significance. Drawing his ideas from the *Book of Changes* and other ancient works, he evolves the theory of multiple correspondences between cosmic order and the human mind, between mind and language, and between language and literature.

Liu continues to draw more analogies between natural and human *wen*:

> Extending [our observation] to all classes of things, [we see that] animals and plants all have their *wen* [patterns/embellishments]: the dragon and the phoenix present auspicious omens with their colorful decorations like elaborate paintings; the tiger and the leopard consolidate their appearances with their 'brilliant' and 'profuse' [patterns];[31] the sculptured colors of sun-

> light-reflecting clouds surpass the painter's wondrous art; the ornate florescence of plants and trees does not need the brocade-weaver's extraordinary skill. Now, how can these be decorations added from without? They are really just so of themselves. As for sounds issuing from woods, which form melodies as do pipes and strings, or fountains striking rocks and evoking resonances as harmonious as those produced by jade chimes and bronze bells—[these show that] when forms are established, then compositions [*chang*] are completed; when sounds issue forth, then *wen* [pattern] is born.[32] Now, if insentient objects have such abundant colorful adornments, how can he that is a vessel with a mind be without his *wen* [embellishments/culture/literature]?[33]

In the next section, Liu Hsieh reiterates the idea that human *wen* originated from the beginning of the universe, and mentions the hexagrams in the *Book of Changes* as the earliest examples of such *wen*:

> The origin of human *wen* [culture/literature/embellishments] began with the Great Primordial [*T'ai-chi*]. In profoundly manifesting the divine light,[34] the signs in the *Book of Changes* were the first. Pao-hsi began [the book] by drawing [the trigrams], and Chung-ni [i.e., Confucius] completed it with the *Wings*. But only on the first two hexagrams, Ch'ien and K'un, did he compose the commentary 'Wen-yen' [patterned/embellished words]. Now, the *wen* [pattern/configuration/embellishment] of words—is this not indeed the mind of heaven and earth?[35]

Again we see how skillfully he shifts the emphasis from *wen* in the sense of "culture" or "embellishment" in general to that of "literature." Actually, the title "Wen-yen" can be and has been interpreted in different ways: either as "words [*yen*] on the text [*wen*]" or as "embellished words."[36] Liu Hsieh naturally took the latter interpretation and neatly turned the compound into *yen chih wen*, the "pattern" or "configuration" or "embellishment" of words—a convenient definition of "literature"! He then fits this in with the multiple correspondences already worked out (universe—mind—language—literature) by repeating the phrase "the mind of heaven and earth" and applying it to literature (*wen*) this time instead of to Man.[37]

He then recounts various legends concerning the invention and development of the Chinese script and enumerates the supposed writings of the sages from the mythical kings of high antiquity to Confucius. This section is of little theoretical interest and will not be given here. However, the concluding section is highly significant:

> From the One Surnamed Feng [i.e., Pao-hsi] to Master K'ung

> [Confucius], from the distant sages[38] who created the Scriptures [*ching*] to the Uncrowned King [i.e., Confucius] who transmitted their teachings, they all, without exception, based themselves on the mind of the Tao to spread their literary compositions [*chang*], and investigated divine principles to set forth their instructions. They took signs from the Yellow River and the Lo River,[39] and divined with milfoil stalks and tortoise shells; they contemplated the configurations [*wen*] of heaven to exhaust all changes, and observed the configurations of man to accomplish cultural transformations.[40] Only then could they bring together the principles of the universe like the warp and woof of weaving,[41] encompass and enwrap permanent rules,[42] expand their deeds and tasks, and make words [*tz'u*] and meanings shine forth brilliantly. Hence we know that the Tao, through the sages, perpetuates [or bestows, *ch'ui*][43] *wen* [literature], and the sages, by means of *wen* [literature], manifest the Tao, so that it can prevail everywhere without hindrance and be used daily without destitution. In the *Book of Changes* it is said, "What arouses the movements of the world lies in the *Words* [*tz'u*]."[44] The reason why the *Words* [or words in general] can arouse the world is that they are the *wen* [configuration/writing] of the Tao.[45]

Here, Liu has summed up his conception of the interrelations among the universe (the Tao), the sage as writer, and literary works, in the circular statement, "The Tao, through the sages, perpetuates literature, and the sages, by means of literature, manifest the Tao,"[46] which may be diagrammatically represented in this way:

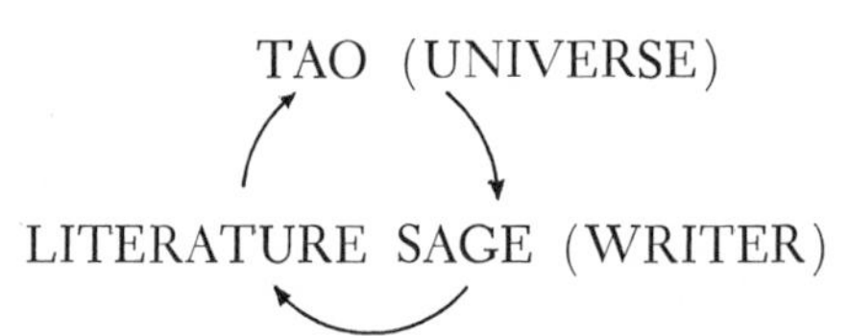

From the passages quoted above, we can see how Liu Hsieh formed his basic conception of literature by amalgamating several concepts all denoted by the word *wen*: (1) *wen* as patterns or configurations of natural phenomena, considered to be manifestations of the cosmic Tao; (2) *wen* as culture, the configuration of human institutions, and a parallel to natural *wen*; (3) *wen* as embellishment; (4) *wen* as the script, which represents language, which in turn expresses the human mind, identified with the mind of the universe. The result of this amalgamation of concepts is the concept of literature as a manifestation of the principle of the universe and a configuration of embellished words.

This conception of literature is of course primarily metaphysical, although it also contains an incipient element of aestheticism, which we shall consider in chapter 5. Meanwhile, it should be recognized that although logically this conception does not necessarily imply any pragmatism, in Liu's actual discussion, as in some of his sources, there is obviously a pragmatic element. However, this is subordinated to the metaphysical concept. As described by him, the sages were sages not so much because of their superior virtues as because of their apprehension of the Tao of Nature, and the Confucian Scriptures were Scriptures not so much because they taught people how to behave as because they embodied the Tao in beautiful language. By praising the sages as the world's first and greatest writers and the Confucian Scriptures as the world's first and greatest literary works, Liu Hsieh can then claim for literature a position of paramount importance in human society without contradicting Confucian orthodoxy. It should further be pointed out that although in other chapters of his book he sometimes emphasizes the expression of personal nature, in the first chapter this is hardly mentioned. The term *ch'ing-hsing* ("emotion and nature," or simply "personal nature") appears only once, in connection with Confucius, who is said to have "sculptured and polished the *ch'ing-hsing*,"[47] where the term seems to refer to human nature in general rather than to the sage's own personal character. In short, the conception of literature described in the opening chapter of Liu's book is predominantly metaphysical.

Liu Hsieh was not unique among his contemporaries in using the metaphysical concept to justify the importance of literature. Hsiao T'ung (501–531), known posthumously as Prince Chao-ming of the Liang Dynasty, who was a patron of Liu's, wrote in the preface to his famous *Literary Anthology* (*Wen-hsüan*):

> Let us contemplate primeval times and view the customs of remote antiquity, when men dwelt in caves in the winter and in nests in the summer, when they ate [raw meat with] furs and drank blood. The world was then in its natural state [*chih*] and people were simple, and no culture [*wen*] had yet arisen. By the time Fu-hsi ruled over the world, he first drew the Eight Trigrams and invented writing [*shu-ch'i*] to replace the system of tying knots with cords. Thereupon literature [*wen*] and books were born. The *Book of Changes* has it: "Contemplate the configurations [*wen*] of heaven to observe the changes of seasons; contemplate the configurations of man to accomplish the cul-

> tural transformation of the world." The significance of literature [*wen*] to the times is far-reaching indeed![48]

In the same preface Hsiao T'ung explains why he has excluded the Confucian Canon, as well as writings of other philosophical schools and historical works, from his anthology, thus revealing that his conception of the scope of literature is a belletristic one. Yet he reverts to the older and broader concepts of *wen* as culture and writings in general, so as to maintain the analogy between the *wen* of heaven and the *wen* of man. In this way he is able to justify the high esteem in which he holds literature, *wen* in the narrower sense.

His younger brother Hsiao Kang (503–551), known posthumously as Emperor Chien-wen of Liang, in his preface to Hsiao T'ung's collected literary works, similarly extols literature by referring to the cosmological analogy. After exclaiming about the great significance of literature and quoting the same remarks from the *Book of Changes* as his brother, he draws the usual analogy between the *wen* of heaven (i.e., celestial bodies) and the *wen* of man, the latter of which he specifically identifies with literature:

> When literature [*wen*] and books were born and when writing [*shu-ch'i*] was invented, when chants and songs arose and odes and hymns began, perfecting filial reverence in human relationships and transforming moral customs in carrying out the Kingly Rule,[49] so that the Tao could extend to the eight extremities of the earth and principles [*li*] penetrate the nine spheres of heaven, manifesting and touching the divine light [or the gods, *shen-ming*] and harmonizing with bells and chimes: this is called the *wen* [literature/culture/configurations] of man![50]

In spite of the pragmatic and aesthetic elements in this passage, its basic concept is metaphysical.

These pronouncements are more in the nature of avowals of pious sentiments or ideals than reflections of contemporary literary trends, which were oriented towards the technical and aesthetic aspects of literature. The Hsiao brothers themselves both wrote in a florid style, and Hsiao Kang in particular was noted for his amorous verse in the "palace style" (*kung-t'i*). Even Liu Hsieh, who attacked excessive ornamentations in literature, still wrote in the medium of the elaborate Parallel Prose. Such discrepancies between theory and practice do not concern us here; I mention them simply to indicate that the metaphysical theories of Liu Hsieh and the Hsiao brothers did not exert great influence at the time. However, during the T'ang period (618–907), their opinions were echoed by many, including poets, prose writers, and historiographers. This is not surprising, since in this period there was a reaction among poets against the poetry of the Six Dynasties (222–589), which they considered frivolous and decadent, and there was a similar reaction among prose writers against Parallel Prose, which they wished to replace with the Archaic Prose (*ku-wen*) modeled on the language of the Confucian Canon and early historical writings. But these T'ang writers tended to place increasing emphasis on the utilitarian functions of literature instead of its metaphysical nature, so that in their theories metaphysical elements became merged with pragmatic ones.

Absorption of Metaphysical Elements by Pragmatic Theories

Among many statements that exhibit a shift from the metaphysical view to the pragmatic I shall cite only a few as examples. First, from two early T'ang historiographers. Li Pai-yao (565–648) begins his preface to the "Biographies of the Literati" section of the *History of the Northern Ch'i* (*Pei-Ch'i shu*) in a metaphysical vein:

> The mysterious signs that display their brightness, with which we may investigate the changes of seasons, are the *wen* [configurations] of heaven; the established words of the sages and enlightened men, which can accomplish the cultural transformation of the world, are the *wen* [literature/configuration] of man. To convey the nature of what is abstruse and what is manifest, to clarify what lies between heaven and man—does this not rest in *wen* [literature]?

But as he goes on, he becomes more pragmatic:

> [The sages] listened to the remote voices of the Three Ancient Ages, and encompassed and enwrapped [the principles for] a hundred generations; they regulated ritual and composed music, so that their true worth rose high and their reputations soared—if their words had not had *wen* [embellishments/patterns], how could they have gone so far?[51]

The rhetorical question at the end is a paraphrase of a remark attributed to Confucius in the historical chronicle, the *Tso-chuan*,[52] or *Tso's Commentary*, so called because it was supposed to be a commentary (*chuan*) on the *Spring and Autumn Annals* (*Ch'un-ch'iu*, the annals of Confucius's native state of Lu for the years 772–481 B.C., which he was believed to have compiled) by one Tso Ch'iu-ming or Tso-ch'iu Ming. The remark, whether or not it was really made by Confucius,[53] may have contributed to the aesthetic concept of literature, but it is quoted here to justify literature as an efficient means to accomplish practical ends.

Another historiographer, Wei Cheng (580–643), is even more pragmatic in his preface to the corresponding section of the *History of the Sui* (*Sui shu*). After quoting the familiar remarks from the *Book of Changes* about contemplating the *wen* of heaven and the *wen* of man, and the remark attributed to Confucius about the necessity for words to have *wen*, he exclaims, "The use of *wen* [literature] is then great indeed!" What this use is will be seen from the following:

> It is the means by which the one above [i.e., the ruler] spreads his moral instructions to those below, and the means by which those below communicate their feelings and intents to the one above.[54]

This is a mere reiteration of an old pragmatic theory,[55] but what interests us is that it appears after a metaphysical introduction.

Similarly, the poet Wang Po (648–675), known as one of the "Four Masters of the Early T'ang" in the history of Chinese poetry, quotes the same remarks from the *Book of Changes* and the *Tso-chuan* and then continues:

> Where a superior man exerts his mind and labors his spirit, he should aim at the great and far-reaching, and not merely at "tracing emotions" and "embodying objects," petty skills comparable to the carving of insects.[56]

Here he is voicing anti-expressive and anti-aesthetic views, for the phrases "tracing emotions" (*yüan-ch'ing*) and "embodying objects" (*t'i-wu*) are taken from Lu Chi:

> Poetry [*shih*] traces emotions and should be exquisite
> as fine patterned silk;
> Expositions [*fu*] embody objects and should be clear
> as limpid water.[57]

Although, as mentioned before, Lu Chi combines various theories of literature in the whole *Exposition on Literature*, the lines just quoted are concerned with expression of emotion and aesthetic qualities of writing. Wang Po shows his disapproval of Lu Chi by identifying "tracing emotions" and "embodying objects" with "petty skills like the carving of insects" (*tiao-ch'ung hsiao-chi*), a phrase used by Yang Hsiung (53 B.C.–A.D. 18) to describe his own works in the form of Expositions which he later regretted after having rejected the aesthetic concept of literature in favor of the pragmatic.[58]

A generation later, another poet, Po Chü-yi (772–846), familiar to many English-speaking readers through Arthur Waley's translations and biography, expressed similar views but, instead of rejecting the expressive and aesthetic concepts totally, assimilated them, together with the metaphysical, into the pragmatic. In his famous letter to his great friend and fellow poet Yüan Chen, Po states that the *wen* of heaven are headed by the Three Lights (*San-kuang*, i.e., the sun, the moon, and the stars), the *wen* of earth by the Five Elements (*Wu-ts'ai*, i.e., metal, wood, water, fire, and earth), and the *wen* of man by the Six Works of the Confucian Canon (*Liu-ching*, i.e., the *Book of Poetry*, the *Book of Documents*, the *Book of Changes*, the *Book of Rites*, the *Book of Music*, now lost, and the *Spring and Autumn Annals*). Among the six works, he continues, the *Book of Poetry* comes first. Why? Because poetry is the most efficient means to move men's hearts:

> The sage moves men's hearts and then the world is at peace. In moving men's hearts, there is nothing that precedes emotion, nothing that does not begin with words, nothing that does not accord with music, and nothing that is deeper than meaning. What we call poetry has emotion as its root, words as its sprouts, music as its flowers, and meaning as its fruit.[59]

Thus, starting from the metaphysical premise, he arrives at a definition of poetry that contains expressive, aesthetic, and pragmatic elements, with its references to emotion, music, and meaning. In what ensues in the letter, he further emphasizes the practical functions of poetry.

It would be tedious to quote more examples, so suffice it to observe that writers of the T'ang and later periods continued to mention the analogy between the *wen* of Heaven and the *wen* of man,[60] but they generally used it to provide a cosmological basis for their pragmatic doctrine, not to justify the exaltation of literature, as did Liu Hsieh and the Hsiao brothers. Accompanying this shift from the metaphysical concept of literature to the pragmatic was a shift from the metaphysical concept of Tao to the moral. The most famous advocate of Archaic Prose and the self-appointed champion of Confucianism against Buddhism and Taoism, Han Yü (768–824), at the beginning of his essay "Tracing the Origin of the Tao" (*Yüan-tao*, the same title as that of the first chapter of Liu Hsieh's *The Literary Mind*), defines the Tao in unequivocally moral terms:

> To love universally is called "benevolence" [*jen*], to act properly is called "rightness" [*yi*]; to proceed from here is called the Way [Tao][61]

The neo-Confucianists[62] who followed in Han Yü's footsteps in subsequent ages belong mainly to the pragmatic tradition, which will be considered in chapter 6. In spite of the shift to pragmatism mentioned above, the term *Tao* in the metaphysical sense did not disappear altogether from critical vocabulary, nor did the metaphysical concept of literature from critical thinking. On the contrary, the metaphysical concept underwent further developments and modifications, thus giving rise to new theories. One major development was the growing interest in the writer's apprehension of and union with the Tao of Nature. To trace the origins of this development, we have to go back in time to the early Taoist works, the *Lao Tzu*, and even more, the *Chuang Tzu*.

Origins of the Concept of Union with the Tao

The identity of Lao Tzu, "Master Lao" or "The Old Master," the putative author of the book called *Lao Tzu*, has never been satisfactorily established, and there is even doubt as to whether such a person ever existed.[63] As for the book so called, which has also been known since the second century A.D. as the *Tao Te Ching* ("The Canon of the Tao and Its Power"), according to recent scholarly opinions it was probably compiled some time during the fourth century B.C., before the compilation of the *Chuang Tzu*.[64] It is generally accepted that Chuang Tzu or "Master Chuang" was Chuang Chou (369?–286? B.C.), who may have written some parts of the book bearing his name, and that other parts were added later on.[65] In fact, in ancient China there was no conception of single authorship, and the label "Such-and-such a *tzu*" signified that a book represented the school of thought reputedly founded by Master Such-and-such, rather than that it was actually written by him.[66] The *Lao Tzu* and the *Chuang Tzu*, then, are anthologies of writings belonging to two schools of thought that flourished during the fourth and third centuries B.C., to which later historians gave the joint name of Tao-chia or "The Taoist School" (not to be confused with the popular religion which is also known as Taoism in English but is called Tao-chiao in Chinese). However, for convenience's sake, we may still sometimes refer to Lao Tzu and Chuang Tzu rather than the *Lao Tzu* and the *Chuang Tzu* when we mean the two books so called, as Arthur Waley and Burton Watson, among others, have done.[67]

Lao Tzu, while maintaining that the Tao is nameless and unnameable, paradoxically has much to say about what it is like, but has relatively little to say about how one is to apprehend it. However, there are at least two remarks in the *Lao Tzu* that bear on this question. One of them is, "In cleaning your mystic vision, can you make it flawless?"[68] The term I have translated as "mystic vision," *hsüan-lan*, has also been taken to mean "mysterious mirror," a metaphor for the mind.[69] In either case, the idea is that one should remove rational knowledge from one's mind so as to contemplate intuitively the Tao of Nature. The other remark runs: "Doing my utmost to attain emptiness, single-mindedly guarding my stillness; when the ten thousand things arise together, I contemplate their return."[70] Here, "emptiness" (*hsü*) also expresses the idea of removing rational knowledge from one's mind, while "return" refers to the return of everything to its basic nature. Much fuller expressions of these ideas of mental emptiness and contemplation of Nature are to be found in the *Chuang Tzu.*

It is no exaggeration to say that the *Chuang Tzu* has influenced Chinese artistic sensibility more profoundly than any other single book. Although not concerned with art or literature but with philosophy, it has inspired poets, artists, and critics for centuries with its ideas about self-oblivious contemplation of Nature leading to intuitive union with the Tao. There are various passages in the book advising one to forget one's self, such as the following:

> Drop your form and body, reject your hearing and eyesight, forget your place in the hierarchy of things, then you may join in great unity with the infinite.[71]
>
> One who forgets about things and forgets about heaven is called a self-forgetter; when one has forgotten one's self, this is called "entering heaven."[72]

When one has forgotten one's self, one will no longer feel the barrier between subjective consciousness and objective reality, but will identify with everything in Nature and "wander in the unitary *ch'i* [air/breath/spirit] of heaven and earth."[73] To lose one's sense of identity and be one with Nature is called "transforming with things" (*wu-hua*),[74] and in order to attain to this transformed state, one must practice what Chuang Tzu calls "mind's abstinence" (*hsin-chai*):

> Don't listen with the ear, but listen with the mind; [better still], don't listen with the mind, but listen with the spirit [*ch'i*]. The ear stops at listening, the mind stops at matching [things with concepts], but the spirit is empty and receives all things. Only the Tao will gather where emptiness is, and emptiness is what is meant by "mind's abstinence."[75]

Here Chuang Tzu is distinguishing three modes of knowing. To him, the lowest mode is "listening with the ear," or sense-perception. Next comes "listening with the mind," which I interpret as conceptual thinking, since it stops with *fu*, which literally means "tally" and which I take to mean "match objects with concepts." (Commentators have explained the word as "to fit" or *ho*, and Burton Watson translated it as "recognition,"[76] neither of which contradicts my interpretation.) The highest mode of knowing is "listening with the spirit," which has been interpreted, rightly I think, as intuitive cognition.[77] However, it should be realized that according to Chuang Tzu this intuitive cognition is not innate but can only be achieved after a long period of intense concentration and self-discipline. To illustrate this point, Chuang Tzu told several parables, which have become not only critical commonplaces but part and parcel of the literary language. The best-known of these tells about a cook who, after nineteen years' experience of cutting up oxen, no longer saw with his eyes but with his spirit (*shen*), and who would still concentrate and move slowly when he came to a complicated joint.[78] Another one tells how a certain woodworker would fast for days and forget about wealth and honor, praise or blame, and even his own body, and then go and contemplate the trees in the woods, before he would select one and make a bell stand.[79]

It should also be realized that Chuang Tzu's conception of intuitive knowledge differs from that of Mencius (Meng Tzu, 371?–289? B.C.), second only to Confucius in importance in the Confucian tradition. Whereas Mencius held the theory that all men have an intuitive knowledge of right and wrong[80]—a theory which was later developed by the Idealistic philosopher Wang Yang-ming (Wang Shou-jen, 1472–1528)—no such moral implications are present in Chuang Tzu's conception of intuitive knowledge. Furthermore, Chuang Tzu's conception of *ch'i* is also different from Mencius's. We have seen that Chuang Tzu uses both *ch'i* and *shen* to signify, among other things, "spirit" or that intuitive, suprarational faculty by which one can apprehend the Tao. And when one has reached this state of intuitive apprehension, Chuang Tzu calls him a "spiritual man" (*shen-jen*, which may also be translated as "god-like man"), or "perfect man" (*chih-jen*), or "true man" (*chen-jen*), or "holy man" (*sheng-jen*, also translated as "sage"). Mencius, on the other hand, conceived of *ch'i* as a kind of vital force which "fills the body" and is "born of an accumulation of rightness."[81] Thus, Chuang Tzu's concept of *ch'i* (or at least one of his concepts of *ch'i*) is metaphysical, and Mencius's is psycho-physiological as well as ethical. Since literary critics used the word in various senses, sometimes more in the Mencian sense and sometimes more in Chuang Tzu's sense, it is important to bear the distinction in mind.

THE CONCEPT OF UNION WITH THE TAO APPLIED TO LITERATURE

We may now consider how Lao Tzu's and Chuang Tzu's ideas about intuitive contemplation of Nature and union with the Tao were applied by literary critics to creative writing. The earlier critics Lu Chi and Liu Hsieh were more interested in the working of the intuitive faculty during the actual process of writing (phase 2) than in the preparation for writing (phase 1), but they did have something to say about the latter. Lu Chi's *Exposition on Literature* begins promisingly with the line, "Standing in the center of the universe to observe its mysteries." The phrase "observe its mysteries" (*hsüan-lan*) is taken from the remark in the *Lao Tzu* quoted above (where I translated it as "mystic vision") but used here verbally. This is, however, immediately followed by, "He nourishes his emotion and will with the Classics and Greats." This anticipates a later tendency, which I shall call "archaism," of substituting ancient literature for Nature as the object of contemplation. Lu Chi then goes on to describe how the writer experiences different emotions in response to changes in the natural world. Since his description is more expressive than metaphysical in character, it will be discussed in chapter 3. But the metaphysical element reappears later:

> At the beginning,
> They all stop their seeing and hold in their hearing,
> To think deeply and search widely;
> Their quintessential spirits [*ching*] gallop to the eight
> extremities of the earth,
> Their minds wander to the region thousands of feet
> above.

Here, the idea of suspending one's sense-perceptions so as to concentrate with one's spirit or intuition is derived from Chuang Tzu. In his descriptions of the writer engaged in the creative process, Lu Chi suggests how, by means of intuition, one can capture eternity and infinity in one's writings:

> He observes past and present in a moment,
> And covers the four seas in the twinkling of an eye.
>
> He encages Heaven and Earth within Form,
> And defeats the myriad things at the tip of his writing brush.[82]

These ideas are echoed by Liu Hsieh in the chapter called "Shen-ssu," which has been translated as "imagination" but which, for reasons to be given in the final chapter, I prefer to translate as "thinking with the spirit" or "intuitive thinking."

At the beginning of the chapter, he explains what he means by this term with a quotation from the *Chuang Tzu*:

> A man of antiquity said, "My bodily form is by the rivers and seas, but my mind is under the watch-towers of the palace of Wei." This is called "thinking with the spirit."

In the *Chuang Tzu*, the remark is made by a certain prince who is unable to forget worldly glories,[83] but Liu Hsieh is borrowing it to illustrate the power of the spirit or intuition to transcend spatial limits. He goes on to show how it can transcend temporal limits as well:

> When a writer is thinking, his spirit travels far. Therefore, when he concentrates his pondering in stillness, his thoughts will touch [what lies beyond] a thousand years; when he quietly moves his countenance, his vision will penetrate ten thousand miles. Amidst his chantings and hummings, sounds of pearls and jades issue forth; before his eyebrows and lashes, colors of wind-swept clouds unfold. Is this not brought about by the natural order of thought? Therefore, when the natural order of thought is subtle and miraculous, the spirit will roam together with external objects. The spirit dwells in the bosom, and the vital force [*ch'i*] and the will [*chih*] master its locks and keys; objects follow the ear and the eye, and eloquent language controls their bolts and triggers. When the bolts and triggers have begun to work, then objects will not hide their forms; when the locks and keys are about to be blocked, then the spirit will seek to escape. Hence, in moulding his thoughts, a writer should value emptiness and stillness: cleanse his five viscera and purify the quintessence of his spirit [*ching-shen*].[84]

The concept of "spirit" or intuition in this passage is obviously derived from the *Chuang Tzu*; in fact, the last sentence quoted is taken almost verbatim from this book.[85] However, it will be noticed that Liu Hsieh does not use *ch'i* as a synonym of *shen*, but in the sense of "vital force," a concept that we shall return to in chapter 3. The idea that language controls the mechanism of sense-perceptions seems to be original and can be interpreted in two ways: either that language is the key to the *depicting* of objects perceived by the senses (and this is how modern commentators have generally interpreted it) or that it is the key to the *understanding* of such objects.[86] If Liu indeed meant the latter, with the implication that we can only understand objects as language presents them to us, he would seem to have anticipated some modern Western philosophers, though he did not go so far as to assert that language is identical with reality, as Ernst Cassirer did.[87]

The tendency among later critics who held metaphysical views of literature to pay increasing attention to the writer's contemplation of Nature and apprehension of the Tao may be said to have begun with

Ssu-k'ung T'u (837–908), who was the first poet to voice explicitly the concept of poetry as an embodiment of the poet's apprehension of the Tao. Before him, poets like Wang Wei (699–759) and Meng Hao-jan (689–740) had embodied their contemplation of Nature in their poetry, but had not explicitly discussed their practice either in poetry or in prose. Ssu-k'ung T'u, on the other hand, expressed his metaphysical conception of poetry in a group of twenty-four poems in tetrasyllabic verse (a verse form which had long become archaic by his time) entitled *Twenty-four Moods of Poetry* (*Erh-shih-ssu shih-p'in*).[88] In each poem, he embodies in concrete imagery a poetic "mood" or "world," and the whole group may be considered descriptions of various poetic styles. However, there is a consistent underlying conception of poetry and there are frequent references to the poet's apprehension of the Tao of Nature. For example, under the heading "Spontaneity" (*Tzu-jan*), he writes, "If you accompany the Tao and go forth with it,/Whatever you touch will come to life as if in Spring"[89] In other words, if the poet identifies with the Tao, everything he writes about will come to life like things in the spring. (I am tempted to say "spring to life," but the pun is purely fortuitous). Again, under "Powerful and Free" (*Hao-fang*), Ssu-k'ung writes: "Follow the Tao and return to the spirit [*ch'i*],/Then you will be able to dwell in abandon."[90] This means, I think, that by following the Tao the poet can achieve spiritual freedom, which will then make his poetry "powerful and free" in style. Finally, under "Embodying and Describing" (*Hsing-jung*), we read:

> The changing appearance of wind-swept clouds,
> The quintessential spirit [*ching-shen*] of flowers
>   and plants,
> The waves and billows of the sea,
> The rugged crags of the mountains—
> All these resemble the great Tao:
> Identify with them intuitively, even to the dust.
> Leave forms behind but catch true likeness,
> Then you will come close to being the right man.[91]

The line that I have translated as "Identify with them intuitively, even to the dust" is ambiguous. The original, *miao-ch'i t'ung-ch'en*, literally means, "miraculously fit, same dust." The last two syllables are derived from the *Lao Tzu*, where the phrase *t'ung ch'i ch'en* ("share its [or their] dust" or "make its [or their] dust the same") has been interpreted and translated in widely different ways.[92] Whatever it may mean in the *Lao Tzu*, as adapted by Ssu-k'ung T'u it seems to mean either that the poet should identify with everything in Nature even down to the smallest particle of dust, or that all things in Nature accord with each other perfectly, even down to the smallest particle of dust. I have chosen the first alternative in the translation above, but the other interpretation need not be excluded. I should also explain that I translated the word *miao*, usually rendered "wonderful" or "subtle," as "intuitively," because it is often used to describe intuitive apprehension or intuitive artistry, which seems to defy rational explanation. In the lines quoted and in others, Ssu-k'ung T'u has conveyed through poetic imagery his conception of poetry as an embodiment of the poet's intuitive apprehension of and identification with the Tao of Nature.

Among poet-critics of the Sung period (960–1279) who shared Ssu-k'ung's views, we may mention the great Su Shih (commonly known as Su Tung-p'o, 1037–1101), who admired the former. In a poem addressed to the Buddhist monk Ts'an-liao, Su writes,

> If you wish to make the words of your poetry subtle
> and miraculous,
> Never tire of emptiness and stillness:
> Being still, one can therefore understand the movements
> of the multitudes of things;
> Being empty, one can therefore receive ten thousand
> worlds.[93]

In another poem, about his deceased friend Wen T'ung's paintings of bamboos, Su stresses the importance, for the artist, of identifying with Nature:

> When Yü-k'o [Wen T'ung] painted bamboos,
> He saw only bamboos but no man;
> Not only did he see no man,
> But he had left his dissolved body.
> His body transformed with the bamboos,
> Producing endless limpidity and freshness.[94]

Although the subject is painting, these words apply equally well to poetry. The idea of identifying with the object of one's contemplation is derived from the *Chuang Tzu*, as is the expression, "left his dissolved body."[95]

RAMIFICATIONS OF THE METAPHYSICAL TRADITION

With Su Shih's disciple Huang T'ing-chien (1045–1105)[96] began a new trend towards the kind of archaism that I mentioned once before

—the kind that substitutes ancient literature for Nature as the object of intuitive contemplation. Of course, the idea of imitating ancient writers was an age-old one in China; what was new and different about the particular form of archaism we are discussing was the idea of meditating on ancient poetry in the same way as in spiritual exercises. This idea was strongly influenced by Ch'anism, the synthesis of Buddhism and Taoism which rose in the seventh century A.D. and which is known to many Westerners by its Japanese pronunciation Zen.[97] The Chiang-hsi (Kiangsi) School of poets, who acknowledged Huang as their "patriarch," were fond of using such Ch'an terms as "commune with" (*ts'an*), "awakening" (*wu*, often translated as "enlightenment"), and "method" (*fa*, the Chinese translation of Sanskrit *dharma*, sometimes translated into English as "law"). By advocating meditation on ancient poetry instead of the Tao, these poet-critics derived a literary theory about how to write poetry from the metaphysical concept of literature.

Both the trend towards archaism and the penchant for using Ch'anist terms in discussing poetry culminated with Yen Yü (fl. 1180–1235), whose work *Ts'ang-lang's Remarks on Poetry* (*Ts'ang-lang shih-hua*)[98] exerted great influence on later critics and also provoked some strong reactions. Actually, Yen has more to say about how to write poetry and how to judge it than what poetry is, and his basic conception of poetry, which is all that we are here concerned with, can only be deduced from a few concise and rather ambiguous remarks. To begin with, he says,

> The ulitmate attainment of poetry lies in one thing: entering the spirit [*ju-shen*]. If poetry enters the spirit, it has reached perfection, the limit, and nothing can be added to it.[99]

The phrase *ju shen* can be interpreted as "entering the realm of the marvelous or divinely-inspired," since in Chinese literary and art criticism, perfect intuitive artistry which seems effortless and natural is often called *shen*, "marvelous," "inspired," or "god-like." It is in this sense that Tu Fu (712–770), the greatest of Chinese poets, used the word in describing his own experience:

> After having read through ten thousand volumes of books,
> I felt, when setting pen to paper, as if aided by
> the gods [*shen*].[100]

However, it is possible that by *ju shen* Yen also meant, as I have suggested elsewhere, entering into the life of things and capturing their spirit or essence.[101] This latter interpretation can be supported by a number of earlier usages of the phrase.[102] In the "Appended Words" to the *Book of Changes*, we encounter the following:

> [Investigate] the quintessence [*ching*] of the principle of things, so as to put it to use. . . . To have exhaustively investigated the spirit [of things] and entered into their transformations is the height of virtue [or power, *te*].[103]

Liu Hsieh, in *The Literary Mind*, characterized the *Book of Changes* itself with the words, "The *Book of Changes* discusses heaven exclusively; it enters the spirit to put it to use."[104] And Liu's contemporary, the art critic Hsieh Ho (fl. 479–532), praised two painters for their ability to "enter the spirit."[105] To these examples we may add the lines previously quoted from Ssu-k'ung T'u, about the "quintessential spirit" (*ching-shen*) of flowers and plants, which resembles the great Tao and with which the poet should identify.[106] Of course, one could argue about the interpretation of these earlier usages too, but whether we take *shen* to mean the "spirit" or "essence" of things or the "divine" and "god-like,"[107] "entering the *shen*" involves reaching beyond or penetrating the material world, and since Yen Yü considers this the ultimate attainment of poetry, his conception of poetry is at least partly metaphysical.

Furthermore, Yen lays great stress on intuitive apprehension which he, like some other critics before him, calls "miraculous awakening" (*miao-wu*):

> In general, the way [*tao*] of Ch'an lies in miraculous awakening alone, and so does the way of poetry. Moreover, Meng Hsiang-yang [Meng Hao-jan] was far inferior to Han T'ui-chih [Han Yü] in learning, and the reason why his poetry nevertheless surpassed the latter's was nothing but his complete reliance on miraculous awakening. Only through awakening can one "ply one's proper trade" and "show one's true colors."[108]

We may ask, when a poet has achieved miraculous awakening or intuitive apprehension, what has he apprehended—the way of writing poetry, or the Tao of Nature, or both? This is in fact the crucial question about Yen Yü's theory of poetry: did he use Ch'an simply as a metaphor for poetry, or did he consider the creative experience of writing poetry and the aesthetic experience of reading poetry to be similar in nature to, if not identical with, the religious experience of spiritual awakening? Yen himself gave no clear indications to the answer, and modern scholars disagree about this question.[109] My opinion is that he used Ch'an primarily as an analogy to poetry, but he also considered intuitive contemplation of Nature a necessary preparation for the intuitive apprehension of the art of poetry. This is suggested by his advocation of *hsing-ch'ü*, which may be translated as "inspired gusto" or "inspired feeling," and which appears to refer to a kind of ineffable feeling or mood inspired by the poet's contemplation of Nature.

Yen came closest to a description of his conception of poetry in the following passage:

> Poetry involves a separate kind of talent, which is not concerned with books; it involves a separate kind of meaning [*ch'ü*], which is not concerned with principles [or reason, *li*]. Yet unless one reads widely and investigates principles thoroughly, one will not be able to reach the ultimate. What is called "not touching the path of reason [*li*] nor falling into the trammel of words" is the best. Poetry is what sings of one's emotion and nature. The poets of the High T'ang [8th century] relied only on inspired feelings [*hsing-ch'ü*], like the antelope that hangs by its horns, leaving no traces to be found.[110] Therefore, the miraculousness of their poetry lies in its transparent luminosity, which cannot be pieced together;[111] it is like sound in the air, color in appearances, the moon in water, or an image in the mirror;[112] it has limited words but unlimited meaning. As for recent gentlemen, they come up with strange interpretations and understandings [of poetry]; and so they take [mere] words as poetry, take talent and learning as poetry, take discussions as poetry. Not that their poetry is unskillful, but it is after all not the poetry of the ancients, because it lacks "the music that one man sings and three men echo."[113] Moreover, in their works they must use many allusions, but pay no attention to inspired moods [*hsing-chih*]; every word they use must have a source, every rhyme they employ must have a precedent. When you read them over and over again from beginning to end, you don't know what they are aiming at. The worst of them even scream and growl, which is much against the principle of magnanimity. They are practically taking abusive language as poetry. When poetry has reached such a state, it can be called a disaster.[114]

Even in this passage Yen Yü says more about what he thinks poetry is *not* than what he thinks it is. However, the negative points he makes will help us reach a kind of definition by elimination. First, according to Yen, poetry is not book learning, although this helps. Second, poetry is not rational discourse, though again a rational knowledge of the principles of things is desirable. Third, poetry is not mechanical imitation of ancient poets. Last, poetry is not unrestrained expression of violent passion. In other words, Yen's conception of poetry is not technical, nor pragmatic, nor expressive in the primitivistic sense. (The term "primitivism" will be discussed in chapter 3.)

Some positive points can also be discerned. First, Yen implies that poetry, or at least the best kind of poetry, is an embodiment of the poet's intuitive apprehension of the reality that lies beyond words. Alluding to Chuang Tzu's saying, "One who has caught the fish can forget the trammel, . . . one who has caught the meaning can forget the words,"[115] Yen Yü hints at the paradox that it is by means of words that the poet reveals the "transformed state of being" (*hua-ching*) in which one is identified with the Tao and has no longer any need for words. Secondly, he observes, albeit somewhat casually and inconsequentially, that poetry "sings of one's emotion and nature," which is an old expressive formula, but the presence of which cannot be ignored. Finally, the images he borrowed from Buddhism—sound in the air, color in appearances, the moon reflected in water, and image in the mirror—appear to have been used in an effort to describe the indescribable and elusive nature of the kind of poetry he held up as the ideal for all poetry, rather than to express the idea that poetry is a reflection of the poet's "mind-picture," as has been suggested,[116] since in Yen's writings there is no word corresponding to "mind-picture." However, we shall consider the significance of these images in greater depth later, in comparison with similar imagery in Western criticism.

In my view, Yen's theory concerning the nature of poetry is mainly metaphysical, although it also contains an expressive element, while his theories about how to write poetry and how to judge it are archaistic. Some later critics influenced by him carried his archaism even further, while others developed the metaphysical strain in his critical thinking.

Since archaism is a literary theory about how to write rather than a theory of literature, we need not concern ourselves with it as such, but since some critics of the Ming period (1368–1644) who advocated archaism also held technical views, we shall discuss them in chapter 4.[117] Meanwhile let us turn our attention to a few other critics who modified the metaphysical concept of poetry in some ways. One of them is Hsieh Chen (1495–1575), who subscribed to archaism but also expressed metaphysical views with an expressive slant in his *Ssu-ming's Remarks on Poetry* (*Ssu-ming shih-hua*):

> The writing of poetry is based on *ch'ing* [emotion/inner experience] and *ching* [scene/external world]: neither by itself can complete [poetry]; neither is in conflict with the other. Whenever we climb high and let our thoughts roam, we communicate with the ancients in spirit [*shen*]; [our thoughts] reach everywhere, far

> and near, and we feel sorrow or happiness accordingly. These things give rise to one another in a chance manner, thereby causing forms to appear where there was no trace of anything, and echoes to be evoked where there was no sound. Now, the *ch'ing* [emotion/inner experience] may be different while the *ching* [scene/external world] is the same, and describing them may be difficult or easy. In poetry, there are two essentials, and nothing is more important than these: what is observed without is the same, but the feelings aroused within may be different. One should exert oneself to make what is within and what is without like one thing, what goes out of one's mind no different from what comes into it. *Ching* [scene/external world] is the matchmaker of poetry, and *ch'ing* [emotion/inner experience] is its embryo. When these fuse to become poetry, one can then sum up ten thousand forms with a few words, and one's poetry will have a primordial vital force [*yüan-ch'i*] which is an indivisible whole and which will overflow without limits.[118]

By laying equal emphasis on *ch'ing* (emotion/inner experience) and *ching* (scene/external world), Hsieh is gravitating from the metaphysical concept of poetry towards the expressive. His idea about causing forms to appear where there was no trace of anything before and echoes to be evoked where there was no sound (an idea probably derived from Lu Chi's lines, "Tax Non-being to demand Being/Knock on silence to seek sound"[119]) also shows affinities with some expressive theories. However, his belief in the fusion of the internal with the external and his reference to the primordial vital force of Nature are consonant with metaphysical theories as well. In another passage he writes:

> The ten thousand scenes [*ching*] and the seven emotions [*ch'ing*][120] fuse with one another as one climbs high and looks afar, as if a row of mirrors were arranged before one and there were nothing that were not truthfully reflected. Sorrow or joy [on the face] would not present a different appearance [in the mirror]; whether it were a side-view or full-faced view, there would be only one mind [behind the face]. A side-view would reveal half [of the mind], a full-faced view, the whole. The mirror is like the mind, and the light is like the spirit [*shen*]. When thought enters the distant and dark realm, then there will be no distinction between the "I" [*wo*] and "things" [*wu*]. The reaches of poetry are mysterious indeed.[121]

We may notice that in both passages Hsieh refers to contemplation of Nature ("climb high and look far") and stresses the identification of subjective consciousness with objective reality by means of intuition (*shen*). These are ideas shared by all metaphysical and some expressive theories. His use of imagery also reflects his partly metaphysical and partly expressive conception of poetry. In particular, his use of the image of the mirror deserves analysis because it is highly complicated and involves two parallel series of operations: just as the physical mirror reflects the human face, which is an expression of the individual's mind, so does the mind, the metaphorical mirror, reflect the external world, which is a manifestation of the cosmic Tao. (Hsieh does not actually mention the Tao, but this seems to be a legitimate inference.) We shall have occasion to discuss the image of the mirror again later.

The fusion of inner experience and external reality is also emphasized by the philosopher and critic Wang Fu-chih (1619–1692):

> *Ch'ing* [emotion/inner experience] and *ching* [scene/external world] are called by two different names but are in fact inseparable. Those who can work miracles in poetry fuse the two naturally and leave no boundary line; those who are ingenious can reveal the one in the other and vice versa.[122]

In this passage Wang makes two significant points. First, he asserts that "inner experience" and "external world" are only two names by which we refer to two aspects of reality and not two separate entities. Second, by distinguishing "those who can work miracles in poetry" (*shen-yü-shih-che*) from "those who are ingenious" (*ch'iao-che*), he implies that only by apprehending reality in its totality can a poet reach the realm of perfect artistry that appears like a natural miracle, but if a poet treats inner experience and external reality as two entities, the best he can attain to is mere "ingenuity."

This emphasis on the fusion of *ch'ing* and *ching* is reiterated by Wang Fu-chih in many other passages, which need not be given here. In addition, he also pays attention to *shen*, which sometimes appears to denote the poet's "spirit" or intuition, and at other times the "spirit" or essence of things. For example, in the following passage *shen* refers to the poet's intuition:

> Why is it that the lines "Green, green, the grass by the river" and "Endlessly, endlessly, longing for the distant road" give rise to and depend on each other, responding to each other breath by breath? It is because when one's spirit [*shen*] and the principles [*li*] of things coincide, then one will naturally hit the mark just right.[123]

Of these two lines, quoted from an anonymous song in which the speaker is a woman longing for her absent husband,[124] the first refers to "things" (*wu*) and the second to emotion. The reason why they form a perfect match is, according to Wang, that the poet has intuitively sensed the underlying affinity between the grass stretching endlessly along the river's banks and the speaker's endless longing for her husband. In other words, perfect poetry results from perfect consonance between the poet's intuition and the underlying principles of things. Here, *shen* is contrasted with *li*. But in another passage, *shen* refers to the essence of things:

> If one harbors emotions [*ch'ing*] and can express them; if one's mind is activated by the scenes [*ching*] that one encounters; if one can empathize with things and capture their spirit [*shen*]; then one will naturally have animated lines and share the marvelousness of Nature's works.[125]

What he means by "capturing the spirit of things" seems to be similar to what Yen Yü calls "entering the spirit" (if my interpretation of the latter phrase is correct), both referring to the identification of the contemplator with the object contemplated. In any case, in spite of changing terminology, Wang Fu-chih consistently advocates the intuitive union of one's mind with the underlying principles of things. Again, like Yen Yü, Wang also condemns mere technical skill in contrast to "inspired encounters" or "what inspiration encounters" (*hsing-hui*).[126] Furthermore, he also admires poetry that has "meaning beyond words,"[127] an idea that is ultimately derived from the *Chuang Tzu*. In brief, Wang Fu-chih shows his affinities with Yen Yü and other metaphysical critics in his preoccupation with phase 1 of the artistic process, conceived of as an intuitive identification of the poet's mind with the underlying principle of the cosmos, in his advocation of inspiration instead of conscious technical skill, and in his admiration of poetry that suggests infinite meanings beyond what is stated. We may therefore justifiably place him in the company of Yen and other metaphysical critics,[128] even though his general philosophical orientation is quite different (whereas Yen and some of the others are influenced by Ch'an Buddhism, Wang Fu-chih is antagonistic to Buddhism and is basically Confucian, but with some Taoist leanings).

The metaphysical concept of poetry enjoyed a temporary vogue during the early part of the Ch'ing dynasty (1644–1911) due to the prestige of Wang Shih-chen (Wang Yü-yang, 1634–1711, not to be confused with the Ming poet and critic Wang Shih-chen or Wang Yüan-mei, 1526–1590), the leading poet of his age. Wang is famous for his advocation of *shen-yün*, a term that he did not define and that has given rise to much controversy. Without attempting a direct definition of the term, we may nonetheless discern in Wang's writings a theory of poetry that has three main aspects: intuitive apprehension of reality, intuitive artistry, and personal tone.[129]

According to Wang Shih-chen, the ultimate aim of poetry is the attainment of spiritual awakening, just as in Ch'an:

> "To discard the raft and climb ashore" is what experts in Ch'an consider to be the "awakened state" [*wu-ching*] and what experts in poetry consider to be the "transformed state" [*hua-ching*]. Poetry and Ch'an are the same and there is no difference between them.[130]

In praising the T'ang poets, he remarks,

> The pentasyllabic Quatrains [*chüeh-chü*] of the T'ang poets often enter [the realm of] Ch'an and have the miraculousness of "catching the meaning and forgetting the words."[131]

Thus, by borrowing terms from Ch'anism and from Chuang Tzu, Wang repeats the paradox hinted at by Yen Yü that it is by means of words that the poet reveals the state of wordless communion with the Tao.

In order to attain to this state, one should encounter the *shen* (spirit or essence) of things with one's own *shen* (spirit or intuition). Like Wang Fu-chih, Wang Shih-chen also emphasizes "what the spirit encounters" (*shen-hui*), or "what the spirit reaches" (*shen-tao*), or "what inspiration encounters" (*hsing-hui*).[132] For instance, in defending ancient poets who mentioned in the same breath places actually hundreds of miles apart, he concludes,

> The ancients, in their poetry, only took what was transcendental and miraculous in their inspired encounters [with Nature], unlike latter-day people whose counting of chapters and verses is merely a mileage-recording drum.[133]

To paraphrase, poetry is not concerned with literal truth but poetic truth, not with empirical knowledge based on sense-perception but intuitive knowledge gained in moments of inspired encounter with Nature. And when one has reached such a state, one's poetry can then enter the realm of *shen*, which, as we have seen before, can mean both "miraculous, inspired" and "capturing the spirit of things." It will be seen, then, that the term *shen* as used by Wang Shih-chen refers both to intuitive apprehension of reality and intuitive artistry that appears like a miracle.

To the word *shen* Wang Shih-chen often adds *yün*, which, as pointed out in chapter 1, has a range of meanings including "tone," "rhyme," "rhythm," "consonance," and "resonance." It has been demonstrated that this word was used to denote personal airs or mien before it was applied to poetry and painting,[134] and Wang Shih-chen's use of the word, either by itself or in the disyllabic compound *shen-yün*, generally means an ineffable personal tone or flavor in one's poetry. This can be corroborated by the following passage, in which he quotes with approval a remark made by the Sung poet, composer, and critic Chiang K'uei (ca. 1155–ca. 1221):

> "The poetry of each master has its own flavor, just as each of the twenty-four modes of music has its own tone, which is where the music comes to rest. Imitators, even though their words may resemble the master's, have lost the tone." These remarks on poetry, though they have not reached Yen Ts'ang-lang [Yen Yü], are worthy to be considered words of subtle understanding.[135]

However, it is possible that by *yün* Wang also meant a kind of resonance between the spirit of things and one's own spirit. If so, then it would seem that both syllables of the compound *shen-yün* in his theory of poetry refer to the poet's relation to the universe as well as his relation to his poetry.

It may be thought that Wang's interest in personal tone makes his theory of poetry an expressive one, but in fact there is a difference between his conception of personal tone and the conception of personal expression in most expressive theories. To Wang, personal tone signifies an individual mode of perception and expression rather than one's personal emotions and nature. In other words, he is concerned with the poet as an artistic *persona* rather than an empirical person.

Wang Shih-chen's influence did not last very long. Those who came after him either reacted against his theory or distorted it into something else. For instance, Weng Fang-kang (1733–1818) turned Wang's metaphysical theory into a partly technical and partly aesthetic one by identifying *shen-yün* with *ko-tiao*, which may be rendered "formal style," as we shall see in chapter 4.

Another ramification of the metaphysical tradition took place among writers of Archaic Prose of the T'ung-ch'eng School (so called because most of the leaders of this school came from T'ung-ch'eng in Anhwei province), which was dominant during the middle and late Ch'ing (eighteenth and nineteenth centuries). One of the leaders of this school, Yao Nai (1731–1815), developed an aesthetic theory of two kinds of beauty in literature from the metaphysical concept:

> I have heard that the Tao of heaven and earth consists in nothing but the *yin* and the *yang*, the gentle and the strong. Literature is the finest essence of heaven and earth, and the manifestation of the *yin* and the *yang*, the gentle and the strong. Only the words of the sages epitomized the conjoining of these two vital principles [*ch'i*] without bias. However, even among the words recorded in the *Book of Changes*, the *Book of Poetry*, the *Book of Documents*, and the *Analects*, we may occasionally distinguish the strong from the gentle. This is because the words differed in character according to the time in which they were said and the person to whom they were addressed. From the philosophers of the various schools [of the fourth and third centuries B.C.] downwards, there has been none whose writing is not biased [in favor of the *yang* or the *yin*]. If one has obtained the beauty of the *yang* and strong, then one's writing will be like thunder, like lightning, like a long wind emerging from the valley, like lofty mountains and steep cliffs, like a great river flooding, like galloping steeds; its light like brilliant sun, like fire, like fine gold covering iron; and compared to human beings, like one leaning from high up and looking afar, like a monarch receiving homage from a multitude of thousands, like one fighting against ten thousand brave warriors aroused by drums. If one has obtained the beauty of the *yin* and gentle, then one's writing will be like the sun just beginning to rise, like cool breeze, like clouds, like vapor, like mist, like secluded woods and meandering streams, like ripples, like water gently rocking, like the sheen of pearls and jade, like the cry of a wild goose disappearing into the silent void; and compared to human beings, like one deeply sighing, or mentally far away and wrapped in thought or warmly happy, or sad with changed countenance.[136]

Both the theory (which reminds one of Hazlitt's theory of masculine and effeminate styles as expressions of two kinds of gusto)[137] and the style (which reminds one of Pater's description of the Mona Lisa) are strongly inclined towards impressionistic aestheticism, and the focus of critical attention has shifted from the writer's relation to the universe (phase 1) to the reader's perception of aesthetic qualities in writing (phase 3).

Yao's theory was inherited by his followers in the nineteenth century. Since then, the metaphysical concept has appeared intermittently in Chinese critical writings. As late as 1910, Wang Kuo-wei (1877–1927) in his *Remarks on Lyrics in the World of Men* (*Jen-chien tz'u-*

hua) advanced his theory of "worlds" (*ching-chieh*), which has much in common with the theories of Wang Fu-chih and Wang Shih-chen.[138] However, since Wang Kuo-wei had been influenced by such Western thinkers as Schopenhauer and Nietzsche, his ideas cannot be said to belong wholly to the indigenous tradition. I have therefore decided not to include a discussion of his theory in this book, but merely point out that he has exerted widespread influence on modern Chinese criticism and that some critical terms and concepts with metaphysical overtones are still current even today.

METAPHYSICAL THEORIES COMPARED WITH MIMETIC AND EXPRESSIVE ONES

We may now consider in what ways Chinese metaphysical theories resemble or differ from Western mimetic theories on the one hand and expressive ones on the other.

Metaphysical theories resemble mimetic ones in so far as both kinds of theories are primarily oriented towards the "universe," but they differ from each other with respect to the identity of the "universe" and the interrelations among the "universe," the writer, and the literary work. In mimetic theories, "universe" may refer to the material world, or human society, or the transcendental (Platonic Ideas or God). For example, Plato conceived artists and poets as imitating natural objects, which according to him, are themselves imperfect imitations of perfect and eternal Ideas, and he therefore assigned art and poetry to a lowly place in his scheme of things.[139] The neoclassicists also regarded art as an imitation of Nature, though they did not share Plato's low opinion of art. Aristotle considered the chief object of imitation in poetry to be human action,[140] so we may say that in the Aristotelian theory of poetry, "universe" means human society. Similarly, Samuel Johnson's well-known praise of Shakespeare's drama as "the mirrour of life"[141] also implies the identification of human society with the artistic "universe." Finally, those who subscribed to the "Transcendental Ideal" of imitation (to borrow M. H. Abrams's phrase), such as the neo-Platonists and some Romantics like Shelley, believed that art imitates the Ideas at first hand, and Blake likewise asserted that the artistic vision or imagination is a representation of what eternally exists.[142]

Of these three ways of identifying the "universe," it is of course the last one that comes closest to the metaphysical, yet even here we may still discern some subtle differences. In mimetic theories that follow the Transcendental Ideal, the Ideas are supposed to exist in some superlunar world as well as in the mind of the artist, but in metaphysical theories the Tao is immanent in everything in Nature. As Chuang Tzu put it, in a remark intended to be funny as well as shocking, though basically serious, the Tao exists even "in shit and piss."[143] Nor does the Tao exist in the individual mind as a distinct concept or image; rather, it absorbs the individual mind. Hence, whereas neo-Platonic asethetics led to an introspective attitude towards art, metaphysical theorists did not advise poets to turn their eyes inward to contemplate their own minds but to contemplate Nature.

It should be obvious that the Tao is not an anthropomorphic deity either. This basic difference in philosophical assumptions can be seen in passages expressing respectively metaphysical and mimetic views, passages that are otherwise strikingly similar. It may be recalled that Liu Hsieh wrote:

> [Man] is the finest essence of the Five Agents, and truly the mind of heaven and earth. When mind was born, then language was established; when language was established, then literature shone forth. This is a natural principle.[144]

With this we may compare what Sir Philip Sydney wrote in his *Apologie for Poetrie*:

> For if *Oratio* next to *Ratio*, Speech next to Reason, bee the greatest gyft bestoweed vpon mortalitie, that can not be praiselesse which dooth most pollish that blessing of speech.[145]

Although in the context Sydney is defending rhetoric and prosody rather than literature itself, his arguments are similar to Liu Hsieh's: both argue that literature or the art of language should be honored because language is a unique human faculty which expresses the equally unique human mind. Beyond this point begins to emerge the difference between the Confucian concept of man[146] and the Christian-humanistic: to Liu, language is a natural manifestation of the human mind, which is in turn a natural manifestation of the cosmic Tao; to Sydney, language and reason are both gifts of God to man. Furthermore, behind Sydney's remarks is the long oratorial tradition that goes back to the Greek Sophists;[147] by contrast, Chinese oratory, which flourished contemporaneously with Greek oratory, declined after the first unification of China and the establishment of a centralized empire in the third century B.C.

As for the interrelations among the universe, the writer, and the literary work, in Western minetic theories the poet is either conceived of as consciously imitating Nature or human society, as in Aristotelian and neoclassical theories, or as being possessed by the Divine and unconsciously uttering oracles, as described by Plato in the *Ion*,[148] whereas in Chinese metaphysical theories the poet is conceived of neither as consciously imitating Nature nor yet as reflecting the Tao in a purely unconscious manner, as if he were a passive, shaman-like, instrument of some supernatural force of which he were unaware and over which he had no control, but as spontaneously manifesting the Tao, in the "transformed state" of consciousness he has attained in which there is no longer any distinction between the subjective and the objective. In the metaphysical view, the writer's relation to the universe is a dynamic one, involving a process of change from conscious effort at contemplating Nature to intuitive identification with the Tao.

In view of the differences between metaphysical and mimetic theories mentioned above, and, further, in view of the literal meaning of the word "mimetic" (even though I am aware that the Greek *mimesis* or its English equivalent "imitation" does not always mean "copying" in the literal sense),[149] I have decided not to apply the word "mimetic" to the theories of literature discussed in this chapter but to call them "metaphysical" instead. However, I do not mean to suggest that the concept of imitation is totally absent in Chinese literary criticism, but only that it did not form the basis of any major theory of literature. On the level of literary theory, the idea of imitation in the secondary sense, that is, imitation of ancient writers, is as prominent in Chinese archaism as in European neoclassicism, but, as has already been pointed out, archaism is not a theory of literature but a literary theory about how to write, and critics who believed in imitating ancient writers did not assert that this constituted the whole nature and function of literature.

Turning to expressive theories, we find that their main difference from metaphysical ones lies in their primary orientation towards the writer, although the two kinds of theories resemble each other with regard to the writer's relation to the universe, both being interested in the identification of the subjective with the objective. However, when it comes to the process by which this identification is to be achieved, expressive critics, such as Coleridge and Ruskin, show a conception different from that seen in metaphysical theories. In expressive theories, this process, whether it is called imagination or Pathetic Fallacy or empathy, is conceived of as one of projection or reciprocity: the poet projects his own feelings into external objects, or interacts with them;[150] in metaphysical theories, the process is conceived of as one of reception: the poet "empties" his mind and keeps it "still" in order to be receptive of the Tao. Here Keats's famous concept of Negative Capability immediately comes to mind as a parallel to the metaphysical concept, but there is still a slight difference: in Keats's theory, as Abrams has pointed out,[151] the poet identifies with individual objects, whereas in metaphysical theories, the poet is generally advised to identify with the Tao, which is the totality of all existence, rather than with individual objects. (There are exceptions, such as Su Shih's poem about painting bamboos quoted above.) Furthermore, expressive theorists generally emphasize heightened sense-perception, but metaphysical ones advocate the suspension of sense-perception, as we have seen.

The similarities and dissimilarities among the three kinds of theories—mimetic, expressive, and metaphysical—are reflected (if I may indulge in using the same metaphor that I am about to discuss) in the various ways in which the metaphor of the mirror is used. In Western mimetic theories, the mirror may represent the work of art, which is conceived of as a reflection of external reality or God, or represent the artist's mind, similarly conceived, whereas in expressive theories the mirror generally represents the artistic work, conceived of as a reflection of the artist's mind or soul rather than of external reality.[152] In Chinese metaphysical theories, the metaphor of the mirror does not occur with such persistency as in Western theories, and therefore does not seem to have played an equally important role in Chinese critical thinking.

Let us examine more closely the two uses of this metaphor that we have seen before. As used by Yen Yü and repeated by several later critics including Wang Shih-chen, "image in the mirror," or "flower in the mirror," together with other images of Buddhist origin free from mimetic overtones ("sound in the air" and "color in appearances"), may have been intended (as I suggested) to describe the elusive nature of poetry, without any deeper significance. However, if we wish to find deeper significance in the metaphor, we should first of all realize that to these critics poetry is not the mirror that reflects reality but an image in the mirror, and if we pursued this analogy ruthlessly, we would have to conclude that since according to Buddhist doctrine "reality" is only an illusion, poetry is an illusion of an illusion —a conclusion even more damning than Plato's that poetry is twice removed from reality. As a matter of fact, the Ch'an masters did reach such a conclusion about language in general, and therefore refused to write anything and even warned their disciples not to remember their words. Fortunately for us, Chinese poet-critics who held metaphysical views of poetry did not go so far; instead, they followed the examples of the Taoists Lao Tzu and Chuang Tzu in accepting the paradoxical nature of language as the inadequate but necessary means to communicate the incommunicable. Lao Tzu remarked, "True words are not beautiful, beautiful words are not true,"[153] but, as Liu Hsieh pointed out, "Lao Tzu disliked artificiality and therefore declared, 'Beautiful words are not true'; yet his 'Five Thousand Words' are refined and subtle, which shows that he did not really reject beauty."[154] Likewise, Chuang Tzu advised us to forget the words once we have caught the meaning, yet he apparently still thought words a necessary "trammel" with which to catch the fish of "meaning."[155] This paradox of trying to communicate the incommunicable, to express the inexpressible, lies at the bottom of all efforts at artistic creation, and has naturally also been perceived by Western poets. Christopher Marlowe, for example, expressed the common experience of all poets when he wrote,

> If all the heavenly quintessence they still
> From their immortal flowers of poesy,
> Wherein as in a mirror we perceive
> The highest reaches of a human wit—
> If these had made one poem's period,
> And all combin'd in beauty's worthiness,
> Yet should there hover in their restless heads
> One thought, one grace, one wonder, at the least,
> Which into words no virtue can digest.[156]

This quotation (without conscious design on my part) brings us back to the metaphor of the mirror, which Marlowe uses to represent poetry as a reflection of the poet's mind, thereby revealing an expressive view of poetry. By a further unconscious association, the next Western poet I wish to quote is Goethe, who shared with Marlowe the interest in the Faust legend, even though the passage just quoted is not from *Doctor Faustus* but from *Tamburlaine* and the one to be quoted is not from *Faust* but from *The Sufferings of Young Werther*:

> . . . if you could breathe on to the paper what lives so fully, so warmly within you, so that it might become the mirror of your soul, as your soul is the mirror of the infinite God![157]

With this passage we may compare the one from Hsieh Chen quoted once before; for convenience I shall repeat the most relevant sentences:

> The ten thousand scenes and the seven emotions fuse with one another as one climbs high and looks afar, as if a row of mirrors were arranged before one and there were nothing that were not truthfully reflected. Sorrow or joy [on the face] would not

> present a different appearance [in the mirror]; whether it were a side-view or full-faced view, there would be only one mind [behind the face]. . . . The mirror is like the mind, and the light is like the spirit.

In the passage from Goethe, the tenor of the metaphor (that which is represented) is at first art, which reflects the artist's soul, and then transferred to the soul, which reflects God. In other words, Goethe seems to be combining the expressive view of art with the transcendental-mimetic. In Hsieh's passage, the imagery is more complex and involves a series of comparisons. First, the tenor of the metaphor of the mirror is the poet's mind, which reflects Nature (and, by implication, the Tao through Nature). This is similar to Goethe's second comparison, since Goethe's concept of God is not the Christian one of God as a transcendent Being but rather the Spinozistic one of God as *Natura naturans.* Secondly, Hsieh sees the face as an expression of the mind, an idea also found in Cicero's remark, "Imago animi vultus [est]" ("the mirror of the mind [is] the face").[158] This idea is not concerned with poetry, but the analogical mode of thinking on which it is based could and did generate both mimetic and metaphysical theories of poetry. Further, Hsieh compares the "spirit" (*shen*) to light, and the "mind" (*hsin*) to the mirror—a combination of images that recalls Hazlitt's use of the same images:

> The light of poetry is not only a direct but also a reflected light, that while it shows us the object, throws a sparkling radiance on all around it.[159]

However, a close comparison of the two passages will reveal their differences in point of view, focus of attention, and implications: Hazlitt, writing from the reader's point of view and focusing attention on the relation between the poem and the reader, uses the images of the mirror and the light to represent two functions of poetry—reflecting and illuminating the sensible world; Hsieh, writing from the poet's point of view and focusing attention on the poet's relation to the universe, uses the same images to represent two mental faculties, the rational and the intuitive, which he, following Chuang Tzu, calls respectively the "mind" (*hsin*) and the "spirit" (*shen*), the latter being the superior one which enables the former to perceive the reality underlying the sensible world. Ultimately, Hsieh's use of the image of the mirror is derived from the *Chuang Tzu,* in which it occurs three times as a description of the mind of the "perfect man" in its tranquility and impartiality towards all things,[160] and possibly also from the *Lao Tzu,* where, as I pointed out before, the expression *hsüan-lan,* which I translated as "mystic vision," could also be interpreted as "mysterious mirror" and a metaphor for the mind.[161] In the context of poetry, the mirror as a metaphor in Chinese criticism signifies mental "emptiness" (freedom from personal emotions and rational knowledge) and stillness rather than reflection of the material world.

In short, metaphysical theories stand somewhere between mimetic and expressive ones, and although these different kinds of theories do not have clear-cut distinctions but shade off into one another like the colors in the spectrum, as long as an area that does not overlap others is large enough to be recognized, we may give it a name of its own. To do otherwise would be like insisting on calling "green" either "yellow" or "blue."

On the other hand, in distinguishing metaphysical theories from other kinds I am not claiming that they embody absolutely unique concepts or ways of thinking. For one thing, the analogical mode of thinking that underlies Chinese metaphysical theories of literature can be easily paralleled in Western philosophical and literary thought: it is present in Platonism as well as neo-Platonism; it is basic to much medieval and Renaissance thought, as can be evidenced by the anagogical (in contradistinction to the allegorical and the tropological) interpretations of the Scriptures and of Dante's *Commedia*,[162] and by the belief in cosmic correspondences;[163] it is an important element of Swedenborgian and Romantic mysticism, and it is also perceptible in such diverse modern intellectual trends as symbolism, archetypal criticism, and structuralism. However, with the possible exception of symbolism, these systems of thought did not give rise to metaphysical theories of literature. The differences between Platonic or neo-Platonic mimetic theories and Chinese metaphysical ones have already been suggested above. The medieval anagogical interpretations constituted a method of practical criticism for a special class of literature; the Renaissance belief in correspondences did not lead to the formulation of a new theory of literature, although it may have reinforced the mimetic (such as in Sydney's *Apologie*); contemporary archetypal criticism and structuralism are concerned with methodologies rather than theories of literature, and when archetypal or structuralist critics do theorize about literature, their theories tend to be mimetic or technical. Only symbolism, influenced by mysticism, offers some interesting similarities as well as contrasts with Chinese metaphysical theories.

Metaphysical Theories Compared with Symbolist Ones

Several symbolist poet-critics, Baudelaire, Mallarmé, and Rimbaud, expressed ideas somewhat similar to those held by Chinese metaphysical poet-critics. For example, Baudelaire's concept of the earth with all its visibilia as a "correspondence of heaven" (*un correspondance du Ciel*), a concept he derived probably from Swedenborg,[164] is comparable to Liu Hsieh's of earthly "patterns" (*wen*) as parallels to heavenly ones. However, whereas Baudelaire sees Nature as "un temple où de vivants piliers/Laissent parfois sortir de confuses paroles,"[165] Liu speaks of "sounds issuing from the woods, which form melodies as do pipes and strings, or fountains striking rocks and evoking resonances as harmonious as those produced by jade chimes and bronze bells" as analogies to literature.[166] In Baudelaire's theory, Nature's secret and confused language awaits the poet's interpretation: "What is a poet, if not a translator, a decipherer?"[167] In Liu's theory, Nature needs no interpretation, and the poet spontaneously manifests the Tao of Nature and parallels its "patterns" with his own.

Furthermore, as pointed out by Marcel Raymond, Baudelaire perceives correspondences on three levels; between the data of the various senses, between the world of the senses and the poet's mind, and between the sensible world and the suprasensible.[168] Of these three levels of correspondences, the first does not involve any conception of poetry but suggests a mode of expression—that which employs synaesthetic imagery. The second implies an expressive concept of poetry rather than a metaphysical one (if Raymond is correct in interpreting Baudelaire's meaning with the words, "From the world of the senses the poet takes the material to forge a symbolic vision of himself or his dream; what he asks of the world of the senses is that it give him the means of expressing his soul").[169] Only the third may be said to be consonant with a metaphysical conception of poetry.

Much deeper affinities with Chinese metaphysical critics and poets are shown by Mallarmé, especially in some statements about poetry that he made in his later years. His letter to Henri Cazalis of 14 May 1867 already indicated his rejection of the expressive concept of poetry in favor of a somewhat metaphysical one:

> I am now impersonal and no longer the Stéphane you knew—but an aptitude of the spiritual universe for seeing and developing itself through what I was.[170]

Some eighteen years later, on 16 November 1885, in his *Autobiographie* addressed to Verlaine, he spoke of "the Orphic explanation of the Earth" as "the poet's sole duty and the literary game par excellence."[171] In the same year, when requested to define poetry, he replied:

> Poetry is the expression of the mysterious meaning of the

> aspects of existence through human language brought back to its essential rhythm: in this way it endows our sojourn with authenticity and constitutes the only spiritual task.[172]

This definition of poetry resembles Chinese metaphysical ones, being concerned with the poet's relation to the universe and its underlying principle.

Naturally, Mallarmé's theory of poetry differs in some ways from Chinese metaphysical ones. In the first place, his preoccupation with Beauty is not paralleled in Chinese theories. This preoccupation found repeated expressions in Mallarmé's letters. For instance, a letter to Cazalis written in May 1866 refers to three short poems which would be unprecedented, "all three for the glorification of Beauty,"[173] and another letter to the same correspondent written about two months later contains the words, "after having found nothingness, I found the Beautiful."[174] Again, in the letter of 14 May 1867 already referred to, Mallarmé reiterates, "I have made a long enough descent into Nothingness in order to be able to speak with certainty. There is nothing but Beauty—and it has only one perfect expression—Poetry."[175] From these statements one might conclude that Beauty was to Mallarmé what Tao was to the Chinese metaphysicals, or at least so it remained for most of his life, until he came to regard the interpretation of cosmic mysteries instead of the glorification of Beauty as the poet's supreme task. Another difference between him and his Chinese spiritual *confrères* is that whereas they thought of poetry as analogous or antecedent to religious enlightenment, he replaced religion with poetry.

In his conception of language Mallarmé also shows some resemblances to Chinese metaphysical critics. Just as Liu Hsieh believed that the prototype of the Chinese script was a manifestation of divine light and claimed, "the reason why words can arouse the world is that they are the *wen* of the Tao,"[176] so did Mallarmé believe in the magic power of words and in the poet's duty to "purify the dialect of the tribe" ("Donner un sens plus pur au mots de la tribu,"[177] as paraphrased by T. S. Eliot) and to restore to language its "essential rhythm." However, with regard to the paradoxical nature of language as the necessary but inadequate means of expressing the ineffable, Mallarmé's attitude differed (at least for most of his life) from the Chinese. This paradox, which the Chinese metaphysical critics and poets accepted with equanimity as an inevitable part of the human condition, was to Mallarmé a source of constant agony and induced in him a sense of impotency and impasse. It was only in his last years that he apparently accepted with good grace the indaequacy of language and the poet's foredoomed failure, as revealed by his remark to Camille Mauclair:

> But we are all failures, Mauclair! How can we be otherwise, when we measure our finiteness against infinity? We place our short life and feeble strength in the balance with an ideal which, by definition, cannot be attained.[178]

Against these words we may juxtapose the following from the *Chuang Tzu*:

> Our lives are finite but knowledge is infinite; to pursue the infinite with the finite is exhausting; to know this and yet still do so will lead to nothing but exhaustion.[179]

Ironically, this warning itself is an attempt to impart knowledge, just as Mallarmé's admission of "failure" is really an acceptance of the challenge of Art to attempt the impossible.

Although Mallarmé could not have known anything about Chinese metaphysical theories of literature, he apparently sensed a spiritual affinity with Chinese artists and poets, for as early as 1864 he wrote in "Las de l'amer repos":

> Je veux délaisser l'Art vorace d'un pays
> Cruel, et, souriant aux reproches viellis
> Que me font mes amis, le passé, le génie,
> Et ma lampe qui sait pourtant mon agonie,
> Imiter le Chinois au coeur limpide et fin
> De qui l'extase pure est de peindre la fin.[180]

One could go on to point out similarities between Mallarmé and Chinese metaphysical critics in their emphases on intuition over reason and on suggestion over description in writing poetry, but these are no longer strictly pertinent to the question of what poetry is.

As for Rimbaud, his concept of the poet as seer (which has been claimed to be the culmination of a long tradition),[181] bears only a superficial resemblance to the Chinese metaphysical concept, for he, together with Baudelaire and other Romantic and Symbolist poets like Novalis and Gérard de Nerval, is interested in delving into the unconscious, whereas the Chinese metaphysicals are not. Furthermore, the heightened state of consciousness, whether induced by drugs or other means, after which Baudelaire, Rimbaud, and other Western poets strove, is quite different from the state of consciousness that the Chinese poets aimed at. Rimbaud's famous "derangement of all the senses" (*dérèglement de tous les sens*)[182] is not at all the same as

Chaung Tzu's "mind's abstinence": the one seeks to descend into the unconscious through synaesthesia, the other to transcend the self-conscious through anaesthesia, on the sensuous level.

Metaphysical Theories Compared with a Phenomenological One

Considerations of space forbid me to discuss other Chinese and Western poets and critics who have written on the relation between poetry and mysticism (and in any case many interesting parallels on this subject have been pointed out by Ch'ien Chung-shu),[183] but I cannot refrain, even though this chapter may already seem inordinately long to the reader, from making a tentative comparison between Chinese metaphysical theories and a contemporary French phenomenological one, that of Mikel Dufrenne, with the awareness that other critics who have also been dubbed phenomenological may have views quite different from his. It goes without saying that it is not my intention to provide a complete and detailed survey or critique of Dufrenne's whole complex system of aesthetics, but only to draw attention to certain elements therein that exhibit remarkable affinities with Chinese metaphysical theories, as seen in three of his works, *Le Poétique* (1963), *Language and Philosophy* (1963), and above all *Phénoménologie de l'expérience esthétique* (first edition, 1953; second edition, 1967). These affinities will appear clearer after we have first realized what Dufrenne's theory, of art in general and poetry in particular, is not.

Dufrenne's theory is not a purely aesthetic (in the sense the word is used in this book) or affective one, for although in discussing the aesthetic object and aesthetic experience he proceeds from the spectator's or reader's point of view, he is not merely interested in how the artistic work affects the reader, but how the reader, through the work, discovers a world, which appears in the natural world but is not of it, and which he finds to be also his own world.[184] In Dufrenne's theory, the reader does not passively let himself be affected by the work; on the contrary, he actively participates in actualizing it. More than once Dufrenne insists that a poem truly exists only when perceived by the reader and consecrated by that perception, and that the aesthetic object needs the spectator in order to be recognized and completed.[185] This conception of the relation between the reader and the work is based on the phenomenological conception of the relation between the subject and the object as one of mutual implication.[186] Speaking of the "poetic state" (*état poétique*), a term that he borrowed from Valéry, Dufrenne describes it as a "mode of being of the subjectivity" which is however "suscitated by the being of the object" and which in turn "actualizes the intention that animates the object."[187] This dialectic relation between the reader and the work parallels that between the author and the world, so that we may say, in our terminology, that Dufrenne's interest in the reader's response to the work (phase 3 of the artistic process) finally leads back to the author's response to the universe (phase 1).

This interest in phase 1 does not render Dufrenne's theory a mimetic one, for he explicitly denies that art copies reality, because, he argues, there is no given reality in a previous perception which the aesthetic perception should equal; instead, it is with art that perception begins.[188] He asserts, "the relation between art and reality is not at all one suggested by an aesthetic realism, according to which art chooses arbitrarily to imitate reality, because reality expects nothing from it; on the contrary, reality expects something from art. . . . it expects its meaning to be spoken. Since art has for its mission the expression of this meaning . . . we should say that reality or nature wants art" (pp. 669–71; my translation). This idea that nature wants art will be considered further below, in comparison with Chinese metaphysical notions. Meanwhile, we should realize that Dufrenne's theory is not an expressive one either, for he rejects the concept of art as self-expression, but states that the artist is forced to create his work by a sense of mission, not by a desire for the simple pleasure of expressing himself (p. 674). Still less is Dufrenne's theory a pragmatic or technical or deterministic one. It seems, then, that his theory has more in common with metaphysical ones than any other kind. In fact, his *Phénoménologie de l'expérience esthétique* concludes with a section entitled "Perspectives métaphysiques" as part of his ontology of art, just as phenomenology itself eventually led to Sartre's phenomenological ontology.

We are now in a position to compare Dufrenne's theory with Chinese metaphysical ones. To begin with, just as Chinese metaphysical critics see both literature and Nature as manifestations of the Tao, Dufrenne sees both art and Nature as manifestations of a "Being of sense" (*un être du sens*), "sense" being identified with "Being," which is "anterior at once both to the object where it manifests itself and to the subject to whom it manifests itself" (p. 667; my translation). This concept of Being is comparable to the Taoist concept of Tao as the totality of all being. Furthermore, Dufrenne emphasizes that this "sense" or meaning of Being is in the principle of Nature and of man, not projected by man into Nature, so that man's mission (and the artist's in particular), is to witness it or speak it, not to invent it (p. 666). This idea is similar to the Chinese metaphysical one that the Tao is immanent in Nature and the writer's task is to manifest it, not to invent it. However, Dufrenne differs from the Chinese metaphysical critics in that he maintains that Nature *wants* its meaning to be revealed by art and therefore needs art, whereas the Chinese critics believe that the Tao is *naturally* manifested in literature, rather than that it wants to be manifested. Apart from this difference, which stems perhaps from the anthropocentrism that characterizes much Western thought, Dufrenne's statement that art "appears at the dawn of history as soon as man has passed beyond the stage of animality" (p. 671; my translation) recalls Liu Hsieh's and Hsiao T'ung's statements that literature (*wen*) originated together with the universe and that it appeared at the beginning of civilization.

Dufrenne's conception of the interrelations among the universe, the artist, and the work of art further resembles the Chinese metaphysical one in that he too conceives of the artist as neither consciously imitating Nature nor revealing its meaning in a purely unconscious and involuntary fashion. To him, there is no contradiction between the voluntary and the involuntary aspects of the artist's vocation, any more than there is between the artist's subjectivity and the truth of the world that he reveals (pp. 674–75). Following the tradition of Husserl, Heidegger, Sartre, and Marleau-Ponty, Dufrenne reaffirms the solidarity of the subject and the object, and the inseparability of noesis (consciousness or perception) from noema (the object of consciousness or perception), or of lived experience (*Erlebnis*) from the experienced world (*Lebenswelt*) (pp. 4–6, et passim, esp. p. 251), just as some Chinese metaphysical critics, as we have seen, affirm the solidarity of the "I" (*wo*) and "things" (*wu*), and the inseparability of "emotion" or "inner experience" (*ch'ing*) from "scene" or "external world" (*ching*). This affinity between Dufrenne and Chinese metaphysical critics springs from an underlying affinity between phenomenology and Chuang Tzu's Taoism, for just as Dufrenne derived his idea of the solidarity of the subject and the object from the phenomenological philosophers mentioned above, the Chinese critics derived theirs from Chuang Tzu, who remarked, "Heaven and earth were born together with me; the myriad things and I are one,"[189] and just as the phenomenologists resolved the subject-object dichotomy by positing a Being that transcends both, so did the Taoists resolve the same dichotomy by positing the Tao, which also transcends both Nature and man. And to say that the Tao transcends Nature is not to say that it is a transcendent entity existing above Nature, but only that it is not confined to any particular thing or class of things in Nature. Indeeed, Heidegger's description of Being could almost serve as one of the Tao:

> Being, as the basic theme of philosophy, is no class or genus of entities; yet it pertains to every entity. Its "universality" is to be sought higher up. Being and the structure of Being lie beyond every entity and every possible character which an entity may possess. *Being is the transcendens pure and simple.*[190]

It is only in this Heideggerian sense that we can speak of the Tao as being transcendent.

The belief in the solidarity of the subject and the object does not lead to the conclusion that artistic and literary works are totally devoid of individuality. Thus, just as Wang Shih-chen sees poetry as an embodiment of both the spirit (*shen*) of things and the poet's personal tone (*yün*), so does Dufrenne see art as both a revelation of the meaning of the world and a self-realization.[191] While denying that the artist is concerned with self-expression, Dufrenne yet declares:

> The less expressive his [the artist's] language—that is to say, the more reticent, more discreet, more impersonal—the better he expresses himself. The less he speaks of himself, the more he reveals of himself. Of what does he speak then? He speaks of the world; and we learn to know him in terms of the world which he talks about and which is one possible type of world among others.[192]

From these and other similar remarks it is evident that Dufrenne, like Wang, is interested in the poet's individual mode of perceiving the world, not in his historical existence.

Some readers may object to my comparison of phenomenological theories to Chinese metaphysical ones on the ground that phenomenologists are metaphysically neutral while metaphysical critics make certain explicit or implicit metaphysical assumptions. To such an objection I would reply that, on the one hand, a phenomenological critic like Dufrenne does make some metaphysical assertions, although not claiming these as absolute truths, and that, on the other, Chuang Tzu's philosophy, which influenced most Chinese metaphysical theories, is also metaphysically neutral, as can be seen from his well-known parable of the dream of the butterfly:

> Once Chuang Chou dreamt of being a butterfly, happily fluttering as a butterfly. Was he/it telling himself/itself how contented he/it was? He/it did not know he/it was Chou. Suddenly he awoke, and there he was, Chou. Was it the butterfly that dreamt of being Chou, or was it Chou that dreamt of being the butterfly—who knows? Between Chou and the butterfly there

> necessarily is a distinction [and yet one does not know which is which]. This is called "transforming with things."[193]

Is Chuang Tzu not "bracketing" the world in Husserl's sense?[194] For he is neither affirming nor denying the reality of either himself or the butterfly, but suspending judgment on both.

This suspension of judgement is called by Husserl ἐποχή (*epoché* or *epokhe*, "abstention"),[195] a term that reminds one of Chuang Tzu's "mind's abstinence" (*hsin-chai*), which we have encountered earlier. There is more than verbal coincidence between these two terms, for both involve the suspension of the "natural standpoint" based on sense-perception, and both aim at an intuitive grasp of the essence (*shen* or *eidos*) of things. The main difference between Husserl and Chuang Tzu seems to be that whereas Husserl's "transcendental-phenomenological reduction" (which is sometimes synonymous with the *epoché*)[196] and "eidetic reduction"[197] are rather deliberate and methodical, Chuang Tzu's "listening with the *ch'i*" is mystical. In spite of this difference, both the phenomenologists and the Taoists, while not relying on primordial intuition, aim at what we may call a "second intuition" achieved after the discarding of empirical knowledge, or a rediscovery of the prereflective and preconceptual state of consciousness in which there is no distinction between the subject and the object. According to Merleau-Ponty, "Husserl's essences are destined to bring back all the living relationships of experience, as the fisherman's net draws from the depths of the ocean quivering fish and seaweed."[198] This is the same metaphor used by Chuang Tzu in the remark, "One who has caught the fish can forget the trammel . . . one who has caught the meaning can forget the words." Is Chuang Tzu's "meaning" not the same kind of meaning of which Mearleau-Ponty speaks, when he remarks, "In the silence of primary consciousness can be seen not only what words mean, but also what things mean: the core of primary meaning round which the acts of naming and expression take shape"?[199]

This brings us back to the paradox of language, which can now be rephrased this way: language is the means by which the poet seeks to convey the preconceptual and therefore prelingual state of consciousness in which the subject and the object, the "I" and the "world," are one, yet as soon as he speaks, he is creating a separation. Thus, Merleau-Ponty states, "It is the office of language to cause essences to exist in a state of separation which is in fact merely apparent,"[200] and Dufrenne likewise remarks, "As soon as man speaks, he is separated," and "The language that binds man to the world is also the language that separatês him."[201] Anticipating both, Chuang Tzu, as soon as he has made (or perhaps quoted) the remark that "the myriad things and I are one," goes on to say,

> Since we are already one, how can I say a word about it? Yet since I have already called it "one," how can I say I have not said a word? "One" and "word" make two; two and one make three. Going on from here, not even a skilled arithmetician could get to the end, let alone an ordinary man.[202]

I may seem to have let Chuang Tzu have the last word every time, but actually he would have been the first to agree with the wise last words with which Dufrenne ends his monumental *Phénoménologie de l'expérience esthétique*: "Perhaps the last word is that there is no last word."[203]

3

Deterministic and Expressive Theories

The Deterministic Concept and Its Development

Some Chinese theories of literature expound the concept of literature as an unconscious and inevitable reflection or revelation of contemporary political and social realities. This deterministic concept is primarily focused on the relation between the artistic universe and the writer, or phase 1 of the artistic process, like the metaphysical and the mimetic concepts, but it differs from the former in that it identifies the universe with human society instead of the cosmic Tao, and from the latter in that it defines the writer's relation to the universe as one of unconscious revelation instead of conscious imitation. Although the deterministic concept is not one that has been greatly elaborated in Chinese literary criticism, it is sufficiently important and distinctive to merit a brief treatment before we turn our attention to expressive theories.

The deterministic concept of literature was closely related to a similar concept of music, as can be witnessed by the following episode recorded in the chronicle, the *Tso-chuan,* for the year 543 B.C. In that year, it is said, Prince Chi-tsa of the state of Wu, while on a friendly mission to the Court of Lu (the native state of Confucius), listened to songs from the *Book of Poetry* and, with uncanny infallibility, identified the period and geographical origin of each song according to the moral character and political sentiments it supposedly expressed.[1] Skeptical as we may choose to be about the credibility of this story, it illustrates well the deterministic concept of poetry, in both its musical and literary aspects.

Elements of determinism are also present in the "Record of Music," which, as we have seen, forms part of the *Book of Rites.* According to this work, music reflects the political conditions of the country:

> The music of a well-governed world is peaceful and happy, its government being harmonious; the music of a disorderly world is plaintive and angry, its government being perverse; the music of a vanquished country is sad and nostalgic, its people being distressed.[2]

These same statements appear in the so-called *Major Preface* (*Ta-hsü*) to the *Book of Poetry*, of controversial date and authorship. Formerly attributed to Confucius's disciple Pu Shang (also known by his courtesy name Tzu-hsia, 507–400 B.C.), it is now believed by many scholars to be by Wei Hung (first century A.D.).[3] If we accepted the later date, it would then seem that the author took the words from the "Record of Music" and applied them to poetry without any change, since the word "music" (*yin*) can refer to poetry as well. The tremendous influence that the *Major Preface* exerted on subsequent literary thought—an influence that we shall consider again later in the chapter—ensured the perpetuation of the deterministic concept contained in the statements quoted above, so much so that the expression "the music of a vanquished country" has remained a stock phrase with which to brand certain kinds of literature that one does not approve.

The *Major Preface* further asserts that poetry changes as society changes. Before quoting the relevant remarks, I should first explain that traditionally the *Book of Poetry* is divided into three main sections, called "Airs" (*Feng*, literally "wind," figuratively "moral influence," "customs," and "admonition"); "Odes" (*Ya*, "elegance" or "rectitude," subdivided into *Ta-ya*, or "Major Odes," and *Hsiao-ya* or "Minor Odes," probably with reference to different types of music, though the terms have been interpreted in other ways); and "Hymns" (*Sung*, which originally referred to dancing that accompanied the ritual hymns).[4] After mentioning these three kinds of poetry, together with three modes of expression, as the "Six Principles" (*Liu-yi*) of the *Book of Poetry*, the *Preface* then states:

> By the time the Kingly Way had declined, and propriety and rightness had been abandoned, [the principle of] government by moral instruction was lost and each state followed a different system of government, each family a different custom. Thereupon the "Changed Airs" and "Changed Odes" arose.[5]

Since the word "changed" (*pien*) often connotes deviation from the norm and even disaster, the statement implies that abnormal times produce abnormal literature, and that it is impossible to produce normal or proper (*cheng*) literature in a time of crisis.

These ideas were developed by the Confucian scholar Cheng Hsüan (127–200) in his *Chronological Introduction to the Book of Poetry* (*Shih-p'u-hsü*), in which he differentiates the "Proper Canon" (*cheng-ching*) from the "Changed Airs" and "Changed Odes" on a chronological basis, the former comprising poetry written under the early, virtuous kings of the Chou dynasty, the latter produced after the decline of the "Kingly Way" and under tyrannical or weak kings.[6] In this way, the contrast between what is considered "proper" (*cheng*, which may also be translated as "normal" or "orthodox") and what is considered "changed" (*pien*, which may also be rendered "abnormal" or "deviating"), both in society and in literature, a contrast implied in the *Major Preface*, is made explicit, and the belief that it is the normality or abnormality of society that determines the normality or abnormality of literature is also clearly shown.

As pointed out by Chu Tzu-ch'ing (1898–1948), from one of whose works much of the material on deterministic theories in the present book is taken, Cheng Hsüan was probably influenced by the theory of "poetic omens" (*shih-yao*) adumbrated by the Confucian scholar Liu Hsiang (77–6 B.C.) and expanded by the historian Pan Ku (A.D. 32–92).[7] According to this theory, when the ruler is tyrannical and the subjects are too frightened to air their grievances, then popular songs and ballads will appear to portend evil, and these are called "poetic omens." The belief in omens was of course not confined to China; one remembers, for instance, Shakespeare's description of the strange omens that preceded Julius Caesar's assassination,[8] but it seems a peculiarly Chinese belief that omens (as distinct from satires) can take the form of anonymous folk songs (as distinct from divine oracles), and Chinese historical works are full of examples of "poetic omens" that augured ill and reflected the abnormality of the times. These may be regarded as a specific illustration of the deterministic concept of poetry.

Cheng Hsüan even implicitly attributed a deterministic conception of poetry to Confucius, when he interpreted the Sage's remark that the *Book of Poetry* "can be used to observe [*kuan*]" as "to observe the rise and decline of moral customs."[9] What Confucius meant by this laconic and ambiguous remark will be discussed in chapter 6. For the present, we shall simply take Cheng's interpretation as another manifestation of his own deterministic conception of poetry.

In the writings of later critics, Cheng's terms "proper" (*cheng*) and "changed" (*pien*) generally assumed meanings different from those he intended, and came to refer to *literary* orthodoxy and innovations respectively.[10] As such, these terms are no longer relevant to the deterministic concept of literature but pertain to concepts of literary history. An exception occurs in the writings of the early Ch'ing critic Wang Wan (1624–90), who applied Cheng Hsüan's theory of "proper" and "changed" poetry to the poetry of the T'ang dynasty (618–907), seeing a close correspondence between the rise and fall of the dynasty and the history of its poetry. Moreover, Wang Wan eloquently expounds his deterministic theory:

> At the height [of the T'ang dynasty], the ruler above exerted his energies, the ministers and officials below hastened about their tasks and spoke without reserve; the administration was simple and punishments were few; the atmosphere among the people was harmonious and peaceful. Therefore, what issued forth in poetry was generally leisurely and refined. Readers regard [such poetry] as "proper" but the authors themselves did not know it was "proper." By the time [the dynasty] declined, then at Court there were factional strifes and in the country military struggles; the administration was complex and punishments were severe; the atmosphere among the people was sorrowful and bitter. Therefore, what issued forth [in poetry] was mostly sad, nostalgic, and urgent. At the very end, [poetry] became superficial and extravagant. Even though there were some virtuous and worthy gentlemen who broadened their learning and lifted up their spirits to seek the florescence of literature, ultimately they could not reach their predecessors. Readers regard [such poetry] as "changed" but the authors themselves did not know it was "changed." Therefore, on the forms assumed by "proper" and "changed" poetry depends the order or disorder of the state; on the growth or diminution of talents depends the rise or decline of moral customs.[11]

This is perhaps the clearest exposition to be found in Chinese literary criticism of the theory that literature is an unconscious revelation of contemporary political and social conditions.

The deterministic concept is often allied to the pragmatic, for it is easy to conclude, from the premise that literature inevitably reflects the society in which it is produced, that it can be used as a historical "mirror" from which practical lessons can be learned. It is also easy to shift from the deterministic position that a writer, willy-nilly, reveals contemporary social and political realities, to the pragmatic one that he *should* consciously do so. However, a distinction exists between the two in basic orientation, the one being focused on phase 1 of the artistic process, the other on phase 4.

It is to be expected that modern critics who are committed to historical determinism will accept the deterministic concept of literature. Thus, for instance, Kuo Shao-yü, in his *History of Chinese Classical Literary Theories and Criticism* (*Chung-kuo ku-tien wen-hsüeh li-lun p'i-p'ing shih*) published in 1959, which is a partial recension of his earlier *History of Chinese Literary Criticism* (*Chung-kuo wen-hsüeh p'i-p'ing shih*, first published in 1948 and revised in 1956), quoted with approval the statements in the *Major Preface* about poetry reflecting political conditions and Cheng Hsüan's interpretation of Confucius's remark that poetry "can be used to observe" as expressions of the "spirit of realism."[12]

Early Expressive Theories: Primitivism

When we turn to Chinese expressive theories, which are primarily focused on the relation between the writer and the literary work, or phase 2 of the artistic process, we find that the object of expression is variously identified with universal human emotions, or personal nature, or individual genius or sensibility, or moral character.

The theory that literature, especially poetry, is a spontaneous expression of universal human emotions and that this actually accounted for the genesis of poetry in antiquity may be called primitivism,[13] origins of which are perceptible in the etymology of the word *shih* 詩 (reconstructed Archaic[14] pronunciation *śi ə g*), the nearest Chinese equivalent to "poetry." This word first appeared in the *Book of Poetry*, in three different poems that date from perhaps the eleventh century to the eighth century B.C.[15] However, the earliest known written forms of the word are in the so-called Small Seal (*Hsiao-chuan*) script of the third century B.C., as recorded in Hsü Shen's *Explanations of Simple and Compound Characters*: 詩 or 𧦅 , the latter being described as an ancient simplified form.[16] In both forms, the part on the left is the "radical" or "signific," which indicates the class of things to which the referent of the word belongs; that on the right is supposedly the "phonetic," which indicates the pronunciation, but may be semantically relevant as well. In the first form, the signific *yen* 言 (modern form 言) means "speech" or "word," and the phonetic *ssu* 寺 (Archaic pronunciation *dzi ə g*; modern written from 寺) now usually means "temple" but in ancient times meant "court" or "attendant." In the second form, the signific is the same *yen*, written differently, and the phonetic is *chih* 之 (Archaic pronunciation *t̂i ə g*), the prototype of both *chih* 㞢 (which means, among other things, "to go") and *chih* 止 (which means "to stop"). As several modern scholars have demonstrated, the characters for *shih* and *ssu* were at one time interchangeable, both being derived from *chih* 㞢 , which was originally written 屮 , a pictogram representing a foot.[17] Thus, the whole composite phonogram[18] (a composite character of which one part indicates the sense and another the pronunciation) for *shih* ("poetry") is seen to consist of *yen* ("word") plus *ssu* ("attendant") or *chih* ("go/stop"), with etymological associations with "foot." The late Ch'en Shih-hsiang suggested that the "syno-antonym" (a word he coined) *chih*, meaning both "to go" and "to stop," here refers to dancing and rhythm;[19] and Chow Tse-tsung has suggested, among a wealth of other suggestions, that *ssu-jen* ("attendant-person") was a disfigured attendant who may have been the same as a *shih-jen* ("poetry-person" or "poet") and who performed such functions as chanting poetry and dancing at ritual ceremonies.[20] Both suggestions are plausible in view of our knowledge of ancient Chinese culture and early Chinese accounts of the genesis of poetry. If we accept the first suggestion, the earliest Chinese conception of poetry will appear to be a primitivistic one: that poetry is a spontaneous expression of emotion in words accompanied with music and dancing. If we accept the second suggestion, this conception will then seem to be partly pragmatic as well, since the ritual ceremonies presumably served some practical purpose.

It has also been suggested that in the composite phonogram for *shih*, the phonetic *ssu* or *chih* was a phonetic loan for *chih* 志 (Archaic pronunciation *t̂iəg*; modern written form 志),[21] which is itself a composite phonogram consisting of the phonetic *chih* 㞢 and the signific *hsin* 心 (modern form 心 , meaning "heart" or "mind"). Traditionally, the word *chih* 志 is interpreted as "where the heart goes" (i.e., heart's wish, or emotional purport) or "where the mind goes" (i.e., mind's intent, will, or moral purpose), though a modern scholar, Wen Yi-to (1899–1946), interpreted it as "what stops or stays in the heart or mind" and discerned three meanings derived from this basic one: "to remember," "to record," and "to cherish [emotion] in the heart."[22] The implications of some of these different interpretations of *chih* for theories of poetry will be discussed later; for the present, suffice it to say that *shih* ("poetry") and *chih* ("heart's wish/mind's intent") were cognate words if not the same word,[23] and that this implies a primitivistic conception of poetry in ancient China.

Further glimpses of the primitivistic concept of poetry can be obtained from the *Book of Poetry*, for though the poets (anonymous for the most part) of this anthology were of course not literary theorists, they sometimes announced their intentions in composing their poems. One poem, for instance, ends with the lines:

> I made this fine song
> To express fully my restless grief.[24]

And another ends:

> A gentleman made this song
> To express his sorrows.[25]

Granted that in these lines the word "song" (*ko*) is used rather than "poem" (*shih*), and further that there may have existed a distinction between the two words *ko* and *shih*, the one referring to poetry when sung and the other to poetry when written down,[26] the underlying conception of poetry, whether sung or written, remains a primitivistic one, not to mention the fact that both words appear side by side in at least one poem in the *Book of Poetry*.[27]

The primitivistic concept of poetry in ancient China crystallized in the statement, *shih yen chih*, which means, literally, "Poetry verbalizes heart's-wish/mind's-intent," and may be more freely translated as "Poetry expresses in words the intent of the heart [or mind]." Traditionally, the *locus classicus* of this laconic and possibly tautological definition of poetry (tautological if the character *shih* indeed consisted of *yen* or "word" plus *chih* or "intent") is a passage in the *Book of Documents*, where the following words are attributed to the legendary sage Emperor Shun (traditional dates 2255–2208 B.C.):

> Poetry expresses in words the intent of the heart [or mind], songs prolong the words in chanting, notes follow the chanting, and pitch-pipes harmonize with the notes.[28]

Although the date of this part of the *Book of Documents* is a matter of dispute among modern scholars, some of whom believe it to be as late as the second century B.C.,[29] the concept of poetry expressed therein was apparently current in the fourth century B.C. and possibly much earlier, since statements almost identical with the first one in the above passage occur in the *Tso-chuan* with reference to an event that took place in 546 B.C., and in the *Chuang Tzu*.[30]

The most famous elaboration of the formula "Poetry expresses intent" is found in the *Major Preface* to the *Book of Poetry*, which, as already mentioned, was formerly attributed to Confucius's disciple Pu Shang, but is now generally believed to be by Wei Hung of the first century A.D.[31] Even if we accept the latter (and later) date, we may still regard the *Preface* as expressing a view of poetry with a long tradition. The *Preface* begins:

> Poetry is where the intent of the heart [or mind] goes. Lying in the heart [or mind], it is "intent"; when uttered in words, it is "poetry." When an emotion stirs inside, one expresses it in words; fiinding this inadequate, one sighs over it; not content with this, one sings it in poetry; still not satisfied, one unconsciously dances with one's hands and feet.[32]

Although the word *chih* ("intent") can be understood in different ways, and although this passage is followed by expressions of other views, it clearly emphasizes the spontaneous expression of emotion and may be regarded as a classic illustration of the primitivistic conception of poetry.

A very similar passage appears in the "Record of Music," which may have been the source of the *Preface*,[33] but the latter is much better-known and has exerted far greater influence on subsequent critical thinking.

The statement *shih yen chih* or "Poetry expresses intent" and its variation as found in the *Preface* have been quoted ad nauseam throughout the centuries and given rise to different theories in accordance with the critic's understanding of the word *chih*, those critics who understood it as "heart's wish" or "emotional purport" developing expressive theories and those who understood it as "mind's intent" or "moral purpose" often combining the expressive concept with the pragmatic.

THE RISE OF INDIVIDUALISM

Beginning with Ts'ao P'i's "Discourse on Literature," expressive theories tended towards individualism, placing more emphasis on individual personality than universal human emotions. We have already encountered Ts'ao P'i's concept of *ch'i* as individual genius based on temperament.[34] Let us now examine more closely the significance and possible sources of this concept. Some modern scholars have assumed that Ts'ao derived his concept of *ch'i* from that of Mencius, but actually there are several differences between the two. Whereas Mencius describes *ch'i* as the result of an accumulation of rightness,[35] Ts'ao's concept of *ch'i* has no moral implications; and whereas Mencius asserts that *ch'i* can be nourished and that it is commanded by the will (*chih*),[36] Ts'ao maintains that it cannot be acquired and implies that it is not subject to the control of the will. In view of these differences, and the known fact that Ts'ao P'i was inclined towards Taoism, it seems likely that he derived his concept of *ch'i* not from the *Mencius* but from other philosophical works, such as the eclectic *Kuan Tzu* (of which the putative author is the statesman Kuan Chung, d. 645 B.C., but which was probably compiled in the fourth century B.C.) and the Taoist *Huai-nan Tzu* (compiled under Liu An, Prince of Huai-nan, d. 122 B.C.).

According to the *Kuan Tzu*, *ch'i* is the force or principle that gives life to everything, and the quintessence of the *ch'i*, called *ching*, becomes spirits and gods when it is freely circulating in the universe, and makes a man a sage when it is lodged in his mind.[37] Furthermore, *ch'i* is the source of thought and knowledge:

> What we call "quintessence" [*ching*] is the finest essence of the vital force [*ch'i*]. When the vital force flows freely, then there is life; when there is life, then there is thought; when there is thought, then there is knowledge; when there is knowledge, then there is an end.[38]

From this it is not a far cry to think of literature, which involves thought and knowledge, as an expression of the *ch'i*, redefined as individual genius based on the writer's temperament, which in turn is based on the amount and kind of vital force (*ch'i*) in his mental and physical constitution.

Turning to the *Huai-nan Tzu*, we find the word *ch'i* used in two different but related senses. In one chapter, *ch'i* refers to the primordial vital force, of which the pure and light kind rose and became Heaven and the heavy and impure kind condensed and formed Earth.[39] Though the subject is cosmogony and not literature, it is possible that this passage inspired Ts'ao P'i to draw a similar distinction between two kinds of genius. In another chapter, *ch'i* denotes vital spirits in a person:

> Blood and vital spirits [*ch'i*] are the flowers of Man, and the five viscera are his quintessence [*ching*]. Now, if the blood and vital spirits can be concentrated within the five viscera and not dissipated outside, then one's bosom will be full [of vitality] and one's desires will become fewer. If so, then one's hearing and eyesight will be clear and far-reaching. This is called "clarity" [of perception]. If the five viscera can be controlled by the mind [*hsin*] and not turn against it, then one's growing will [*chih*] can prevail and one's action will not be perverse. If so, then one's quintessential spirit [*ching-shen*] will flourish and one's vital spirits [*ch'i*] will not disperse.[40]

This psycho-physiological concept of *ch'i*, which somewhat resembles the Renaissance concept of "spirits" with its related concepts of "humors" and "complexions,"[41] was quite well known in China in the first two centuries of the Christian era, and was mentioned by one writer in discussing calligraphy,[42] but Ts'ao P'i was the first to apply it to literature. In so doing he made two significant modifications. First, he conceived the difference in *ch'i* between individuals to be not only quantitative but also qualitative, for he remarked that the *ch'i* could be pure [or light] or impure [or heavy]; secondly, he rejected the idea (shared by Mencius and the compilers of the *Huai-nan Tzu*) that the *ch'i* is subject to the control of the will (*chih*). The resultant theory of literature emphasizes individuality and its spontaneous expression, uncontrolled by conscious will.

It may also be pointed out that Ts'ao P'i's idea that literary genius cannot be passed on even from father to son is ultimately derived from Chuang Tzu's famous parable about the wheelwright who said he could not teach his son how to make a wheel even though he himself knew exactly how,[43] though here again Ts'ao was not the first to echo Chuang Tzu but was the first to apply the idea to literature.[44]

Important contributions to the development of expressive theories were made by Lu Chi in his *Exposition on Literature,* which, as mentioned in chapter 2, also contains metaphysical ideas. We shall now direct our attention to Lu's expressive views. In the first place, to the idea that literature is a spontaneous expression of emotions he adds the more sophisticated one that the emotions thus expressed are the results of the writer's sensitive response to Nature:

> Following the four seasons, [the writer] sighs
> over the passage of time;
> As he observes the myriad things, his thoughts
> rise in profusion.
> He laments the fallen leaves in stern autumn,
> And rejoices over the tender twigs in fragrant spring.[45]

This concept of the writer's relation to Nature differs from the metaphysical in that it sees the writer as reacting emotionally to external stimuli instead of seeking to identify intuitively with the cosmic Tao.

Secondly, Lu Chi does not consider emotion to be the only substance of literature, for though he asserts, as we have seen, that "poetry traces emotions and should be exquisite as fine patterned silk,"[46] he does so while enumerating ten literary genres, each with its own function and appropriate style. Moreover, in other parts of the *Exposition on Literature,* he repeatedly emphasizes *li,* which covers a range of meanings including "reason," "principles of things," and "order." Thus, even though the expression *shih yüan ch'ing* (which is here translated as "Poetry traces emotions" but can also be interpreted as "Poetry originates from emotions") has been singled out as a catchword and raised to the same level of importance as the earlier formulation *shih yen chih* ("Poetry expresses intent"),[47] Lu Chi's conception of literature is in fact not exclusively emotive.

詩原情

Furthermore, he describes writing as not only an expressive act but also a creative one:

> Tax Non-being to demand Being,
> Knock on silence to seek sound;
> Contain what is endless within a foot of
> white silk;

Utter what is boundless from the square-inch
of the heart.[48]

These lines contain in rudimentary form the concept of literature as creation and that of the literary work as "heterocosm,"[49] but Lu Chi did not develop them much further, probably because of the absence in traditional Chinese philosophy of the concept of a personal Creator, with whom the writer could be compared.

Perhaps Lu Chi's most remarkable critical insight is shown in the passage on inspiration:

As for the encounter with inspiration,
The law governing its flow or obstruction—
When it comes, it cannot be checked;
When it goes, it cannot be stopped.
Sometimes it hides itself like light vanishing;
Sometimes it stirs like sound arising.
When the natural trigger is fast and sharp,
What confusion will not be put in order?
Gusts of thought issue forth from the breast,
Fountains of words flow from the lips and teeth;
Luxuriant profusion and powerful splendor
Are captured by the writing brush and white silk;
Words, brilliantly shining, innundate the eye;
Music, richly sounding, fills the ear.
But when the six emotions run sluggish,[50]
When the will strives forward but the spirit delays,[51]
Then [the mind] is unfeeling like a withered tree
And empty like a dried-up stream;
Though one may concentrate one's soul to search
the mysteries
And lift up one's spirits to seek by oneself,
Order, lying in the dark, becomes even more submerged;
Thoughts, obstinately recalcitrant, refuse to be
drawn out.
Therefore, sometimes one may exhaust one's feelings
but achieve regrettable results;
At other times one may follow one's ideas freely yet
commit few faults.
Even though this matter rests with myself,
It is not within my power to control it.
Thus, often I stroke my empty bosom and sigh,
For I have not understood the causes of its ebb and flow.[52]

This eloquent passage speaks for itself and hardly needs exegesis.

Both Ts'ao P'i's and Lu Chi's ideas were developed or modified by Liu Hsieh, whom we have discussed at some length as a leading exponent of the metaphysical concept of literature. We shall defer consideration of the question how far Liu succeeded in synthesizing the metaphysical concept with the expressive (and indeed other concepts as well) until the final chapter; nor shall we discuss his expressive views related to literary theories, but concern ourselves only with such of his expressive views as belong to the level of theory of literature.

Liu Hsieh postulates the expressive concept of literature at the beginning of the chapter entitled "Style and Personality" (*T'i-hsing*):

> When emotion moves and is given shape by words, when reason issues forth and is revealed in writing, this is [a process of] following the hidden to reach the manifest, originating from the internal to seek its external correspondence.[53]

We notice that, like Lu Chi, Liu does not confine literary expression to emotion alone, but places emotion and reason side by side.

In another chapter, "Emotion and Ornamentation" (*Ch'ing-ts'ai*), he again lays equal emphasis on emotion and reason:

> Emotion is the warp of literature, and diction is the woof of reason. It is only when the warp is straight that the woof can be completed; only when reason is established that diction can be fluent. This is the basic source of writing.[54]

As a matter of fact, though he frequently mentions "emotion" (*ch'ing*) throughout *The Literary Mind*, the word "reason" (*li*) occurs with even greater frequency. Moreover, *ch'ing* itself does not always mean "emotion" but sometimes denotes the prevailing condition or basic nature of a thing (a common enough usage). For instance, when he quotes from the *Huai-nan Tzu* the remark that when a man plants an orchid it will not have fragrance, he explains, "This is because he does not have its nature [*ch'ing*]."[55] (The orchid being supposedly feminine by nature, only when planted by a woman, so the saying goes, will it be fragrant.) Here, and in other passages, the word *ch'ing* is really synonymous with *hsing* (which is generally translated as "nature," and when referring to personal nature may also be translated as "personality"). Indeed, Liu Hsieh often uses the two words together as a disyllabic compound, either *hsing-ch'ing* or *ch'ing-hsing*, signifying "personal nature" rather than "emotion *and* personal nature."

With regard to the writer's response to Nature, Liu Hsieh expresses views similar to Lu Chi's. In one passage he writes,

> Man is endowed with seven emotions, which are moved in response to objects. It is only natural to be moved by objects and sing one's heart's intent.[56]

Here he appears to be following the *Major Preface* to the *Book of Poetry* in not making a distinction between "emotion" (*ch'ing*) and "heart's intent" (*chih*), and following Lu Chi in thinking that emotions arise in response to external objects. In two other passages he reiterates, "Emotion is aroused by objects. . . . objects are viewed with emotion,"[57] and again, "Emotion changes because of objects, and words issue forth because of emotion."[58]

When it comes to individual genius, Liu's ideas are more complicated than those of his predecessors. We have seen, in chapter 2, his ideas that the spirit or intuition (*shen*) is controlled by the vital force (*ch'i*) and the will (*chih*) and that objects are perceived by the ear and the eye, the workings of which are controlled by language.[59] These ideas, which concern perception, may be diagrammatically represented this way:

PERCEPTION

Vital force (*ch'i*), Will (*chih*) → Spirit or Intuition (*shen*) → Objects

Language ↓ → Senses → Objects

As for the process of expression, the following two passages from the "Style and Personality" chapter of *The Literary Mind* are of great importance:

> Talent [*ts'ai*] may be ordinary or outstanding, the vital force [*ch'i*] may be strong or gentle, learning [*hsüeh*] may be superficial or profound, practice [*hsi*] may be refined or vulgar: all these are what one's personality [*ch'ing-hsing*] has smelted or what gradual cultivation [*t'ao-jan*, literally "moulding and dyeing"] has crystallized.[60]
>
> . . . .
>
> The strength of talent [*ts'ai*] dwells within, and originates from the blood and vital force [*ch'i*]; the vital force is what substantiates the will [*chih*], and the will is what determines lan-

guage. The utterance of [verbal] flowers is due to nothing but personality [*ch'ing-hsing*].[61]

Combining the ideas from the above two passages, we may illustrate them by the following diagram:

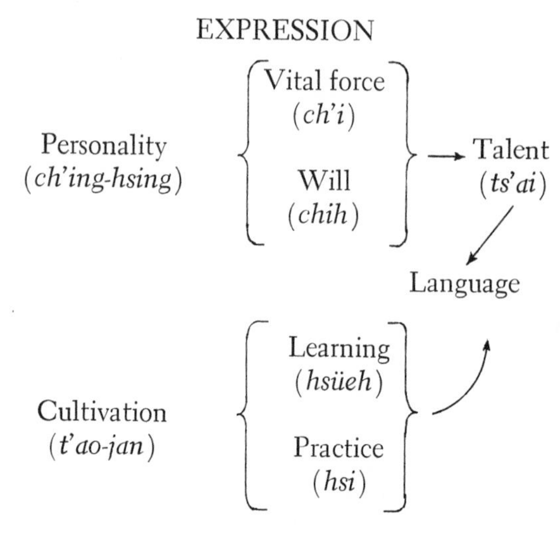

When we compare the two diagrams, we discover that "spirit" (*shen*) in perception corresponds to "talent" (*ts'ai*) in expression; in other words, the former refers to the intuitive faculty of perception and the latter to the intuitive power of expression, both of which Liu conceives of as being controlled by the will and the vital force. In this he seems to have been influenced by Mencius and differs from Ts'ao P'i and Lu Chi. He further follows Mencius and differs from Ts'ao in thinking that the vital force can be cultivated, for he has a chapter called "Yang-ch'i" or "Nourishing the Vital Force," in which he advises writers on how to conserve the *ch'i* and not overtax it. However, he agrees with Ts'ao that talent or genius (which he calls *ts'ai* and Ts'ao calls *ch'i*) differs from one writer to another, being part of each individual's nature.

Incidentally, Liu's remark that the vital force may be strong or gentle apparently influenced Yao Nai in formulating his theory of two kinds of beauty in literature, but Liu is referring to the writer's personality while Yao is concerned with aesthetic qualities in writing.[62]

Liu Hsieh's contemporary Chung Hung (*fl.* 483–513) also affirms the expressive concept of poetry, at the beginning of the preface to his *Classes of Poetry* (*Shih-p'in*, completed after 513):[63] "The vital force [*ch'i*] stirs objects, and objects move people; hence one's nature is agitated, and this is embodied in dancing and singing."[64] Here, *ch'i* refers to the vital force in Nature, not such force in an individual, and the idea that poets respond emotionally to external objects and then express such response in poetry agrees with Lu Chi's and Liu Hsieh's. Although the statement just quoted is followed by others that express metaphysical and pragmatic views, the fact that the expressive concept is mentioned first suggests that it was central to Chung Hung's critical thinking. However, he was mainly concerned with practical criticism and literary history and contributed little to general theories of literature.

Eclipse of Expressive Theories

For the next millennium, the expressive concept of literature was usually subordinated to the pragmatic. For example, the early T'ang historiographer Yao Ssu-lien (d. 637) in the preface to the "Biographies of the Literati" section of the *History of the Ch'en* (*Ch'en shu*) praised writers with these words: "With regard to great things, they composed charters and edicts in classical style to assist the Kingly Way; with regard to small things, the principles of their literary works are clear and correct, expressing their personal natures."[65] The compound here translated as "personal nature," *hsing-ling*, had previously been used by Liu Hsieh to denote either the spiritual powers of Nature or such powers when endowed in man,[66] but Yao used it, I think, as a synonym for *hsing-ch'ing*. We shall see below how the term *hsing-ling* acquired new significance in later expressive theories.

Yao Ssu-lien apparently thought that the expression of one's personal nature was irrelevant to morality, for he quoted his father Yao Ch'a's words at the end of the "Biographies of the Literati" section of the *History of the Liang* (*Liang shu*):

> Emperor Wen of Wei [Ts'ao P'i] remarked, "Literary men, ancient and modern, have seldom been able to keep their reputations and integrity intact." Why is this so? Now, literature is what miraculously expresses one's personal nature, and uniquely draws forth what lies in one's bosom. [Literary men] are apt to despise their peers, and are thus bound to reveal their arrogance. In major cases, they offend lords and princes; in minor ones, they insult their friends and associates. This is what causes them to bring resentment and incur blame.[67]

Yao obviously regarded the expression of personal natures as less important than assisting government, although he anticipated some later expressive theories of an extremely individualistic and antimoralistic kind by separating moral character from a writer's works.

In contrast, the Sung neo-Confucian philosopher Shao Yung (1011–77) subjected the expressive concept of poetry to a moral interpretation. In the preface to his own collected poems, Shao quotes the familiar words from the *Major Preface* to the *Book of Poetry* and then adds, "When one cherishes thoughts about the times, this is called 'intent' [*chih*]; when one is moved by objects, this is called 'emotion' [*ch'ing*]."[68] Unlike the author of the *Major Preface* itself or Liu Hsieh, Shao Yung draws a distinction between *chih* and *ch'ing*, the former referring to intellectual reflection, the latter to emotional response to external stimuli. Furthermore, he relates even emotions to "the times" or contemporary social and political conditions:

> There are seven emotions, which depend on two essentials: personal life and the times. The former refers to joy or sorrow in one's personal life, the latter to fortune or misfortune of the times. Joy or sorrow in one's personal life merely concerns poverty or wealth, high or low station, but fortune or misfortune of the times concerns the rise and fall [of the state], order or disorder [in the country].[69]

He therefore condemns poetry that only expresses personal emotions and advocates poetry that shows concern for "the times," or what some modern critics would call "social consciousness."

Revival of Expressive Theories

In later periods, the expressive concept of literature continued to appear from time to time, but it was not until the late Ming period (late sixteenth and early seventeenth centuries) that it received uncompromising advocation and formed the basis of a "movement." A precursor of this movement was the eccentric and iconoclastic thinker Li Chih (1527–1602), who belonged to what is sometimes called the "Left Wing" of Wang Yang-ming's school of Idealistic philosophy.[70] Li Chih asserted in his essay, "On the Childlike Heart" (*T'ung-hsin shuo*), that the "childlike heart" is the "true heart," and whoever retains it is a "true man" and will be able to produce great literature, whether it is poetry, prose, fiction, drama, or examination essays. According to him, "all the best literature of the world has always come from the childlike heart," whereas the works in the Confucian Canon do not represent the true words of the sages but only provide "pretexts for the moralists and gathering places for false men."[71] As far as his concept of the "childlike heart" was concerned, he could have cited Mencius and Lao Tzu as his authorities, for the former said, "A great man is one who has not lost the heart of the new-born child,"[72] and the latter asked, "In concentrating your vital force and attaining gentleness, can you be like a baby?"[73] However, Li Chih was the first to apply this concept of the "childlike heart" to the writer, and to maintain that it is the sole source of all great literature. In doing so, he may be said to have revived the primitivistic concept of literature. He was also the first to regard popular works of drama and fiction as great literature, thereby extending the scope of the traditional concept of "literature."

In another essay entitled "Miscellaneous Remarks" (*Tsa-shuo*), Li again expresses the primitivistic view:

> Those who can truly write never intended to produce literature in the first place. In the bosom [of a true writer], there are so many indescribable, strange things, in his throat there are so many things he wants to utter yet dare not, in his mouth there are often so many words he wants to say but has nowhere to say—when these have been stored up to the limit and accumulated for so long that they can no longer be checked, then, one day, when he sees a scene that arouses his emotions, when what touches his eye draws a sigh from him, he will "grab someone else's winecup to pour over his own grievances," give vent to his feelings of injustice, and lament the ill fates of a thousand years.[74]

The idea that literature is the involuntary outpouring of pent-up grievances could be traced back to the *Book of Poetry*, but Li Chih gave it an especially dramatic expression.

Notable as his contributions were to literary criticism, Li Chih was not primarily interested in literature. It was left to the three Yüan brothers of Kung-an (in Hupeh province) to launch a conscious movement against the archaism that had been the literary orthodoxy for a long time.

The three brothers who formed the Kung-an School, Yüan Tsung-tao (1560–1600), Yüan Hung-tao (1568–1610), and Yüan Chung-tao (1570–1623), were influenced by Li Chih but held less radical views. Even among the brothers themselves there were naturally some differences of opinion, though they all emphasized individuality and spontaneity, while attacking imitation of ancient writers.

The eldest one, Yüan Tsung-tao, wrote a "Discourse on Literature" (*Lun-wen*) in two parts, in which he set forth his views on literature. At the opening of the first part, he writes:

> The mouth and the tongue are what represent the heart [or mind, *hsin*], and literature is what in turn represents the mouth and the tongue. Being twice removed, even if it is fluently written, it will not, one fears, be as good as the mouth and the tongue. How can it then be like what lies in the heart [or mind]?

From this somewhat skeptical restatement of the old concept that literature expresses what lies in the heart or mind, he derives the conclusion that the primary function of literature is communication (*ta*):

> Therefore, Confucius, in discussing literature, said, "Words communicate; that is all."[75] The difference between what is literature and what is not lies in whether it communicates or not.[76]

As for what is to be communicated, Tsung-tao stresses the intellectual rather than emotional aspect of the writer's personality. In the second part of his "Discourse on Literature" he remarks:

> When burning incense, if you use aloeswood, the smoke will smell like aloeswood; if you use sandalwood, the smell will be that of sandwood. Why? Because each kind of incense has a different nature [*hsing*]. In music, the bell does not rely on the drum's sound, nor does the drum borrow the bell's tone. Why? Because each instrument is different. It is the same with literature. If you have a certain kind of learning, then this will brew a certain kind of opinion; and if you have a certain kind of opinion, then you will originate a certain kind of language.

Consequently, though he opposes imitation of the ancients, he does not reject learning. Instead, he advocates "producing reason [*li*] from learning and producing literature from reason."[77]

The second and most famous of the three brothers, Yüan Hung-tao, paid more attention to emotion and personal nature (*hsing-ling*), as may be witnessed by these words from his preface to the collected poems of his younger brother, Chung-tao:

> Most of his works uniquely express his personal nature and are not restricted by conventions. Unless it is what flows from his bosom, he will not write it down. Sometimes, when his emotion encounters the right environment, he can write a thousand words in a moment, like water pouring eastwards [into the sea].[78]

In the same preface, Hung-tao gave as his opinion that the only contemporary writings that had a chance of survival were the folk songs sung by women and children in the streets, the reason being as follows:

> These are still the works of "true people," who are without

> knowledge or learning; hence, they are full of true voices. Not affecting the manners of the Han and Wei, nor following in the footsteps of the High T'ang, they are words uttered in accordance with the free bent of one's nature, and can express people's joy, anger, sadness, pleasure, appetites, and desires.[79]

In this passage, which is remarkable for its inclusion of "appetites and desires" (*shih-hao ch'ing-yü*) among legitimate subjects for literary expression, Yüan Hung-tao shows his agreement with Li Chih. In another preface, written to introduce a friend's collected works, he echoes Li's concept of the "childlike heart" in even more explicit terms, while emphasizing another concept, "gusto" (*ch'ü*):

> What is rarest in people is "gusto," which is like color on mountains, flavor in water, light on flowers, or airs of women. . . . Now, what gusto owes to Nature is profound, but what it owes to learning is superficial. When one is a child, one does not know there is such a thing as gusto, yet wherever one goes, gusto abounds: with a face free from serious expressions, eyes whose pupils are never fixed, a mouth ever mumbling and muttering, and feet leaping and jumping without stop—there is no other time in life comparable to this for perfect happiness.[80]

As described above, "gusto" appears to mean both an ineffable air or flavor in a person's nature (and hence in his writings), and an instinctive joy commonly seen in children but rarely kept by adults. This concept of gusto may therefore be considered a dimension of "personal nature," differing from Yen Yü's concept of "inspired gusto" (*hsing-ch'ü*, mentioned in chapter 2), which is the result of one's contemplation of Nature. It was Yüan Hung-tao's nostalgia for this instinctive "gusto" that led him to distrust learning and to recommend reliance on spontaneous feelings.

The youngest of the Yüan brothers, Chung-tao, took a more moderate stand than his brothers and adopted a kind of historical relativism. To him, it was a historical necessity to advocate individualism as an antidote against imitation and preoccupation with technical rules, but he also believed that when individualism was carried to excess, it would then become necessary to advocate the observance of technical rules as a remedy.[81] In other words, he did not regard self-expression as the sole purpose of literature at all times, only as one of the two extremes between which the literary pendulum was bound to swing.

Later Expressive Theories

The Kung-an School achieved great success for a time in discrediting archaism and promoting individualism, but its influence soon waned, so that at the beginning of the Ch'ing dynasty (1644–1911), most influential figures in the literary "establishment" rejected the views espoused by the Yüan brothers. However, Li Chih and the Yüan brothers had a spiritual heir in the unorthodox critic Chin Jen-jui, better known as Chin Sheng-t'an (1610?–61), who also expressed strong individualist views on literature and esteemed works of popular fiction and drama as highly as the most venerated classics.[82] Although as a practical critic Chin is much concerned with technical details, his basic conception of literature is an expressive, even a primitivistic, one. For example, in a letter he wrote:

> Poetry is only a sudden cry from one's heart; everyone, even a woman or a child, has it, in the morning or at mid-night. Now, suppose here is a new-born baby whose eyes cannot yet turn and whose fists cannot yet open, but who, stretching its arms and twisting its feet, utters a sound from its mouth. When I look at it carefully, I find this is really poetry. There is no one in the world who, not having been moved in the heart, will utter a sound from his mouth, nor is there anyone who, having been moved in the heart, will not utter a sound from his mouth. What moves the heart and is uttered from the mouth is called poetry.[83]

Elsewhere he reiterated this extreme view of poetry. However, the preface he wrote to his selection of T'ang poetry has a slightly more moderate tone.[84] Written in elegant Parallel Prose, in contrast to the semicolloquial style he often employs in his letters and critical commentaries, the preface contains echoes of the metaphysical ideas of Liu Hsieh as expressed in the opening chapter of *The Literary Mind*,[85] but its main arguments are expressive, as the following excerpt will show:

> The power of poetry is great indeed! It was created when heaven and earth began, and it will perpetuate itself beyond the end of eternity [*sic*], continuing and lasting, dim and dark, for we know not how many ages. The void, which has no special nature, moves and stirs of itself. When it moves and stirs for a cause, then music arises. Now, the woods, when shaken by the wind, will produce harmony like pipes and mouth-organs; the fountains, when obstructed by rocks, will resound like bells and drums; when the spring sun shines in the air, flowers will blossom in wild profusion; when the autumn chill sweeps the steps, the insects will chirp urgently. If even such insentient objects cannot help doing so, how can man be without poetry? When one is surrounded by words, at the moment of reaching the limit of sorrow, one's nature and emotion become what one draws from and pours forth; past and present, what one bids farewell and welcome to. Since not only is what one bids farewell to vaguely distant and

> irretrievable, but what one welcomes is also all too quick to disappear, thereupon what one pours forth from one's emotion will be endless, and what is drawn from one's nature will likewise be inexhaustible.[86]

Though in the first part of this passage Chin is following the metaphysical tradition, he soon turns his attention to the expression of personal nature (*hsing*) and emotion (*ch'ing*), instead of the manifestation of the cosmic Tao. He goes on to say that the poet does not need the aid of either Nature or Art:

> All this [the writing of poetry] is neither what Primordial Transformation [*yüan-hua*] has moulded, nor what mountains and rivers are able to aid in time. For as soon as one's eyebrows and lashes move, it is already completed within; as soon as one's throat turns, it is thoroughly described without. How should one need to borrow from the forest of writing brushes in order to brandish [the brush] and sprinkle [the ink], or seek moisture from the river of ink?[87]

Furthermore, he claims that before the invention of the script, music and poetry already existed. Thus, when "a boy with his hair done up in two buns" chanted a ballad, or when "a girl laid down her pretty basket and heaved a sigh," these became the songs that Confucius did not delete from the *Book of Poetry* and that Tzu-hsia, the reputed author of the *Major Preface*, prostrated himself to read.[88] What Chin Sheng-t'an is suggesting is that genuine emotion is sufficient to make anyone a poet, without the benefit of either genius or artistry—a theory that his own practical criticism of what he considered works of genius rather belies.

An early Ch'ing critic who did not rebel against orthodoxy but nevertheless voiced some independent opinions on poetry was Yeh Hsieh (1627–1703), whose *On the Origins of Poetry* (*Yüan-shih*, a treatise in two parts, each comprising two subsections) is one of the few systematic works on poetry in Chinese. His conception of poetry appears to be primarily expressive, for he states: "The foundation of poetry is the poet's mental capacity [*hsiung-chin*, literally, 'bosom and lapel']. If he has this mental capacity, he can then express his personal nature and intelligence, his perceptivity and talent."[89] From the examples he gives (the great poet Tu Fu who, Yeh believes, was moved to thoughts about the sovereign and the state by everything he encountered, and the great calligrapher Wang Hsi-chih who lamented human mortality in an essay written on a festive occasion), it is clear that by "mental capacity" he means the writer's intellectual capacity and moral character, rather than his emotional or aesthetic capacity. This is corroborated by another passage, in which Yeh declares:

> "The purpose of writing poetry is to express one's personality." This is something that everyone knows and everyone can say, but not everyone can do. "In writing poetry, if one has a personality, one will inevitably have a visage." This is something that not only not everyone can do, but not everyone even knows or can say. For instance, take any one of Tu Fu's poems, or even one line, and everywhere you will see his worries for the country and his love for his sovereign, his compassion for the times and his sadness over disorder, his refusal to compromise in adversity, his integrity in poverty, his way of expressing his indignations and refining his nature by means of enjoying the landscape and drinking with friends, even though he had traveled through rugged, war-torn, bandit-infested terrain: this is Tu Fu's visage. Whenever I read him, his visage leaps before my eyes.[90]

This "visage" (*mien-mu*), then, refers to the expression of the writer's moral character in his works.

Yeh's expressive conception of poetry can be further attested by remarks like the following: "Poetry is the voice of the heart. It may not be uttered against the heart, nor can it be uttered against the heart."[91]

However, he does not neglect the importance of the universe, which, according to him, can be summed up in three words: "principle" (*li*), "event" (*shih*), and "manner" (*ch'ing*). What he means by these terms is explained in this passage:

> What I call "principle," "event," and "manner" are the principles by which the Ch'ien [the masculine, creative, or *yang*] and the K'un [the feminine, receptive, or *yin*] fix their positions, the sun and moon revolve; and even down to such things as grass, trees, flying birds and running beasts, if one of the three is lacking, then nothing can be complete. Literature is what expresses the manners [*ch'ing-chuang*] of all things in the universe. Yet there is something else that controls these three principles and strings them together: this is the vital force [*ch'i*]. The functions of "principle," "event," and "manner" are due to the function of the vital force. Take, for example, a tree or a plant. What enables it to come into being is the "principle"; once it comes into being, it then becomes an "event"; and after having come into being, it flourishes and multiplies, presenting a myriad different manners and appearances, all giving one the feeling that they are contented with their own nature: these constitute its "manner."[92]

In this passage, Yeh is using the term "principle" (*li*) in the same sense as in neo-Confucian metaphysics, where *li* ("principle" or "reason") and *ch'i* (often translated as "ether" in this context) correspond to "form" and "matter" in Greek philosophy,[93] but instead of contrasting *li* with *ch'i*, he contrasts it with both *shih* ("event," which refers to the actualization of the "principle" of a thing) and *ch'ing* (which does not mean "emotion" here but the manner in which a thing appears), while subordinating all three to the *ch'i*, which does not seem to denote "matter" but cosmic vital force, as in the *Kuan Tzu*.[94]

To grasp and express these three principles of the universe, the poet should, Yeh believes, possess four inner qualities: talent (*ts'ai*), daring (*tan*), judgment (*shih*), and strength (*li*):

> These four qualities are what exhaustively bring out the spiritual light [*shen-ming*] of the mind. All forms, colors, sounds, and appearances await these to be made manifest and clear. . . . If one uses the four qualities that lie within one and measures the three principles that lie in things so as to produce the literary works of a true writer, then from the great principles of heaven and earth, down to such small things as an animal or a plant, there is nothing about which one can sing and chant apart from this.[95]

In spite of certain metaphysical ideas in the passages just quoted, Yeh's conception of poetry is ultimately more expressive than metaphysical, for his theory is primarily oriented towards the writer:

> The "intent" [*chih*] is explained as "where the heart [or mind] goes"; and it is what the Buddhists call the "seed." When this intent first occurs, there are indeed differences between high and low, great and small, far and near. But as long as one has this intent, and fills it with what I call "talent," "judgment," "daring," and "strength," then when one observes what is above and investigates what is below, when one encounters objects and is touched by scenes, one's feelings will spring up abundantly and spread all over, and one's talent and thoughts will overflow beyond the words written down.[96]

In this account of the writer's relation to the universe, instead of "emptying" his mind to be receptive of the Tao, as in metaphysical theories, the writer, equipped with certain mental qualities, responds to the universe and then expresses his response.

The last critic I shall discuss in this chapter is Yüan Mei (1716–

98), who refined the concept of *hsing-ling*, and, because of his great popularity as a poet, gave the term wider currency than it had ever enjoyed before. It may be recalled that some of his predecessors used this term as a synonym for *hsing-ch'ing* or "personal nature," but in Yüan Mei's usage the two terms do not denote identical concepts, the one, *hsing-ch'ing*, referring to one's personal nature in general, and the other, *hsing-ling*, to a special kind of artistic sensibility ingrained in one's nature.[97] I have therefore translated the latter term as "native sensibility."[98] It is true that he did not explicitly define these two terms, but the following remarks, with which he criticized some of his contemporaries, suggest that he did make a distinction between the two:

> People nowadays force themselves to write poetry out of a desire for the reputation of being a poet; not only do their poems depart from their personal natures [*hsing-ch'ing*], but they also lack the working of sensibility [*ling-chi*].[99]

What he calls *ling-chi* here signifies the functioning (*chi*, literally, "trigger" or "mechanism") of the sensibility (*ling*), which is part of one's nature (*hsing*). Elsewhere he often praises other poets for the "native sensibility" (*hsing-ling*) their works reveal. In this respect he differs from Li Chih and Chin Sheng-t'an, who claim that genuine emotion alone is sufficient for the creation of poetry.

On the other hand, Yüan Mei does stress the importance of personality and emotion. Again and again he repeats that poetry is an expression of "personal nature" (*hsing-ch'ing*) or of emotion (*ch'ing*), especially love, or that it is "the voice of the heart."[100] His advocation of love poetry, even that which expresses homosexual love, brought him into sharp conflicts with Confucian moralists like Shen Te-ch'ien (whom we shall discuss in chapter 6), and has won him somewhat excessive acclaim as a great free thinker from some modern scholars.[101] The fact is, Yüan Mei did not formulate a systematic theory of poetry, and most of his ideas were not original. However, he did elaborate some of the ideas he had inherited from earlier critics, especially the Yüan brothers of Kung-an of the previous dynasty (even though he never mentioned them by name),[102] and his views were not as one-sided as those of Li Chih or Chin Sheng-t'an, though basically he shared with them the expressive conception of literature. Since Yüan Mei's time, there have been no major developments in Chinese expressive theories, but the expressive concept of literature has remained widely held, implicitly if not explicitly, by Chinese critics, as can be seen from frequent uses of such phrases as "expressing emotion" (*shu ch'ing*) and "genuine emotion" (*chen ch'ing*) as criteria for literature.

Chinese and Western Expressive Theories Compared

The similarities between the theories discussed in this chapter and Western expressive ones will be apparent to anyone familiar with the latter, and need not be pointed out. Instead, a few differences may be mentioned. First, whereas in Western expressive theories the creative character of the imagination is of central importance, Chinese expressive theorists, with a few exceptions like Lu Chi and Liu Hsieh, seldom emphasize creativity. For example, whereas Coleridge describes the "secondary Imagination" (the artistic imagination) as the faculty that "dissolves, diffuses, dissipates, in order to recreate,"[103] and Wordsworth likewise asserts, "The Imagination also shapes and *creates*,"[104] similar statements are hardly ever found in Chinese expressive theories. This difference may be due to, as I suggested earlier, the absence in traditional Chinese philosophy of the concept of an anthropomorphic deity as the Creator of the world, in contrast to the Judaeo-Christian concept of God the Creator, which provided a model for the concept of the artist as creator. Coleridge's description of the "primary Imagination" (which is the "prime Agent of all human Perception" and is similar in kind to the secondary or artistic imagination) as "a repetition in the finite mind of the eternal act of creation in the infinite I AM"[105] clearly illustrates this.

Secondly, Chinese expressive theorists, except one or two radicals like Li Chih and Chin Sheng-t'an, do not value intense emotion or passion as a prerequisite for artistic writing, as their Western counterparts tend to. Most Chinese expressive critics would readily accept Wordsworth's theory that poetry is "the spontaneous overflow of powerful feelings"[106] with the proviso that "sincere" or "genuine" be substituted for "powerful."

Finally, again with the exceptions of Li Chih and Chin Sheng-t'an, Chinese expressive critics, while agreeing with both Chinese metaphysical critics and Western expressive ones that spontaneity and intuition are more important than technique, would not go so far as Croce in identifying intuition with expression,[107] but would rather concur with Joyce Cary that the passage from intuition to expression is an arduous one that requires hard work.[108] Most Chinese expressive theories, although placing primary emphasis on spontaneous expression, do not exclude conscious artistry altogether.

4

Technical Theories

The Technical Concept of Literature: Earlier Examples

The technical concept of literature, according to which literature is a craft much like other crafts such as carpentry except that it uses language as its material instead of physical substances, resembles the expressive concept in so far as it too is primarily focused on phase 2 of the artistic process, but differs from the latter in so far as it construes the process of writing not as one of spontaneous expression but as one of deliberate composition. In Chinese criticism, this concept is more often implied in practice than stated in theory; for example, writers of erudite Expositions, ornate Parallel Prose, and other forms of literature regulated by strict technical rules, who were preoccupied with prosodic and rhetorical details often at the expense of the expression of thought or feeling, may be said to have subscribed to the technical concept of literature, even if they did not explicitly state it and may have paid lip service to other concepts such as the pragmatic or the expressive. However, some examples of overt statements of the technical concept can be found in Chinese literary criticism.

One such statement was made by Shen Yüeh (441–513), one of the first to expound the theory of the "Four Tones" (*ssu-sheng*) and to formulate prosodic rules based on tonal distinctions in the Chinese language. This is not the place to go into details about the nature of the four tones in Chinese and the prosodic rules derived from them; it is sufficient for our present purpose to realize that, since the fifth century, Chinese phonologists and prosodists have recognized four tones, called "Level" (*p'ing*), "Rising" (*shang*), "Falling" (or "Departing," *ch'ü*), and "Entering" (*ju*), the last three known collectively as "Oblique" (or "Deflected," *tse*), and that conscious exploitation of tonal variations and contrasts formed the basis of various Chinese verse forms.[1]

To return to Shen Yüeh: in his biography of the poet Hsieh Ling-yün (385–433) in the *History of the Sung* (*Sung shu*), he writes:

> When the five colors set each other off, or when the eight notes harmonize with each other, it is because each color, or each note on the pitch-pipe, has its suitable place. [In writing,] if you

> wish to make the *kung* [the first note of the pentatonic scale] and the *yü* [the last note] modify each other, the high and the low modulate each other, then when there is a "floating sound" [i.e., Level Tone?] before, it must be followed by a "cut-off sound" [i.e., Oblique Tone?]. In the same line, the tones of the syllables must all be different; in two consecutive lines, light syllables and heavy ones must not be repeated. Only when one has a subtle understanding of these principles can one discuss literature.[2]

The precise meanings of Shen's terms "floating sound" (*fu-sheng*), "cut-off sound" (*ch'ieh-hsiang*), "light," and "heavy" have been variously interpreted but do not concern us here. What does concern us is the last sentence, which postulates that knowledge of prosodic niceties is the sine qua non of literature.

Shen Yüeh's view was shared by many, though not everyone thought it wise to express it as openly as he did. Even his great contemporary Liu Hsieh, whose metaphysical and expressive views we have dealt with, did not totally reject the technical view: he devoted several chapters to considerations of such technical features of literature as prosody and parallelism, and in the chapter entitled "General Principles" (or "Artistry in General," *Tsung-shu*),[3] he stressed the importance of artistry: "Therefore, one who holds artistry [*shu*] as the reins to control his composition is like a good player of checkers who knows all the moves; one who rejects artistry is like a player of backgammon who seeks lucky chance."[4] In other words, good writing requires conscious artistry as well as natural talent and inspiration.

CONTINUATION OF THE TECHNICAL VIEW

Passing over a host of compilers of prosodic and rhetorical manuals, who implicitly held the technical concept of literature but did not formulate theories, we shall now turn our attention to some poets and prose writers who expressed technical views on literature. One of these is the early Ming poet Kao Ch'i (1336–74), who stated: "The essentials of poetry are three: 'formal style' [*ko*], 'meaning' [*yi*], and 'gusto' [*ch'ü*]: that is all. Formal style is that by which one distinguishes the form [*t'i*]; meaning is that by which one conveys the feeling; gusto is that by which one reaches the miraculous."[5]

The word here rendered "formal style," *ko*, is used either by itself or in disyllabic compounds to denote various concepts: on its own, or in compounds such as *feng-ko* and *ch'i-ko*, it usually denotes "style," especially when this is conceived in formal terms, whereas in other compounds like *ko-lü* and *ko-tiao* it denotes "form" or "prosodic rules." At the same time, the word also has the implication of "standard."

Judging by the fact that Kao Ch'i considered *ko* the means by which one distinguishes the form (*t'i*) of a poem, we may conclude that he used the term to refer to style in its formal aspect, and further that he attached great importance to form and technique, although his theory of poetry is not purely technical but partly expressive.

Another Ming poet and critic who paid great attention to the formal and technical aspects of literature is Li Tung-yang (1447–1516), who wrote in a preface: "Words that form patterns [*chang*] become prose literature [*wen*], and prose literature that forms musical sounds becomes poetry [*shih*]. Poetry and prose literature are both called 'words,' yet each has its own form [*t'i*] and should not be confused."[6] In another preface, he reiterated the idea that the distinction between prose literature and poetry is a formal one: "What makes poetry different from prose [*wen*] is that it possesses regulated sounds and can be recited and chanted."[7] Furthermore, he insists that formal distinctions between different kinds of verse must be kept: "Ancient Verse [*ku-shih*] and Regulated Verse [*lü-shih*] are different forms; each must be written according to its own form before it can be considered proper."[8] This strong insistence on formal distinctions is matched by an equally strong insistence on adherence to rules and standards:

> What we call "prose literature" [*wen*] consists of words that form patterns; and what we call "poetry" is prose literature that forms musical sounds. In using patterns, one should value extended narrative and description, expanding and embellishing, letting go or holding back, doing what one wishes, yet there must be fixed standards. As for the use of songs and chants, sighs and exclamations, which are flowing and stirring, this rests with musical sounds, yet the regulation of high and low, long and short, must also be clear-cut and not confused.[9]

Underlying the above statements is the concept of literature as a craft with definite rules and methods.

The Technical Concept Combined with Archaism

As already indicated in chapter 2, some critics who advocated archaism held the technical concept of literature. Li Meng-yang (1472–1529), one of the "Former Seven Masters" of the Ming dynasty, defended his own practice of imitating the ancients in a letter written in reply to Ho Ching-ming (1483–1521)—another of the "Former Seven Masters," who had accused Li of being a "mere shadow of the ancients" and of having failed to "build one hall or open one door of his own"—by arguing that it was not the words or the ideas of the ancients but the rules or methods (*fa*) of literary craftsmanship embodied in their works that he imitated:

> Ancient craftsmen ilke Ch'ui and Pan built different halls and dissimilar doors, but when it came to making a square or a circle, they could not do without the carpenter's square or the compasses. Why? Because these represent the rules [*fa*]. When I follow the ancients foot by foot and inch by inch, I am really following the rules. If I had stolen the ideas of the ancients, or pilfered the forms of the ancients, or cut and tailored the words of the ancients to be my own literary works, then you could certainly call me a "shadow." But if I take my own feelings and describe contemporary events while following the rules of the ancients foot by foot and inch by inch, without plagiarizing their words, this is comparable to Pan making a circle like Ch'ui's circle or Ch'ui making a square like Pan's square, while Ch'ui's wood was not the same as Pan's wood. Why should this not be allowed?[10]

By drawing an analogy between building houses and writing, without showing any awareness that there might be basic differences between the two activities, Li Meng-yang reveals his technical conception of literature. He draws a further analogy between literature and calligraphy, the latter of which he also conceives as a craft with definite rules or methods:

> Composing literature is like calligraphy: the characters written by Ou [-yang Hsün], Yü [Shih-nan], Yen [Chen-ch'ing], and Liu [Kung-ch'üan] are all different, but their strokes are the same. If the strokes were not the same, then they would no longer be proper characters. What are their differences? These lie in their thickness or thinness, length or shortness, density or sparseness. Therefore, these six qualities are the force [*shih*] or the style [*t'i*] of the characters, not the essence [*ching*] of the strokes. What then is the essence? It is that which responds to one's mind and is based on rules [*fa*]. (p. 8b)

He goes on to observe:

> The ancient writers brandished their writing brushes and at once achieved all the excellent qualities [of literature], but their developments and conclusions, pauses and restraints, were never without rules, foot by foot and inch by inch. These are what I call the compasses and the square. (p. 9a)

The same ideas are reiterated in two other letters, one addressed to a Mr. Chou, the other to one Wu Chin:

> Literary works must have rules and models, for only then can they harmonize with musical measures, just as squares and circles need the carpenter's square and the compasses. (pp. 13 a-b)
>
> Literature has its own formal styles [*ko*]; one who does not follow the formal styles of the ancients will never be able to understand literature. (p. 11 b)

These quotations should be sufficient to show how the technical concept of literature led Li Meng-yang to believe in archaism and the observance of rules and methods.

The writers quoted so far were mainly concerned with poetry. One who was mainly concerned with prose was T'ang Shun-chih (1507–60), a master of Archaic Prose. He too believed in the observance of rules or methods, though conceived in more flexible terms:

> The prose literature before the Han period was never without method, yet never had methods; since its method lies in the absence of methods, the method is esoteric and cannot be espied. The prose literature of the T'ang and later periods cannot do without method but can observe methods without missing a centimeter or millimeter; since its method lies in having methods, the method is strict and must not be broken. When it is esoteric, then people suspect that there is no method; when it is strict, then people suspect that there are methods that can be espied. However, it is indisputable that literature must have methods which come into existence naturally and cannot be altered.[11]

In the original passage the word *fa* (which I translated in previous quotations as "rules") is sometimes used in the sense of "method" or "methodology" in general and at other times in the sense of definite "methods"; I have translated it in the singular or the plural accordingly, even though in Chinese there is no formal indication of number. Whether *fa* refers to method in general or to particular methods, T'ang's emphasis on *fa* suggests a technical conception of literature.

A TECHNICAL VIEW OF DRAMA

One writer primarily concerned with dramatic literature is the early Ch'ing dramatic poet and critic Li Yü (1611–80?), whose dramatic criticism is distinguished for its attention to structure, in contrast to that of most other Chinese dramatic critics, who are chiefly interested in prosodic, rhetorical, and musical details. (It should be explained that traditional Chinese drama is written partly in prose and partly in verse, the latter invariably intended for singing.)[12] Li Yü's basic conception of dramatic literature may be deduced from the following passages. To begin with, he poses the question why writers are reluctant to discuss dramaturgy:

> I have often wondered why it is that, since whenever there is a kind of literature there will be rules and standards for that kind of literature, written down in books and as good as personal instruction, when it comes to the art of writing lyrics and composing dramatic works, this has not only not been treated in detail but has been left aside as a subject of discussion.[13]

He answers the question himself by giving three reasons: first, the secret of playwriting is too subtle to be conveyed in words; second, the principles of dramatic writing vary constantly; finally, successful dramatists are rare and those who have mastered the difficult art of playwriting wish to keep their "trade secrets." He then refutes the first two reasons by arguing that though the highest reaches of drama may be beyond verbal communication, this is not true of dramaturgy as a whole, and that it is true of all literature, not only drama, that the principles must vary. He therefore comes to the conclusion that it is really the last reason which accounts for the lack of discussions of dramaturgy, and declares his intention to reveal all he knows about the art of playwriting. This passage shows that Li Yü believed in technical rules and methods, though he realized that these must not be rigidly followed but applied with infinite variety.

The next passage I shall quote gives further indications of Li's conception of drama through two telling analogies:

> As for "structure" [*chieh-kou*], this refers to the time before one works on the musical notes and is just beginning to choose the rhymes and put down the writing brush on paper; it is like Nature [*tsao-wu*] giving form to a human being: when the semen and blood are first joined together and before the foetus has taken complete shape, It first plans the whole form, so that this drop of blood will have the potentialities of the five organs and the hundred bones. If It had no such total plan at first but produced the body from top to toe, section by section, then the human body would have numberless marks of breaks and junctures, and the flow of blood and vital spirits would be obstructed. It is the same with a craftsman building a house: when the foundation has been laid but before the frame has been put up, he must first plan where to build a hall, where to open a door, what kind of wood is needed for the lesser beams, what kind for the greater; only when the whole plan is clear can he wield his axe and adze.[14]

In the first analogy, in which playwriting is compared to the formation of the human body before birth, the term here translated as "Nature," *tsao-wu*, literary means "that which produces things," and can also be translated as "creator," but I have chosen not to do so, for I think that Li Yü, like many other Chinese writers, did not mean by this term a personal deity but rather an impersonal power, or Tao, which is responsible for the creation of all things. His analogy, therefore, is not quite the same as the Western analogy between the artist and Deus Creator.[15] That Li Yü conceived the process of creation in Nature as a mechanical one is suggested by his statement that this process is the same as that of building a house. To him, the process of creation in Nature, that of artistic creation, and that of mechanical production, are all basically the same.

This technical concept of art is revealed once more by another analogy he draws, one between playwriting and tailoring: "Composing a play is like making clothes: at first you take what is whole and cut it into pieces, then you take the pieces and put them together."[16] In fact, it is to the technique of drama, rather than its relation to reality or to the playwright's personality, or its effect on the spectator or reader, that Li Yü directs his main attention.

Later Technical Theories

Among later Ch'ing critics who expressed technical views and whom I shall discuss here, one was mainly interested in poetry and three were mainly interested in prose. Rather than dealing with them in strictly chronological order, I shall discuss first the one interested in poetry and then the others.

The critic mainly concerned with poetry is Weng Fang-kang (1733–1818), who, as I already mentioned in chapter 2, turned Wang Shih-chen's metaphysical theory of "spirit and tone" (*shen-yün*) into a technical-aesthetic one by identifying *shen-yün* with *ko-tiao* or "formal style."[17] His understanding of *shen-yün* may be seen in the following words from his essay "On Spirit and Tone" (*Shen-yün lun*): "*Shen-yün* is all-embracing: it may be seen in formal style [*ko-tiao*], or in intonation and rhythm [*yin-chieh*], or in diction and syntax [*tzu-chü*, literally, 'words and sentences or lines']; one cannot name it by holding to only one aspect."[18]

This interpretation of *shen-yün* leaves out all the metaphysical implications of the term as used by Wang Shih-chen and confines it to the formal and technical elements of poetry. Weng Fang-kang's technical conception of poetry is also expressed in other essays in which he emphasizes what he calls the "flesh texture" (*chi-li*) of poetry and the rules (*fa*) of poetic composition. In the essay "On the Rules of Poetry" (*Shih-fa lun*), he writes,

> When literature is formed, then rules are established. In the establishment of rules, there are those which are established at the beginning or at the center: this is the way the rules establish the correct basis [of poetry] and trace its source. Then there are those which are established about the details, about the flesh texture or the seams: this is the way the rules exhaust all forms and all possible changes. Tu [Fu] wrote, "The rules [of poetry] are naturally what we Confucians possess"[19]—this refers to the rules that establish the basis [of poetry]. Again he wrote [in a poem addressed to Kao Shih], "In your fine lines, what are the rules like?"[20]—this refers to the rules that exhaust all possible changes. Now, since the rules that establish the basis do not originate with oneself but are like rivers flowing into the sea, some forming the source and others the stream, they must be sought from the ancients. And since the rules that exhaust all possible changes, from major ones concerning the principles of beginning and ending, down to such details as the grammatical nature of a word or the tone of a syllable, as well as those governing continuation or transition, development or conclusion, normalcy or deviation, must all be sought from the ancients, one then realizes that everything must be measured by the ruler and the compasses and must conform to the musical measures regulated by the five notes and the six pitch-pipes, and that one must not allow one's own wishes to intrude to the slightest degree.[21]

This is an uncompromising exposition of the technical concept, diametrically opposed to the expressive concept, and although Weng does recognize the importance of the poet, he is concerned with the poet only as a craftsman and not as a personality, as shown by the following words from the same essay: "In writing poetry, who is it that writes? In using rules, who is it that uses them? In poetry, there is a self; in rules, there is a self to operate them" (p. 1 a). Furthermore, although he insists on the necessity of seeking the rules of poetry from the ancients, he disapproves superficial imitation of the style and diction of the ancients. To him, following the ancients does not mean copying the appearance of their works, but following the rules that these exemplify. In this respect he is in fact voicing the same opinion as Li Meng-yang, whose defence of imitation we have seen, even though, ironically, Weng condemns Li as a superficial imitator of the ancients.

The three critics mainly interested in prose all belonged to the T'ung-ch'eng School, and one of them, Yao Nai, we have discussed in chapter 2 with regard to his aesthetic theory derived from the metaphysical concept of literature. Yao's elder contemporary, fellow townsman, and mentor, Liu Ta-k'uei (1698–1780), may be considered an exponent of the technical concept. In his *Casual Notes on Literature* (*Lun-wen ou-chi*) he writes, "In the way of writing, the spirit [*shen*] is the main thing, and the vital force [*ch'i*] supports it."[22] His use of the terms *shen* and *ch'i* should not mislead us into thinking that his conception of literature is metaphysical or expressive, for his concept of *shen* is not metaphysical like Liu Hsieh's or Yen Yü's, nor is his concept of *ch'i* expressive like Ts'ao P'i's, even though he mentions Ts'ao's advocation of *ch'i* with approval. A clue to what he means by these terms is contained in these words: "The spirit [*shen*] is the master of the vital force [*ch'i*], and the vital force is the function of the spirit. The spirit is only the fine essence of the vital force."[23] This is admittedly still rather vague, but when he writes in more concrete terms, his concepts of *shen* and *ch'i* emerge more clearly:

> Literature must, above all, attempt to be strong in vital force [*ch'i*], but if there is no spirit [*shen*] to control the vital force, it will run wild, not knowing where to settle down. The spirit and the vital force are the finest essences of literature; intonation and rhythm [*yin-chieh*] are the somewhat coarser elements of literature; diction and syntax [*tzu-chü*] are the coarsest elements of literature. However, I assert that in discussing literature, when one comes to diction and syntax, one has exhausted the skills of literature. This is because intonation and rhythm are the outward traces of the spirit and vital force, and diction and syntax are the regulations of intonation and rhythm. The spirit and vital force [as such] are invisible, but one can see them in intonation and rhythm; intonation and rhythm [as such] cannot be regulated, but one can regulate them by diction and syntax.[24]

From this passage it appears that Liu Ta-k'uei's "spirit" (*shen*) and "vital force" (*ch'i*) have little if anything to do with the writer's intuitive apprehension of reality or intuitive expression of his personality, but are the forces controlling such technical elements of writing as intonation, rhythm, diction, and syntax. The word "coarse" (*ts'u*) is used here not in a pejorative sense but to refer to the more palpable, formal, outer elements of literature, in contrast to the impalpable, supraformal, inner elements which he calls the "finest essences" and which consist, according to him, of the "spirit" and "vital force." Since he believes that the inner elements can be controlled by the outer, his conception of literature is primarily technical.

This technical concept is also shown in another passage, which contains the familiar analogy between writing and craftsmanship: "A literary man is like a master craftsman: what we call 'spirit,' 'vital force,' 'intonation,' and 'rhythm' are the skills of the [literary] craftsman; what we call 'principles,' 'reason,' 'book learning,' and 'knowledge of state affairs' are the materials of the [literary] craftsman."[25]

Liu's theories exerted some influence on Yao Nai, who wrote in the preface to his *Classified Anthology of Ancient Prose Literature* (*Ku-wen-tz'u lei-tsuan*):

> In general, there are thirteen classes of prose literature, but what makes them literature consists of eight elements: spirit, principles, vital force, flavor, formal style, rules, sound, and color. The former four are the essences of literature; the latter four are the coarser elements of literature. However, if one discards the coarser elements, then wherein can the essences rest? Those who learn from the ancients must first encounter their coarser elements, then encounter their essences, and finally control the essences and leave the coarser elements behind.[26]

Although Yao did not define each of the eight elements of literature he postulated, it is clear that he agreed with Liu that the inner essences or supraformal elements of literature can be controlled by the formal and more tangible ones.

A follower of Liu and Yao was Tseng Kuo-fan (1811–72), who was an important member of the T'ung-ch'eng School, although he was not a native of that district and is now chiefly remembered as a political and military leader. He wrote in his journal in the Seventh Month (July-August) of 1851: "In writing, all depends on the flourishing of the vital force [*ch'i*], and if you wish the vital force to flourish, it all depends on the clear division of sections."[27] And again in the Eleventh Month (December) of 1861: "The method of Archaic Prose lies wholly in exerting oneself with regard to the 'vital force' " (p. 52). And in a letter to his son Chi-tse written on 13 February 1861, he wrote: "The powerful and extraordinary [*hsiung-ch'i*] qualities of literature lie in the operation of the vital force for their fine essences; as for their coarser elements, these depend wholly on syntax and diction."[28] These remarks obviously echo Liu Ta-k'uei and Yao Nai and reflect a technical conception of literature.

SOME WESTERN PARALLELS

The technical concept of literature is as familiar in Western theories of literature as in Chinese ones; as a matter of fact, it has had a longer history in the West, from the ancient Greeks, especially Aristotle, through such medieval and Renaissance rhetoricians and critics as

Donatus, Scaliger, Sir Thomas Wilson, and Puttenham, down to twentieth-century critics as diverse as the Russian Formalists, the Chicago neo-Aristotelians, and some French and American structuralists, who, despite their avowed and genuine differences of outlook and opinion, have some affinities with one another, and with the Chinese critics discussed in this chapter, in their preoccupation with the technique of writing and their tacit if not overt acceptance of the concept of literature as a craft, a concept that, one would have thought, R. G. Collingwood had refuted once for all[29] but that seems by no means dead.

5

Aesthetic Theories

Origins of the Aesthetic Concept of Literature

The concept of literature as beautiful verbal patterns, on which Chinese aesthetic theories of literature are based, is closely related to the technical concept, so much so that one may say that they are two sides of the same coin. Their basic difference lies in that the aesthetic concept is primarily focused on the immediate effects of a literary work on the reader (phase 3 of the artistic process), whereas the technical concept is focused on the writer's relation to his work (phase 2). When a critic discusses literature from the writer's point of view and prescribes rules for composition, he may be said to expound a technical theory, but when he describes the beauties of a literary work and the pleasures it affords the reader, then his theory may be called aesthetic.

In Chinese literary criticism, the origins of the aesthetic concept can be traced back to the etymology of the word for "literature," *wen*, which, as was pointed out in chapter 1, probably had the original meaning of "pattern" or "marking" (see notes 20–25 to chapter 1). That literature should have been called "patterns" suggests an aesthetic concept of literature, though not necessarily an exclusively aesthetic one.

Various early Chinese (pre-Han) texts contain remarks that can be, and have been, interpreted as expressing an aesthetic conception of literature. In the chronicle, the *Tso-chuan*, for the year 547 B.C., is recorded a saying of Confucius: "If words do not have *wen* [patterns/embellishments], they will not go far."[1] Even if, as some modern scholars think,[2] the remark was not really made by Confucius, the fact that it was attributed to him gave it immense prestige and lent support to those inclined to an aesthetic view of literature. Likewise, the title of one of the *Commentaries* on the *Book of Changes* (traditionally attributed to Confucius), "Wen-yen," as mentioned once before,[3] has been interpreted as "embellished words" and used as evidence that the Sage regarded embellishments as a necessary element of literature. In another of the *Commentaries*, the "Appended Words," the *Book of Changes* itself is praised with these words: "Its meaning is far-reaching; its words are embellished [*wen*]."[4]

The aesthetic concept became more clearly recognizable during the

Han period (206 B.C.–A.D. 220), when the elaborate Exposition was the most highly valued literary genre, and when a narrower, "purer," conception of "literature" (*wen*), as distinct from culture or learning in general, was gradually emerging.[5] This can be seen in the use, as a synonym for *wen*, of the disyllable *wen-chang*, to the second syllable of which we shall now direct our attention. As a word in itself, *chang*, modern form 章, has various meanings including "pattern," "decoration," "illustrious," "manifest," "stanza," and "statute." Its earliest known written form, as found in the inscription on a bronze vessel of the Shang or Yin period (pre-twelfth century B.C.), is , which, according to the modern scholar Chu Fang-p'u, represented the ring of light surrounding a burning faggot.[6] This seems more likely to be the true etymology of the word than the traditional interpretation as given by Hsü Shen in his *Explanations of Simple and Compound Characters*: "*Chang* means the end of a piece of music; the character consists of *yin* [music] and *shih* [number ten], the latter signifying the end of a series of numbers,"[7] since Hsü's interpretation is obviously a piece of ingenious and fanciful rationalization based on the much later Small Seal form of the word, , which indeed consists of "music" plus "ten." In pre-Han and early Han texts, *chang* sometimes denotes "illustrious" or "to manifest," but as a noun it generally denotes some kind of pattern, whether physical or metaphorical.[8] For instance, in the *Book of Poetry* the word *chang* occurs altogether eleven times (not counting repeated lines), four times meaning "patterns" with reference to woven material, once referring to "patterns" formed by stars in the sky, three times meaning "outward adornments" (once with reference to speech), once meaning "model," once "statutes," and once "splendid" or "shining."[9] More interesting still is a passage in the *Rituals of Chou* (*Chou li*, which was said to be a record of the ritual and government systems of the Chou but which modern scholars believe to have been compiled by early Han scholars in the second century B.C.),[10] which states, "In colored weaving, blue interwoven with red is called *wen*, red with white is called *chang*."[11] Thus, the  disyllable *wen-chang* can be explained as "pattern-pattern," or as "verbal pattern" (if we take *wen* to be the modifier of *chang*), in either case implying formal pattern and beauty. The fact that, as mentioned in chapter 1, *wen-chang* was used to denote cultural refinement before it was applied to literature suggests that it was intended to be, originally at any rate, a pleonastic compound consisting of two synonyms. (Such compounds are common in Chinese.) Furthermore, although *chang* sometimes means "manifest" in early texts, it is used in this sense only verbally, not substantively, so that the possibility that *wen-chang* meant "verbal manifestation" seems remote. We may therefore conclude that in using the compound *wen-chang* to refer to literature, writers of the Han and later periods had in mind chiefly its formal and aesthetic qualities.

The analogy between literature and weaving or embroidery implied in the compound *wen-chang* is often made explicit. The past master of the Exposition *par excellence*, Ssu-ma Hsiang-ju (179–117 B.C.), is reported to have said:

> To join together different colored silk strands to form patterns [*wen*], to array brocades and embroideries as the substance, to [interweave] each warp with a woof, to [alternate] each *kung* [the first note of the pentatonic scale] with a *shang* [the second note]: these are the outward traces of the Exposition. As for an expert Exposition-writer's mind, which encompasses the universe and surveys all kinds of people, this is something obtained within which cannot be communicated.[12]

Although the second half of the quotation embodies a metaphysical conception of literature, the first half is definitely aesthetic-technical in its emphasis on the sensuous beauties of literature, on the one hand, and the technical means to achieve such beauties, on the other; and although the book in which this quotation is found, *Miscellaneous Records of the Western Capital* (*Hsi-ching tsa-chi*), is of controversial date and authorship,[13] the views contained therein are such as might have been expressed by Ssu-ma Hsiang-ju, judging by his practice as a writer.

An even more unmistakable expression of the aesthetic concept is the definition of *wen* given by Liu Hsi (early third century)[14] in his lexicographical work, *Explanations of Names* (*Shih-ming*): "*Wen* means assembling various colors to form brocade or embroidery, assembling various words to form phrases and meanings like patterned embroidery."[15]

Aestheticism in the Theories of Various Critics

Elements of aestheticism are also discernible in the writings of several critics we have discussed in previous chapters, namely, Lu Chi, Liu Hsieh, Hsiao T'ung, and Shen Yüeh. Lu Chi's dictum that poetry should be "exquisite as fine patterned silk" has already been quoted twice (chapter 2, note 57, and chapter 3, note 46). The following lines from his *Exposition on Literature* may further illustrate the aesthetic element in his critical thinking:

> As an object, literature presents many appearances;

> As form, it undergoes constant changes.
> In joining ideas together, one should esteem skill;
> In choosing words, one should value beauty.
> As for the alternation of sounds and tones,
> They should be like the five colors enhancing each
> other.[16]

Liu Hsieh, whose metaphysical theory also contains an aesthetic element, as we noted in chapter 2, suggests a balance between inner substance (*chih*) and outward beauty (*wen*) in literature, as demonstrated at the beginning of the "Emotion and Ornamentation" chapter of *The Literary Mind*:

> The writings of the sages and enlightened men are known collectively as "literary patterns" [*wen-chang*]: what are they if not ornamentations! Now, water, which is by nature mobile,[17] forms ripples; trees, which are solid in substance, give forth blossoms: these are examples of outward beauty [*wen*] attaching itself to inner substance [*chih*]. If the tiger and the leopard had no beautiful patterns [*wen*], their hide would be no different from a dog's or a sheep's;[18] the rhinoceros has hide, but this relies on vermilion varnish for color [when made into armour]:[19] these are examples of inner substance awaiting outward beauty.[20]

Having made his position clear, Liu Hsieh then proceeds to elaborate his aesthetic theory:

> Therefore, the basic way of literature consists of three principles: the first is called "formal pattern" [*hsing-wen*], which refers to the five colors; the second is called "auditory pattern" [*sheng-wen*], which refers to the five notes [of the pentatonic scale]; the third is called "emotional pattern" [*ch'ing-wen*], which refers to the five temperaments.[21] The five colors, when interwoven, form embroidered patterns; the five notes, when arranged, form music such as the Shao and the Hsia;[22] the five temperaments, when expressed, form literary compositions: this is the inevitable working of divine principles.[23]

The analogies with music and embroidery are also drawn by Hsiao T'ung in the preface to his *Literary Anthology*, in which, after enumerating various genres, he comments: "These are like different kinds of musical instruments which, whether made of earthenware or gourds, together delight the ear, or the embroidered patterns *fŭ* [black and white] and *fú* [black and blue] which, though differing in color combinations, both provide enjoyment for the eye."[24] It may be recalled that Shen Yüeh, too, drew these analogies in his remarks on literature, which I have quoted in chapter 4 as an example of the technical concept but which can also be considered an expression of aestheticism.

The same applies to some of the other critics quoted in the chapter on technical theories, and I shall not repeat the quotations and discussions, but give examples of aestheticism from the writings of various other critics of the T'ang and later periods, to whom the aesthetic concept may or may not be central.

Aestheticism and Sensuous Experience

Ssu-k'ung T'u, whose metaphysical theory of poetry has been discussed in chapter 2, shows a streak of aestheticism when he compares the "taste" or "flavor" (*wei*) of poetry to that of food, in a letter addressed to a Mr. Li:

> In my humble opinion, only when one can distinguish flavors can one speak of poetry. South of the [Yangtze] River and the [Five] Ranges [regions then considered semibarbarian], when it comes to condiments that make food tasty, it is not that their vinegar is not sour, but it is *merely* sour, not that their salt is not salty, but it is *merely* salty. The reason why people from the Central Realm [China proper] stop eating [Southern food] as soon as they have satisfied their hunger is that they know there is something lacking—the pure beauty that lies beyond saltiness and sourness.[25]

This concept of the "flavor that lies beyond sourness and saltiness" or the "flavor beyond flavor," which has been much admired by later poet-critics including Su Shih and Wang Shih-chen, is based on an analogy between literary and sensuous experiences, similar to the analogies with music and embroidery.

An appeal to the sense of taste is also made by the famous Sung poet and prose writer Ou-yang Hsiu (1007–72), when he praises his fellow-poet Mei Yao-ch'en by saying that reading the latter's poetry is like eating an olive: at first it tastes bitter, but the longer one chews it, the more one appreciates its true flavor.[26] As a matter of fact, the quality that has been generally recognized as typical of Sung poetry, especially the kind represented by Mei, is known as "dryness" (*se*), another aesthetic concept based on sensuous experience.

Later Advocates of the Aesthetic Concept

Other examples of aestheticism expressed in terms of sensuous experience are too numerous to mention. Naturally there are also aesthetic theories that do not resort to analogies with sensuous experience. A salient example is that of the Ch'ing scholar Juan Yüan (1764–1849), who maintained that only writings employing rhyme and parallelism could be called "literature" (*wen*), thus reviving the Six Dynasties concept of literature (*wen*) as belles lettres, in contradistinction to "plain writing" (*pi*).[27] In his essay "An Interpretation of *Wen-yen* [literary/embellished language]," he writes:

> Confucius himself gave the title "Embellished Words" [*Wen-yen*] to his commentary on the hexagrams Ch'ien and K'un [in the *Book of Changes*]: this is the ancestor of the literary compositions [*wen-chang*] of all ages. Those engaged in literary composition, who do not concern themselves with harmonizing sounds to form rhymes or polishing words and phrases to make them go far[28] so that what they write should be easy to recite and easy to remember, but merely use single [i.e., non-parallel] sentences and write in such wild abandon that, as soon as they begin, they will not stop until they have reached thousands of words, do not realize that what they write is what the ancients called "speech" [*yen*], which means "straightforward speech," or "talk" [*yü*], which means "argument," but not language [*yen*] that has embellishments [*wen*], not what Confucius called *wen* [embellished words/literature].[29]

This aesthetic theory of literature is reiterated in Juan's "Postface to Prince Chao-ming's Preface to His *Literary Anthology*," in which he further argues that since Prince Chao-ming (Hsiao T'ung) explicitly excluded from his "literary" anthology the Confucian Canon, the histories, and the philosophers, these are not to be regarded as "literature," a name that should be bestowed only on writings embellished with such formal beauties as parallelism and rhyme.[30]

The influence of Juan Yüan's theory, with its concommitant advocation of Parallel Prose as the only legitimate literary medium (in direct opposition to the advocates of Archaic Prose), lasted well into the twentieth century, through such noted scholars as Liu Shih-p'ei (1884–1919) and Huang K'an (1886–1935). Liu, for instance, stated categorically in the "general introduction" to his *History of Medieval Chinese Literature* (*Chung-kuo chung-ku wen-hsüeh shih*) that only writings employing parallelism deserve to be called literature (*wen*).[31] Similar ideas can be seen in Huang's commentaries on *The Literary Mind*.

SOME WESTERN PARALLELS

The aesthetic theories of literature described above have many Western parallels, whether these are labeled "hedonism," "formalism," or "aestheticism." To mention only a few of the most famous theories,

Aristotle's theory of catharsis, half of the Horatian formula that poetry both instructs and delights (the other half being pragmatic), Longinus's theory of the sublime, and Plotinus's theory of beauty, all have this in common with the Chinese aesthetic theories: they are all primarily focused on the immediate effects of a literary work on the reader or spectator. Sometimes we find striking similarities between Chinese and Western theories. For instance, Liu Hsieh's three kinds of patterns—"formal," "auditory," and "emotional"—are similar to the three kinds of rhetorical figures mentioned in Puttenham's *The Arte of English Poesie* (1588) ("sensible," "auricular," and "sententious"[32]) as well as to Ezra Pound's "Phanopoeia," "Melopoeia," and "Logopoeia."[33] On the other hand, there are naturally some differences. In general, Chinese aesthetic theorists were not wont to discuss Beauty in the abstract or to categorize aesthetic effects, as did Aristotle, Longinus, and Plotinus, but were content with impressionistic descriptions of aesthetic experience, often drawing analogies with sensuous experience. In this respect they resemble the nineteenth-century Western aesthetes, but they never went so far as to advocate "art for art's sake" or to declare that all art is amoral or immoral, as Oscar Wilde did.

6

Pragmatic Theories

Early Pragmatic Views

Pragmatic theories, which are primarily concerned with phase 4 of the artistic process and are based on the concept of literature as a means to achieve political, social, moral, or educational purposes, have been the most influential ones in traditional Chinese criticism, because they were sanctioned by Confucianism. Expressions of the pragmatic concept of poetry can be found in the *Book of Poetry,* which Confucius was said to have compiled and which became the first work in the Confucian Canon. The authors of several poems in this anthology announced that their intention was to admonish a ruler or an official. For instance, one poem, believed to be directed against an official,[1] contains the lines,

> This man is not good;
> I wrote this song to admonish him.[2]

Another poem, written by a certain Chia-fu, who may have lived in the early eighth century B.C.,[3] concludes with the words:

> Chia-fu composed this poem
> To investigate the causes of the King's troubles;
> May you change your heart,
> In order to cherish all the states.[4]

Yet another poem, addressed by one official to another, has a similar ending:

> The King wishes to value you as jade,
> Therefore I offer you this great admonition.[5]

Occasionally the poets announced their intention to praise a noble lord instead of admonishing him. One poem eulogizing the Earl of Shen, a maternal uncle of King Hsüan (reigned 827–782 B.C.), ends:

> Chi-fu composed this song,
> With its grand verse,
> And its fine tune,
> To present to the Earl of Shen.[6]

Another eulogy presented by Chi-fu to Chung-shan-fu expresses similar sentiments.[7] Whether the intention was to admonish or to praise a feudal lord or an official, the underlying assumption was that poetry should be concerned with government.

This assumption continued to be held by Confucius and the early Confucians. Before considering Confucius's views on literature, we should realize that Confucius was not a literary critic, any more than was Plato, and that the remarks made by M. H. Abrams about Plato could be applied, *mutatis mutandis,* to Confucius:

> neither the structure of Plato's cosmos nor the pattern of his dialectic permits us to consider poetry as poetry—as a special kind of product having its own criteria and reason for being. In the dialogues there is only one direction possible, and one issue, that is, the perfecting of the social state and the state of man; so that the question of art can never be separated from questions of truth, justice, and virtue.[8]

Fortunately, however, Confucius did not banish the poet from *his* ideal society, for he believed in the beneficial effects of poetry.

Since Confucius was not a literary critic, it is pointless to argue, as some have done,[9] over the question how good a critic he was. Nonetheless, the scattered remarks made by or attributed to him about language and about poetry have exerted such a profound influence on critics who came later that they must be considered. As for his remarks about *wen,* which, as mentioned in chapter 1 (see notes 27–29), meant to him "culture," "learning," or "refinement," rather than "literature" as we now understand the term, they will not be discussed, even though some of them have been applied to literature.

Two apparently contradictory remarks about language, both attributed to Confucius, have been quoted in different chapters of this book but may be repeated here. The one is, "Words communicate; that is all." And the other is, "If words do not have *wen* [patterns/embellishments], they will not go far." As we have seen, the former remark was cited by a critic to support an expressive theory of literature, and the latter by another critic to support an aesthetic one (see notes 75 and 76 to chapter 3, and chapter 5 at note 23). Can we accept both remarks as authentic sayings of Confucius? If so, can they be reconciled? Furthermore, do they really imply, respectively, an expressive concept of literature and an aesthetic one? Lo Ken-tse accepted the former remark as authentic and concluded that the latter could not have been made by Confucius, since it contradicted the former.[10] Actually, even if we accept the latter also, it can be interpreted as revealing not an aesthetic concept but a pragmatic one, for it does not claim that verbal patterns or embellishments are the very end of literature, but emphasizes these as a means to make words "go far" or render them more effective, probably in achieving practical purposes. As for the former remark, it is more likely that by "communicate" (*ta*) Confucius meant the communication of ideas or intentions in a social context than that he was referring to self-expression on the part of the literary artist.

The remarks Confucius made on various occasions about poetry have also been interpreted in different ways and cited as the final authority for very different theories of poetry. It will be convenient to quote below all the remarks about poetry recorded in the Confucian *Analects*, except those on particular poems or lines, and discuss them one by one. But first it should be explained that when Confucius spoke of "poetry" (*shih*) he was referring to the *Book of Poetry*, which was all the poetry that was available to him, or at least all that he would have accepted as such.[11] We are therefore justified in taking what he said about this anthology as representing his views on poetry in general.

> The *Three Hundred Poems* may be summed up in one phrase: "No evil thoughts."[12]

This remark obviously shows a pragmatic concern with the moral contents and effects of poetry.

> Be inspired by *Poetry*, confirmed by ritual, and perfected by music.[13]

The word translated here as "inspire," *hsing*, can also be taken to mean "begin"[14] or "exalt,"[15] and the words "ritual" (*li*) and "music" (*yüeh*) may also refer to particular books, but no matter how we interpret these words, it is clear that the whole remark describes a program for self-cultivation and is concerned with the practical effects of poetry.

> Though a man can recite the *Three Hundred Poems*, if he cannot carry out his duties when entrusted with affairs of state, and cannot answer questions on his own when sent on a mission abroad, what is the use of having studied the poems, no matter how many?[16]

This passage refers to the practice, common in the time of Confucius, of quoting lines from the *Book of Poetry*, often out of context, as an oblique way of expressing one's intentions on diplomatic or state occasions. The extremely pragmatic attitude in this passage is self-evident.

> If you do not study *Poetry*, you will not be able to speak [properly].[17]

Addressed to his son, this remark shows that Confucius regarded the *Book of Poetry* as a model of eloquence as well as a source of moral inspiration. The concern is still a pragmatic rather than aesthetic one, and the suggestion made by a recent writer that Confucius is stressing here the "artistic character of language"[18] is questionable.

> Young men, why do you not study *Poetry*? It can be used to inspire, to observe, to make you fit for company, to express grievances; near at hand, [it will teach you how] to serve your father, and, [looking] further, [how] to serve your sovereign; it also enables you to learn the names of many birds, beasts, plants, and trees.[19]

This is by far the fullest statement Confucius made about poetry, and also the most problematic, since most of the key words are not explained. However, judging by the opening remark, "why do you not *study Poetry*," we may conclude that Confucius is speaking of poetry from the reader's point of view, not the poet's. Furthermore, the phrase "can be used to" (*k'o-yi*) is another indication that he is concerned with the *uses* of poetry, not its genesis or nature. We can now consider the problematic terms in this passage.

Let us begin with the word *hsing*, here rendered "inspire," which, as mentioned above, can also be taken to mean "begin" or "exalt." In addition, it is also a technical term in Chinese literary criticism, one that appears in the *Major Preface* to the *Book of Poetry* as the name of one of three modes of expression in that anthology. When used this way, its precise meaning has been a subject of much controversy, which we cannot discuss in detail here; briefly, *hsing* may be explained as the "associational mode," in which the poet begins (*hsing*) by presenting a natural phenomenon and then expresses the human emotion inspired (*hsing*) by or associated with that phenomenon, instead of directly expressing himself (*fu*, the "expository" or "descriptive" mode) or making an explicit comparison between the natural phenomenon and the human situation or emotion (*pi*, the "comparative" or "analogical" mode).[20] This is a necessarily oversimplified interpretation of the three modes, and other interpretations, especially of *hsing*, are possible.[21] Further, the distinction between *pi* and *hsing* has by no means been clearly established, and traditional critics tend to lump the two together as *pi-hsing*, meaning loosely any kind of analogical way of expression. To return to the passage from the Confucian *Analects*, commentators on and translators of this passage fall into two groups: those who interpret *hsing* as "arouse," "inspire," or "incite," and those who take it in the technical sense. Among the former group some assume the object of "inspire" or "incite" to be emotions;[22] others assume it to be moral intents or sentiments.[23] It is impossible to be certain which Confucius meant; if the former, his conception of poetry would seem to be partly aesthetic, since the immediate emotional effect of poetry on the reader belongs to phase 3; if the latter, then his conception would seem to be totally pragmatic. As for those who take *hsing* as a technical term, their interpretation seems untenable since, as already pointed out, Confucius is speaking from the reader's point of view and not the poet's, and it does not make good sense to say that poetry (or the *Book of Poetry*) can be *used* to draw analogies or "make metaphorical comparisons."[24] If Confucius had really meant by *hsing* a mode of poetic expression, he would have said "*hsing* can be used to compose poetry" (*hsing k'o-yi shih*) instead of the other way round.

Next, we may consider the word "observe" (*kuan*), which has been variously interpreted as "observe the rise and decline of moral customs,"[25] "observe the successes and failures [of government],"[26] "self-contemplation,"[27] "observe people's feelings,"[28] "observe the myriad things in the universe,"[29] and "observe a man by seeing what lines he quotes from the *Book of Poetry*."[30] Again, it is impossible to ascertain which meaning Confucius intended, but in the light of Confucius's general interests and his other remarks on poetry, it seems likely that he is referring to poetry as a practical aid to one's observation (whether of the morals and mores of society or of the character of an individual) rather than as a means of self-contemplation or contemplation of the universe.

The third key word in the passage, *ch'ün*, literary means "crowd" or "community," and here probably refers to elegant speech as a social accomplishment. This interpretation is supported by the remark quoted earlier that without studying poetry one would not be able to speak. However, the word has been given a moralistic interpretation: "attempting to improve each other in company."[31] In either case, the concern remains pragmatic.

Next comes the word *yüan*, "complain" or "express grievances," which may seem to imply an expressive concept of poetry, if by this Confucius meant "express one's grievances by composing poetry." However, this would involve a sudden shift of point of view from the reader's to the poet's, which seems unlikely. What he probably meant is that one can rid oneself of grievances by *reciting* appropriate lines of poetry, in which case the underlying concept of poetry may be called partly aesthetic (in so far as it is concerned with the immediate emotional effects of poetry) and partly pragmatic (in so far as it has a practical purpose in view). It has also been suggested that *yüan* here refers to grievances against the government.[32] If this is true, the concept of poetry underlying the remark would be even more pragmatic.

The remaining remarks in the passage quoted above, about serving one's father and sovereign and learning the names of flora and fauna, are so obviously pragmatic as to need no comment.

In sum, I think Confucius's conception of literature was predominantly pragmatic, and even though he was aware of both the emotional effects and the aesthetic qualities of literature, these were to him subordinate to its moral and social functions.

Development of Confucian Pragmaticism

From the time Confucianism was established as the orthodox ideology of China in the second century B.C. down to the early twentieth century, the pragmatic concept of literature remained practically sacrosanct, so that critics who basically believed in other concepts rarely dared to repudiate it openly, but paid lip service to it while actually focusing attention on other concepts, or interpreted Confucius's words in such a way as to lend support to nonpragmatic theories, or simply kept silent about the pragmatic concept while developing others. As for those who did subscribe to the pragmatic concept, their theories of literature differed from one another in emphasis only: some emphasized the political functions of literature, either as an aid to government from the ruler's point of view, or as a means of criticism and protest from the subject's; others emphasized the effects of literature on personal morality. Although in the Confucian scheme of things sociopolitical and moral issues are closely interrelated, we can still recognize on which ones a critic lays his chief emphasis. Since it would be boring to quote a long succession of critics who expressed the same ideas and repeated the same quotations from the Confucian Canon throughout the centuries, only some of the most prominent ones will be mentioned.

The *Major Preface* to the *Book of Poetry*, from which statements embodying deterministic and expressive concepts have been quoted in chapter 3, also contains some strongly pragmatic pronouncements. On the one hand, it stipulates the political functions of poetry from the ruler's point of view:

> Therefore, nothing approaches the *Book of Poetry* in maintaining correct standards for success or failure [in government],

> in moving Heaven and Earth, and in appealing to spirits and gods. The Former Kings used it to make permanent [the tie between] husband and wife, to perfect filial reverence, to deepen human relationships, to beautify moral instruction, and to improve social customs.[33]

On the other hand, it also describes the political functions of poetry from the subject's point of view, in explaining the meaning of the word *feng* (which, as mentioned previously in chapter 3, means literally "wind" and figuratively "moral influence," "customs," and "to admonish") as the name of one of the three main categories of poetry in the *Book of Poetry*:

> The one above uses *feng* [airs/moral influence] to transform those below, and those below use *feng* [airs/admonition] to criticize the one above; when the main intent is set to music and the admonition is indirect, then the one who speaks does not commit any offense, while it is enough for the one who listens to take warning. Therefore, it is called *feng* [airs/moral influence/admonition].[34]

The independent-minded thinker Wang Ch'ung (A.D. 27–?), who held many unorthodox views on other subjects, nonetheless expressed the pragmatic concept of literature. His emphasis is a moral one, for he sees literature as a means to encourage good and deter evil:

> How can literature be merely a matter of playing with ink and toying with the writing brush? It is that which records men's deeds and passes on men's names [to posterity]. Good men wish [to have their deeds] recorded, and so exert themselves to do good; wicked men dislike [to have their deeds] recorded, and so make efforts to restrain themselves. Therefore the writing brush of the literary man is that which encourages good and warns against evil.[35]

Cheng Hsüan, whose deterministic conception of poetry has been described in chapter 3, reveals the pragmatic aspect of his theory of literature when he stresses the admonitory function of poetry:

> Poetry is the sound of admonition set to music. When writing was first invented, men were simple and esteemed plain substance. When a man praised [the ruler] to his face, it was not considered flattery, and when a man admonished [the ruler] face to face, it was not considered slander. The ruler and the subjects treated each other like friends, and everything depended on sincerity. When this principle declined somewhat, treachery and deceit thereby grew, and the one above and those below offended

> each other. By the time the rules of propriety [*li*] were regulated, the ruler was exalted and the subjects were degraded, the way of the ruler [being supposed to be] hard and severe, and that of the subject pliant and obedient. Thereupon few offered admonition, and the feelings and intents [of the subjects] were not communicated [to the ruler]. Therefore those who wrote poems used them to praise the ruler's virtues and to criticize his vices.[36]

This pragmatic concept of poetry does not necessarily contradict the deterministic, for one could conceive a poet as consciously attempting to admonish the ruler and unconsciously reflecting contemporary political conditions at the same time. The two concepts are related to different phases of the artistic process: the pragmatic to phase 4, the deterministic to phase 1.

Critics who did not openly reject the pragmatic concept of literature even though it was not primary in their theories include Ts'ao P'i, Lu Chi, and Liu Hsieh. Ts'ao, in the concluding passage of his "Discourse on Literature," declares, "For literature is a great task [that concerns] the governing of the State, a splendid enterprise that will never perish."[37] Likewise, Lu Chi, after stating that literature manifests universal principles in the final section of his *Exposition on Literature* (as we have seen in chapter 2), goes on to mention its political and moral functions: "It saves [the way of] Kings Wen and Wu from falling,/And propagates moral teaching so that it will not vanish."[38] As for Liu Hsieh, we have noted in chapter 2 that the pragmatic element in the opening chapter of *The Literary Mind* is subordinated to the metaphysical concept. However, in the final chapter of his book (which sets forth his intentions in writing it and is in fact like a preface although it is placed at the end of the book, as was often done in ancient Chinese books), the pragmatic concept becomes more prominent:

> The functions of literature [*wen-chang*] are really ramifications of the Scriptures: the Five Rites[39] rely on it for their completion, and the Six Codes[40] are put into effect by means of it. It is that by which [the principles governing the relationship between] the sovereign and the subjects are enabled to shine brilliantly, and [those governing] military and state affairs are made bright and clear.[41]

How Liu Hsieh attempted to reconcile this pragmatic concept with other concepts will be considered in the next chapter.

Examples of the assimilation of the metaphysical concept by the pragmatic have been given in chapter 2 and will not be repeated here.

Instead, we may turn our attention to critics who stressed the moral effects of literature. Beginning with Han Yü, whose moralistic definition of the word *Tao* we have seen, neo-Confucians generally conceived of literature as a means of propagating the Tao or Way, understood as the epitome of moral rather than cosmic principles. By far the most famous formulation of this moralistic conception of literature is that made by the philosopher Chou Tun-yi (1017–73):

> Literature is that by which one carries the Way. If the wheels and shafts [of a carriage] are decorated but no one uses it, then the decorations are in vain. How much more so in the case of an empty carriage! Literature and rhetoric are skills; the Way and virtue are realities. When someone devoted to these realities and skilled [in writing] writes down [the Way], if it is beautiful, then [people] will love it, and if they love it, then it will be passed on.[42]

In this passage, although the author begins by considering literature from the writer's point of view, by the end his attention has shifted to the moral effects of literature on the reader. We may therefore conclude that Chou Tun-yi's conception of literature is a pragmatic one, being concerned primarily with phase 4 of the artistic process.

Chou's formulation of the moralistic conception of literature was so influential that the slogan "Literature is that by which one carries the Way," or "Literature is a vehicle of the Way" (*wen yi tsai Tao*), became one of the two most often-quoted platitudes in Chinese literary criticism (the other one being the expressive formula "Poetry expresses intent," mentioned in chapter 3). Chou's followers, the two brothers Ch'eng Hao (1032–85) and Ch'eng Yi (1033–1107), went even further by asserting that literature is harmful to the pursuit of the Way.[43] Thus, the pragmatic concept of literature, when pushed to the extreme, led to what is in fact not a theory of literature, but an anti-theory.

Continuation of the Pragmatic Tradition

Later Confucian pragmatic critics on the whole did not develop theories basically different from those described above. However, to illustrate the continuity of the Confucian pragmatic tradition in Chinese literary criticism as well as its lack of innovations, I shall quote from the writings of the Ch'ing critic Shen Te-ch'ien (1673–1769) and the modern scholar Huang Chieh (1874–1935).

Shen Te-ch'ien, the favorite poet and literatus of the Manchu Emperor Ch'ien-lung, studied under Yeh Hsieh, whose views on poetry we have discussed in chapter 3. However, he did not inherit any of Yeh's expressive views but adhered staunchly to the pragmatic concept. In his *Miscellaneous Remarks on Poetry* (*Shuo-shih tsui-yü*), he begins by saying,

> The way of poetry is such that it can be used to regulate one's nature and emotions [or personality, *hsing-ch'ing*], to improve human relationships and [understanding of] things, to move the spirits and gods, to spread [moral] teaching in the states, and to deal with feudal lords. So important are its uses![44]

And in his preface to the revised edition of his anthology of T'ang poetry, he says much the same thing: "The exaltation of poetry as [moral] teaching is [due to the fact] that it can be used to moderate one's nature and emotions, to deepen human relationships, to aid government, and to move the gods and spirits.[45] Again, in his preface to his anthology of Ch'ing poetry, he reiterates: "Poetry must be based on one's nature and emotions, and concern itself with human relationships, everyday uses, and the causes of the rise and fall [of the state] in ancient and modern times. Only such poetry may be preserved."[46] These remarks, being mere echoes of the *Analects*, the *Major Preface* to the *Book of Poetry*, and other Confucian texts, contain nothing new.

The last Confucian pragmatic critic I shall quote, Huang Chieh, was for many years a professor of Chinese poetry at National Peking University. In the opening section of his *Poetics* (*Shih-hsüeh*) he announces his conception of poetry thus:

> The greatness of poetry as [moral] teaching is related to the rise or decline of the state, but those who discuss poetry to-day do not regard this as an urgent concern. Some there may be who hum and ponder over this [i.e., poetry], but then they let themselves go amidst rivers and lakes or skirts and clogs. Or there may be some who use it as a means to praise others or as friendly exchange. The reason why poetry has declined is that the principle of poetry is no longer clear.[47]

And, in his preface to his annotated edition of the poetry of Juan Chi (210–263), he repeats his pragmatic views:

> Since the abnormal conditions of the world have become a crisis, men's hearts have deteriorated even further. The Way and virtue [or morality, *tao-te*], propriety and rules [or the rules of propriety, *li-fa*], have all been usurped by wicked men. Some cunning ones then use this as an excuse to attempt to destroy them [*tao-te* and *li-fa*]. Only poetry as a form of [moral] teaching can penetrate men's hearts most deeply, and only in a time like this

> do students seek poetry as if hungry and thirsty. My duty lies in interpreting poetry, and I desire to make students understand clearly the intents [*chih*] of the poets so as to regulate their own nature and emotions [*hsing-ch'ing*], in the hope that this may be beneficial to people in the way they behave as people.[48]

Pragmatic Theories Distinguished from Other Kinds

It may be pointed out that although pragmatic critics sometimes employ the same critical terms as metaphysical ones on the one hand and expressive ones on the other, the underlying ideas are quite different. For instance, both metaphysical and pragmatic critics speak of literature in relation to the Tao, but whereas the former conceive of literature as a manifestation of the Tao, the latter conceive of it as a vehicle for the propagation of the Tao, let alone the difference between the metaphysical concept of Tao as cosmic principle and the pragmatic one as the moral Way. As for the difference between expressive and pragmatic critics when discussing literature in relation to personal nature and emotion (*hsing-ch'ing*), the former see literature as an expression of the writer's personal nature and emotion, while the latter see it as a means to regulate or moderate the reader's. In pragmatic theories, the focus of attention inevitably rests on the long-term effects of literature on the reader.

Parallels between Chinese pragmatic theories and Western ones, such as those of Horace, Sydney, and the Marxist critics, are too obvious to need elaboration.

7

Interactions and Syntheses

In discussing the six kinds of theories of literature in the preceding chapters, I have isolated each kind so as to exhibit clearly its distinctive features, although at times I have indicated interrelations among different kinds of theories. In this chapter I shall deal in greater detail with interactions among different kinds of theories and give some examples of contradictions between critics, self-contradictions or illogicalities in the writings of individual critics, and attempts at reconciling and synthesizing different theories. To use a metaphor with a traditional Chinese flavor, having separated different colored strands of silk from a piece of brocade, we may proceed to put them back together and see what patterns they make. Furthermore, since I have allocated space to the different kinds of theories according to what seemed to me their intrinsic interests and what promised to offer the most revealing and suggestive comparisons with Western theories rather than their relative historical importance, I hope to make amends now for any misleading impressions I may have created and to restore a proper historical perspective by recapitulating chronologically the developments of the various kinds of theories in broad outline.

Emergence of Different Theories

Let us begin with the earliest period (ca. 1000–722 B.C.), when rudimentary concepts of literature, or at least of poetry, first appeared. As we have seen in chapter 3, the etymology of the word for poetry, *shih*, suggests that the earliest Chinese concept of poetry was an expressive one, or possibly a partly expressive and partly pragmatic one. The expressive concept is also evidenced by some declarations of purpose in poems dating from about the elventh century to the eighth century B.C., and the pragmatic one by similar declarations in other poems dating from the ninth century B.C. (see notes 24 and 25 to chapter 3; notes 2 and 4 to chapter 6). As for the etymon of the word *wen*, although it has aesthetic implications, we cannot assume on this basis the existence of an aesthetic concept of literature in the earliest period of Chinese literary thought, since the word was not used until the second century B.C. to denote "literature."[1]

During the Ch'un-ch'iu, or Spring and Autumn (the period covered by the *Spring and Autumn Annals*, 722–481 B.C.), and the Chan-kuo, or Warring States (403–221 B.C.) periods, the pragmatic concept of literature was endorsed by Confucius and the early Confucians, although some of Confucius's remarks were later cited by different critics to lend support to nonpragmatic theories.[2]

It was during this period that the expressive concept of poetry became succinctly embodied in the statement *shih yi yen chih*, or "Poetry is that by which one expresses intent," as recorded in the *Tso-chuan* (probably compiled in the fourth century B.C.) for the year 546 B.C. Later, further abbreviated as *shih yen chih*, or "Poetry expresses intent," this formula became one of the two most often quoted slogans in Chinese literary criticism (see note 32 to chapter 3). (The attribution of this statement to the legendary sage Emperor Shun cannot be accepted.)

Meanwhile, the deterministic concept made its first appearance in the *Tso-chuan* with reference to an event that took place in 543 B.C., and the chief sources of metaphysical theories, the *Commentaries* on the *Book of Changes*, the *Lao Tzu*, and the *Chuang Tzu*, were probably produced during the fourth and third centuries B.C. (see chapter 2).

With the official recognition of Confucianism as the orthodox ideology in the Han period (206 B.C.–A.D. 220), the pragmatic concept of literature assumed supremacy, at least nominally, although in fact the aesthetic concept was quite widely held, judging by the use of the terms *wen* and *wen-chang* (both meaning literally "patterns") to denote writings marked by formal aesthetic qualities,[3] and the emergence of the ornate Exposition as the most highly esteemed literary genre. Attempts were made to reconcile the pragmatic concept with the aesthetic by claiming for works written and enjoyed largely for aesthetic reasons a didactic function. For instance, Ssu-ma Hsiang-ju's pyrotechnic description of the imperial hunting park entitled *Shang-lin fu* was written ostensibly to admonish the emperor against extravagant hunts.[4] That such attempts did not convince everyone may be deduced from the case of Yang Hsiung, who at first admired Ssu-ma greatly and wrote Expositions himself but later despised the genre as a "petty skill like the carving of insects," fit only for boys but unworthy of mature men.[5] His rejection of the aesthetic concept of literature in favor of the pragmatic has at least the merits of intellectual honesty and logical consistency, whether one approves or deplores his change of attitude.

INCONSISTENCIES IN THE MAJOR PREFACE

Among writings of the Han period, the *Major Preface* to the *Book of Poetry* is the fullest exposition of a theory of poetry, but it also presents the most glaring non sequiturs. I have quoted three statements from the *Major Preface* in different chapters; however, to show its inconsistencies I shall quote again in toto the passage in which all three statements occur:

> Poetry is where the intent of the heart [or mind] goes. Lying in the heart [or mind], it is "intent"; when uttered in words, it is "poetry." When an emotion stirs inside, one expresses it in words; finding this inadequate, one sighs over it; not content with this, one sings it in poetry; still not satisfied, one unconsciously dances with one's hands and feet. Emotions are uttered in sounds, and when sounds form patterns [*wen*], they are called music. The music of a well-governed world is peaceful and happy, its government being harmonious; the music of a disorderly world is plaintive and angry, its government being perverse; the music of a vanquished country is sad and nostalgic, its people being distressed. Therefore, nothing approaches the *Book of Poetry* in maintaining correct standards for success or failure [in government], in moving Heaven and Earth, and in appealing to the spirits and gods. The Former Kings used it to make permanent [the tie between] husband and wife, to perfect filial reverence, to deepen human relationships, to beautify moral instruction, and to improve social customs (Cf. note 32 to chapter 3.)

It will be observed that after announcing the expressive concept in the first three sentences, the author, either consciously or unwittingly, introduces an aesthetic element in the next sentence when he speaks of "patterns" of sound; then, after expressing the deterministic concept in the sentence beginning "The music of a well-governed world...," he shifts to the pragmatic in the last section of the passage, "Therefore, nothing approaches. . . ." In spite of the ingenuous (or perhaps ingenious) use of "therefore," no logical explanation is given as to how and why the spontaneous expression of one's emotion will necessarily reflect political conditions, or how and why such expression will fulfill moral, social, and political purposes. To accept this passage as a whole, one would have to assume that there are no human emotions other than those induced by political conditions and that all emotions thus induced are necessarily moral and conducive to better political conditions. One would also have to refrain from raising the question whether all spontaneous expressions of emotion will somehow acquire auditory patterns that can be called musical.

These illogicalities are not resolved in the remainder of the *Preface*. It may be recalled that its author stated that after the decline of the Kingly Way the "Changed Airs" and "Changed Odes" arose.[6] He further comments:

> The historiographers who understood the marks left by success or failure [in government], who lamented the abandonment of propriety and rightness, and who grieved over the harshness of punishments, sang their emotions and natures in order to admonish the one above [i.e., the ruler]: they were those who understood [the causes of] change in [political] affairs and nostalgically remembered old customs. Therefore, the "Changed Airs" issued forth from emotion and stopped at propriety and rightness. What issued forth from emotion is the nature of the people; what stopped at propriety and rightness is the remaining beneficial influence of the Former Kings. (Cf. note 32 to chapter 3.)

This attempt to reconcile the expressive concept of poetry with the deterministic and the pragmatic is not successful. In the first place, there is an apparent discrepancy between the statement that the historiographers "sang their emotions and natures" and that what issued forth from emotion was "the nature of the people." Even if we accept the explanation of the sub-commentator K'ung Ying-ta (574–648) that the author did not mean that the historiographers expressed their own emotions and natures in poetry but that they collected songs that expressed the emotions of the people (cf. note 32 to chapter 3), we may still doubt whether the expression of the people's emotions would necessarily "stop at propriety and rightness."

Florescence of Different Theories

During the Wei (220–265), Chin (265–420), and Southern Dynasties (420–589), when Chinese literary criticism attained its richest and most varied florescence, expressive as well as technical and aesthetic theories were prominent, while the metaphysical concept of literature became for the first time fully articulated, and the pragmatic received nominal homage. We have already discussed various theories of these periods, including those of three critics of major importance, Ts'ao P'i, Lu Chi, and Liu Hsieh; it is now time to examine how far each of them succeeded in synthesizing different concepts.

Ts'ao P'i is predominantly an expressive critic, since he considers *ch'i*, or individual talent based on temperament, the most important element of literature. The pragmatic concept is introduced towards the end of his essay on literature, perhaps simply to pay lip service to it. In order to realize the relative importance of the expressive concept and the pragmatic in his thinking, let us see the passage in which the pragmatic concept makes its sole appearance:

> Literature is a great task [that concerns] the governing of the State, a splendid enterprise that will never perish. Our life span will come to an end; glory and happiness will cease with one's person. These have their inevitable limits in time, and cannot compare with the endlessness of literature. Therefore the writers of antiquity dwelt among the writing brushes and ink and expressed their meanings in chapters and volumes; without depending on the words of good historians or relying on the influence of high positions, their fame naturally passed on to posterity.[7]

It is obvious from this passage that the pragmatic concept is not integrated with the rest of Ts'ao's theory of literature, which is expressive, as further evidenced by his idea that through literature one can gain immortal fame. This idea, which he inherited from the *Tso-chuan*,[8] can be called an extension of the expressive concept of literature, for it suggests that literature is not only self-expression but also self-perpetuation.

LU CHI'S ECLECTICISM

Lu Chi, from whose *Exposition on Literature* I have quoted lines revealing metaphysical, expressive, aesthetic, and pragmatic concepts, appears to be eclectic rather than syncretic, for he makes no attempt to integrate these different concepts into a single system, but expresses them at different points in his work (see note 23 to chapter 2, note 45 to chapter 3, note 16 to chapter 5, and note 38 to chapter 6). However, these concepts are of varying degrees of importance in his thinking. The expressive is by far the most important, for his attention is primarily focused on phase 2 of the artistic process, and his most penetrating observations concern the creative process and the working of inspiration. Next in importance seems to be the metaphysical concept, for he sees the manifestation of universal principles as the primary function of literature, and envisages the writer as contemplating the mysteries of the universe before he begins to write. Less important appear to be the technical and aesthetic concepts, for although Lu Chi pays considerable attention to the conscious artistry of writing and the aesthetic qualities to be aimed at, to him these are secondary to inspiration, which is beyond conscious control. The pragmatic concept is only introduced at the end of the work, perhaps to forestall possible criticism from Confucian moralists. It would be fair to say that while Lu Chi did not formulate a consistent system out of the various concepts of literature he adopted, neither did he contradict himself blatantly.

Liu Hsieh's Syncretism

Now we come to Liu Hsieh, whose magnum opus, *The Literary Mind*, takes into account all the four phases of the artistic process and contains elements of all the six kinds of theories of literature found in Chinese criticism except the deterministic. As I attempted to demonstrate in chapter 2, Liu's basic conception of literature, which he describes in his first chapter, is primarily metaphysical, although other concepts assume prominence in some other chapters of his book. Liu does not explicitly explain the interrelations among the different concepts; however, it is possible to discern, through analysis, how the other concepts are related and generally subordinated to the metaphysical.

We have already seen, in chapter 2, how Liu subordinates the pragmatic concept to the metaphysical by stressing the sage's role as one who manifests the cosmic Tao in literature rather than one who teaches moral lessons. To Liu, the moral Tao is based on the cosmic Tao, and since literature manifests the former, it can serve moral purposes. In other words, it is from the metaphysical nature of literature that its pragmatic functions are derived, not the other way round. His theory thereby differs from purely pragmatic ones, according to which the pragmatic purposes of literature dictate its nature.

As for the expressive concept, although this is emphasized in various places in Liu's work, it is demonstrably subordinated to the metaphysical through the concept of "naturalness." More than once Liu states that it is "natural" for a man to reveal his nature in literary works (*wen*), just as it is natural for flora and fauna to manifest their natures through their outward beauty (*wen*).[9] The analogy between tiger's and leopard's skins, on one hand, and literature, on the other (an analogy that Liu adopted from Confucius's disciple Tuan-mu Ssu, known by his courtesy name Tzu-kung—see note 18 to chapter 5), points at a crucial difference between Liu's conception of literature and the purely expressive one: whereas Liu sees literature as part of the cosmic process of natural manifestation of inner qualities through outward patterns, purely expressive theorists see it as self-expression intended by the writer. To ignore this vital difference and call Liu Hsieh a primarily expressive theorist is to confuse manifestation with expression,[10] which would lead to the absurd conclusion that tigers and leopards consciously *express* their natures by means of stripes and spots.

At the same time, this concept of natural manifestation of inner qualities through outward patterns, illustrated by the above analogy and many others, also accommodates the aesthetic concept of literature, for if it is natural for every object to have its own outward beauty (*wen*), it is equally natural for man to manifest his nature in beautiful language (*wen*). Thus the aesthetic concept is also justified by an appeal to the metaphysical. In Liu's system as a whole, the aesthetic concept is relegated to a secondary position, as is the technical. To him, literature should have formal beauty, but not *merely* formal beauty; it involves technique, but is not *merely* technique.

The technical concept may seem to contradict that of natural manifestation, but it can be argued that there is no real contradiction between, on the one hand, the assimilation of technique as a preparation for writing, and, on the other, the natural and intuitive character of the actual process of writing. In other words, if one gradually absorbs artistic technique until it becomes second nature, then the process of writing will not be a deliberate but a spontaneous one. That this is what Liu meant can be seen from his allusions to Chuang Tzu's parables about the cook and the wheelwright (in a passage to be quoted below): both have reached a state of intuitive control over technique after years of concentrated effort. Hence, Liu concludes, "if one holds one's mind and cultivates artistry [*shu*], there will be no need to engage in painful thinking."[11]

The seeming contradictions among the various kinds of theories involved in Liu's work, as well as their possible resolutions, can be illustrated by an analysis of his varying accounts of the relation between the writer's mind and the universe. In several places, as pointed out in chapter 3, he describes this relation as a reciprocal one: objects move the writer, who responds to them emotionally. This description is in accordance with the expressive concept of literature. However, in the passage from the "Intuitive Thinking" (*Shen-ssu*) chapter quoted in chapter 2 of the present book, he advises the writer to empty his mind and keep it still. This idea that the mind should be receptive is consistent with metaphysical theories. Yet immediately after the passage in question, he goes on to say:

> Accumulate learning to store up treasures, draw from reason to enrich your talent, investigate experience to exhaust enlightenment, tame your feelings to put words in order.[12]. Then, let the

> "cook of mystical understanding"[13] seek the rules of music so as to fix the ink on paper,[14] and let the "wheelwright of unique enlightenment"[15] espy mental images so as to wield his axe. This is the first skill to be mastered in controlling writing, and the main principle in planning a piece.[16]

Here, the four activities enumerated, which correspond to what he calls "learning" and "practice" in the "Style and Personality" (*T'i-hsing*) chapter (see chapter 3 of this volume), as well as the references to "rules" (*lü*), "skill" (*shu*), and "controlling" (*yü*), all seem to contradict the concept of mental emptiness and describe what we may term an "investigative" state of mind, which is more in tune with a technical theory of literature than a metaphysical or expressive one. To complicate matters further, Liu follows this passage with another one in which he describes first a creative and then a projective mental process:

> Now, as soon as the intuitive thinking [*shen-ssu*] has begun to operate, a myriad paths will vie with one another in sprouting up [*sic*]; one can then apply the compasses and the square to empty space, and carve and engrave what has no form.[17] If one climbs a mountain, one's feelings will fill the mountain; if one observes the sea, one's ideas will overflow the sea. No matter how much talent I may have, it will gallop together with the wind and clouds.[18]

Both the idea of giving form to non-existent things and that of projecting one's mind into Nature are consonant with expressive theories, and so we seem to have come full circle. Actually, the seeming inconsistencies can be resolved by pointing out that the different kinds of relation between the writer and the universe, and the different mental processes involved, pertain to different levels of experience and may occur at different times. For the sake of clarity, we may summarize the different mental processes roughly in the order in which they may be supposed to occur:

1. The investigative: writer accumulates knowledge and investigates experience. This refers to experience at the rational level, and to long-term preparations for writing.
2. The reciprocal: objects appeal to writer's senses; writer responds emotionally. This refers to experience at the sensuous-emotional level and to the time before writing.
3. The receptive: writer empties mind and keeps it still to be receptive of cosmic Tao. This refers to intuition in its quiescent mode, and to the time immediately before writing .
4. The projective: writer projects own feelings into objects. This

refers to intuition in its active mode, and to the time immediately before or during the process of writing.

5. The creative: writer creates imaginary objects that do not exist in real world. This also refers to intuition in its active mode, and to the time of writing.

As interpreted above, the different mental processes do not necessarily contradict each other, for a writer can engage in rational investigation of things and be emotionally responsive to them in his daily life, and then, just before he begins to write, free his mind from its ordinary preoccupations so as to be ready for intuitive encounter with Nature and for the creative act itself. To be sure, Liu has modified the Taoist concept of mental emptiness and combined it with other concepts, thus making it possible to admit expressive and technical views into his metaphysical theory. Although he has departed from Lao Tzu and Chuang Tzu to the extent that he does not reject rational knowledge or emotional rapport with objects, it seems unlikely that in quoting Chuang Tzu's words Liu actually had in mind the Confucian Hsün Tzu's idea of being "empty, single-minded, and still" (which apparently refers to concentration and riddance of preconceptions), as has been suggested.[19]

Liu Hsieh also departs from Chuang Tzu somewhat in his conception of intuition: he conceives of it as having both an active or projective mode and a quiescent or receptive mode, instead of being only receptive. (However, it should be realized that Chuang Tzu's concept of mental emptiness is not the same as Locke's concept of the mind as a tabula rasa, which passively receives impressions; that is why I have avoided describing this mental state as "passive.") Various modern scholars have identified Liu Hsieh's "intuitive thinking" (*shen-ssu*) with "imagination" or its modern Chinese equivalent, *hsiang-hsiang*,[20] but in fact it is only the active mode of *shen-ssu* that corresponds to "imagination," as the word has been used by Coleridge and most critics writing in English since. Moreover, whereas Coleridge asserts that the imagination is "essentially *vital*, just as all objects (*as* objects) are essentially dead,"[21] Liu, in common with practically all other Chinese critics, does not regard things as "dead" but as possessing their own "spirit" (*shen*). It is therefore somewhat misleading to translate *shen-ssu* as "imagination."

It would be pleasant if we could claim on Liu Hsieh's behalf that his attempts to reconcile different theories of literature are totally successful, but such a claim would hardly be true. I have pointed out elsewhere instances of his apparent inconsistencies due to his efforts to reconcile the pragmatic (or didactic) and the expressive (or individualist) theories,[22] and I shall mention them again briefly, while adding a few details and revising some of my previous translations of his remarks. One instance occurs when, after quoting the definition of poetry attributed to the sage Emperor Shun, "Poetry expresses intent" (*shih yen chih*), Liu goes on to quote another definition from the *Apocryphal Commentary on the Book of Poetry*, "Poetry [*shih*] means 'hold' [*ch'ih*]," and elaborates:

> Poetry is what holds one's emotion and nature [within the bounds of propriety]. In summing up the *Three Hundred Poems* [Confucius] described their general principle with the phrase, "No evil thoughts." The interpretation of "poetry" as "hold" finds here its corroboration.[23]

Ingenious as it may be, this attempt to reconcile the pragmatic concept with the expressive fails to explain how the expression of one's intent will necessarily have a morally beneficial effect on the reader. If it is implied that it is because the poets' intents are moral that their expressions will have such effects, then the question may be raised as to why the poets' intents are always moral. If it is further argued that only those intents that are moral should be expressed in poetry, then this is no longer saying the same thing as that poetry is the spontaneous expression of one's intent. In other words, the pragmatic and prescriptive doctrine that poetry *should* exert moral influence and the expressive and descriptive statement that poetry *is* the expression of the heart or mind simply cannot be reconciled without drastic modifications.

Similarly, when Liu Hsieh praises the poets of the *Book of Poetry* with the words taken from the *Major Preface* that they "sang their emotions and natures so as to admonish the one above,"[24] he perpetuates the omission of any logical explanation of the connection between the expressive nature ascribed to poetry and the pragmatic functions it is supposed to serve. Despite such inconsistencies or omissions of explanations, Liu's work remains a tour de force unique in Chinese literary criticism.

The Dominance of Pragmatism and Some Deviations

The T'ang dynasty (618–907), which succeeded the short-lived Sui (589–618), witnessed unprecedented and unsurpassed developments in literature, especially poetry, but no correspondingly remarkable developments in criticism. This is not surprising, for an age of great creativity is not necessarily also an age of great critical sophistication. Nevertheless, it is still disappointing that most of the great T'ang poets either kept silent about the nature of literature (as Wang Wei did), or, when they did speak on the subject, expressed rather conventional views (as Li Po and Tu Fu did).[25]

Through most of the T'ang period, the pragmatic concept of literature prevailed, sometimes absorbing other concepts, especially the metaphysical, as described in chapter 2, while the technical concept, though not explicitly expounded, was the tacit assumption underlying many manuals of poetics, which often purported to be the works of famous poets. However, during the late T'ang and the subsequent Five Dynasties (907–959) periods, deviations from the pragmatic view became more common. An example is the poet Li Shang-yin (813?–858), who, as a young man, wrote in a letter to a would-be patron:

> At first, when I heard my elders say that in learning the Tao one must seek it from the ancients and in composing literature one must follow rules, I felt greatly unhappy. Then I withdrew and thought to myself: How can what we call the Tao be something that only the ancients called the Duke of Chou and Confucius were capable of? For, inferior as I am, I can personally partake in it together with the Duke of Chou and Confucius. Therefore, I have tried to practice the Tao without depending on the moderns or the ancients, and in writing I have directly wielded my brush, being loathe to plagiarize the Scriptures or the histories, or to avoid what may cause offense to the contemporary world.[26]

This passage has been cited as evidence of Li's frontal attack on the moralistic view of literature,[27] but actually he is not repudiating the moralistic interpretation of Tao or challenging the theory that literature should propagate the Tao, but merely denying that the only way to acquire the Tao is by studying the writings of the ancient sages and the only way to expound the Tao is by imitating their words. By claiming that anyone can partake in the Tao and freely express himself in writing, Li introduces an expressive element of an individualistic kind into the pragmatic view of literature.

His subscription to both the pragmatic and the expressive concepts can be further attested by another letter, written to accompany a collection of his own poems being presented to a high official. He begins the letter with a statement that shows an unmistakably expressive view: "Man is endowed with the finest essences of the Five Agents and furnished with the capacity of being stirred by the seven emotions. Therefore, he must chant and sigh to communicate his personal nature [*hsing-ling*]."[28] Then, after praising the poets of the *Book of Poetry* and some later poets and comparing their works to music and embroidery, he concludes, "[Poetry that] criticizes the times and [that which] reveals one's intent each has its own points." This indicates that he regarded both the expressive and the pragmatic concepts of poetry as valid, without attempting to integrate the two or distorting either one to fit the other. At the same time, his comparisons of poetry to music and embroidery suggest an aesthetic element in his theory as well.

Another late T'ang poet who departed from the pragmatic tradition was Ssu-k'ung T'u, whose metaphysical and aesthetic views have been discussed in chapters 2 and 5 respectively.

During the Sung dynasty (960–1279), the pragmatic concept was again dominant, while other concepts appeared occasionally. This does not mean that opinions on literature were unanimous; on the contrary, there were disagreements among three groups: the neo-Confucian philosophers known as *tao-hsüeh-chia* ("experts in the study of the Tao or Way," not to be confused with the Taoists), the expert writers of Archaic Prose (*ku-wen-chia*), and the experts in Confucian Scriptural scholarship (*ching-hsüeh-chia*).[29] Members of the first group, such as the Ch'eng brothers and Chu Hsi (1130–1200), regarded literature (*wen*) as subsidiary or even detrimental to the Way (Tao); the second group, represented by Ou-yang Hsiu, justified their interest in literature by subscribing to the theory that literature is a means of expounding the Way; the third group, represented by Wang An-shih (1021–1086), identified literature with the study of the Confucian Scriptures and the application of their principles to statecraft. Basically, all three groups accepted the pragmatic concept of literature, their differences being concerned with the questions of how much attention one should devote to literature as a means of propagating the Way, and of what kind of pragmatic purpose literature should primarily serve, whether moral or political. Since no basically conflicting conceptions of literature were involved in these disagreements, we need not discuss them. Instead, we shall briefly review the varying degrees of exclusiveness and rigidity with which certain writers adhered to the pragmatic concept, and consider what other concepts some of them admitted into their thinking.

The extreme position taken by the Ch'eng brothers, that literature is harmful to the Way, has already been mentioned in the preceding chapter. A little less extreme are the attitudes of Chou Tun-yi, who raised the banner of "Literature is a vehicle of the Way" (*wen yi tsai Tao*, as described in chapter 6), and of Shao Yung, who subordinated the expressive concept to the pragmatic by interpreting "intent" (*chih*) as moral purpose and social concern (as described in chapter 3). One may add the comment that Shao, and many others who interpreted *chih* in a similar fashion, were able to avoid the difficulty that Liu Hsieh was apparently unable to solve, but they did so only at the cost of distorting the expressive concept embodied in the hallowed formula "Poetry expresses intent" (*shih yen chih*). They did not effect a genuine reconciliation between these two different concepts of literature, but merely subverted the one to fit the other.

Still less strictly pragmatic is Ou-yang Hsiu, the spiritual heir of Han Yü and the leader of the second Archaic Prose movement (the first being that led by Han himself in the T'ang). As a writer, Ou-yang wrote serious essays and official historiography in Archaic Prose, adopting a high moral tone and an archaic and relatively plain style; poems in traditional meters (*shih*) in a similar style; official documents in the ornate Parallel Prose; and lyrics or songs (*tz'u*) that are highly romantic or even erotic in a refined or colloquial style.[30] One can explain such seeming inconsistencies, as indeed he himself did to some extent, by saying that in using Parallel Prose he was only making concessions to contemporary practice and taste,[31] and that the lyrics were mere entertainment,[32] not to be considered "literature." Even so, his conception of literature seems to change when it comes to poetry. When discussing *wen* either in the broader sense of "literature" in general or in the narrower sense of "prose," particularly Archaic Prose, he maintains a pragmatic attitude and follows the doctrine that literature should propagate the Way,[33] but when he praises Mei Yao-ch'en's poetry for its "olive-like" taste (as mentioned in chapter 5), and when he expresses special admiration for Han Yü's dexterity in rhyming,[34] he betrays aesthetic and technical concerns. Moreover, in developing an idea of Han Yü's and proposing that "poetry improves with adversity" (*shih ch'iung yü kung*),[35] he reveals an expressive view of poetry as the expression of pent-up grievances and frustrations. Ou-yang Hsiu was not the first to adopt this dualistic attitude to prose and poetry; some T'ang writers had already shown a tendency to treat the two separately.[36] However, the tendency became more pronounced in Sung times and persisted in later periods, perhaps because this dualism provided a conscious or unconscious outlet, or rather inlet, for nonpragmatic views.

Even more liberal than Ou-yang's views are those of Su Shih, whose metaphysical ideas of identifying with Nature and of mental emptiness and stillness have been mentioned in chapter 2. His metaphysical leanings can be further seen in the way he tried to reconcile the two apparently contradictory remarks about language attributed to Confucius:

> Confucius said, "If words do not have *wen* [patterns/embellishments], they will not go far." He also said, "Words communicate; that is all." Now, if words should only communicate, we may suspect that they are not *wen* [embellished/literary]. It is not so at all. To seek the subtleties [or wonders, *miao*] of things is like trying to tie up the wind or capture shadows; we can hardly find one man out of thousands who can make things appear clearly in the mind, let alone making them appear clearly from the mouth and the hand [i.e., in speech and writing]. This is what is meant by "words communicate." If words can reach such a state of communicativeness, there will be more than sufficient *wen* [embellishments/literature].[37]

This interesting and highly individual interpretation of the remarks attributed to Confucius throws more light on Su Shih's own conception of literature than the Sage's. Apparently taking these two remarks as expressions of an aesthetic concept and a pragmatic one respectively, Su attempted to reconcile them by interpreting both "literariness" (*wen*) and "communication" (*ta*) as the ability to capture the subtleties or wonders of things and to express them in words—an idea in accordance with metaphysical theories of literature. Thus, he reconciled the aesthetic and the pragmatic concepts and transcended both by means of the metaphysical.

Somewhat different views were held by Su Shih's younger brother Su Ch'e (1039–1112), who incorporated pragmatic, metaphysical, and aesthetic elements into a mainly expressive theory of literature, while rejecting the technical concept. As a very young man, he wrote in a letter presented to Grand Marshal Han Ch'i:

> I consider writing [*wen*] to be an embodiment of one's vital force [*ch'i*]. However, writing is not something that one can learn to become capable of, while the vital force is something that one can acquire by cultivation. Mencius said, "I am good at cultivating my overflowing *ch'i*." Now, when we observe his writing, it is wide and deep, vast and grand, filling the space between heaven and earth, and matching the magnitude of his vital force. The Grand Historiographer [Ssu-ma Ch'ien] travelled over the world, surveying all the famous mountains and great rivers within the four seas, and associating with the heroic and outstanding men of Yen and Chao. Hence his writing is spacious and free, possessing to a remarkable degree an extraordinary air [*ch'i*]. Did these two masters ever, writing-brush in hand, *learn* to produce such writings? The vital force of each filled his inside, overflowed his countenance, stirred up his words, and manifested itself in his writing, without his knowing it himself.

> I have lived for nineteen years. When I lived at home, those with whom I associated were only neighbors and fellow villagers, and what I saw was confined to a few hundred *li*, without high mountains that I could climb or vast wilderness that I could view so as to broaden myself. And although among the books of the "hundred schools" there was none that I did not read, these were all old traces left by the ancients, not sufficient to stimulate one's will and vital force. For fear these might trickle away, I left with determination, to seek the extraordinary events and grand views of the world, so that I might realize the greatness of the universe.[38]

Allowing for a certain amount of youthful bravado, we may still see in this letter Su Ch'e's conception of literature, which is chiefly expressive, as witnessed by the first sentence quoted. However, his concept of *ch'i* differs significantly from Ts'ao P'i's. Whereas Ts'ao regards the *ch'i* as an innate quality that cannot be acquired, Su Ch'e expresses the opposite view that it can be acquired by "cultivation" or "nourishing" (*yang*). What he means by "cultivating one's *ch'i*" is not quite the same as what Liu Hsieh means by the same expression: as used by Liu, the phrase refers to the conservation of creative energy, but in Su's usage it refers to a more positive process of expanding and enriching one's vital force. He appears to suggest two ways of doing this: first, by cultivating one's moral force, as implied by his quotation of Mencius, who, it may be recalled, conceived of the *ch'i* as being "born of an accumulation of rightness," and secondly, by assimilating the cosmic vital force (*ch'i*), as suggested by the emphasis on observing the grandeurs of Nature. These two ways would seem to reconcile Su Ch'e's expressive concept of literature with the pragmatic on the one hand and the metaphysical on the other. At the same time, since he describes the extraordinary *ch'i* of Ssu-ma Ch'ien's writing as a perceptible quality, he shows some aesthetic concern as well. As for his rejection of the technical concept, this is clearly shown by his remarks that writing is not something that one can learn, and that all books are only old traces of the ancients.

Other Sung writers and critics who held nonpragmatic views include members of the Chiang-hsi School (mentioned in chapter 2), whose preoccupations with "method" and imitation of ancient poets imply a technical conception of literature, and Yen Yü, whose mainly metaphysical theory of poetry has been discussed in some detail. It is ironic that Yen criticized poets of the Chiang-hsi School severely, for he was influenced by them in the application of Ch'an terminology to poetry. A further irony occurred later when some of Yen's followers reverted largely to the technical concept, as we shall see below.

ARCHAISM AND ITS REACTION

During the Yüan, or Mongol, Dynasty (1280–1368) and the early part of the Ming (1368–1644), the pragmatic concept of literature remained the orthodox one, although other concepts sometimes became noticeable, such as Kao Ch'i's technical and expressive ones mentioned in chapter 4. However, from about the middle of the fifteenth century to the late sixteenth, the position of literary orthodoxy was assumed by archaism, which, as pointed out before, is not a theory of literature but a literary theory about how to write. Therefore, those who subscribed to archaism may differ in their basic conceptions of literature. Broadly speaking, writers and critics who accepted archaism (that is, the contemplation and imitation of the works of ancient writers as a means to achieve mastery of literary technique) fall into two groups: those who apparently considered mastery of technique as an end in itself and whose concept of literature may therefore be called technical, and those who considered the process of acquiring intuitive mastery of technique as a means of attaining spiritual enlightenment[39] and whose concept of literature may therefore be called primarily metaphysical. The former group may be represented by Li Tung-yang and Li Meng-yang, both discussed in chapter 4; the latter group by Hsieh Chen, discussed in chapter 2.

A critic who struck a balance between the metaphysical and the technical concepts was Hu Ying-lin (1551–1602), who acknowledged that he derived his two main ideas about poetry, intuitive "awakening" or enlightenment (*wu*) and "method" (*fa*), from Yen Yü and Li Meng-yang respectively. His reconciliation of the two concepts can be seen clearly from the following passage:

> The essentials of writing poetry do not go beyond two principles: [the first consists of] formal style [or form and style, *t'i-ko*] and musical tone [or sound and tone, *sheng-tiao*]; [the second of] inspired imagery [*hsing-hsiang*] and personal airs or spirit [*feng-shen*]. With regard to formal style, there are rules that one can follow; but with regard to inspired imagery and personal airs or spirit, there are no ways that one can adhere to. Hence, a writer need only seek to make his form correct and his style lofty, his sound powerful and his tone flowing; after he has accumulated practice for a long time, all his careful attentions will melt away and all outward traces will dissolve. Then his inspired imagery and personal airs or spirit will naturally become transcendent.

> To draw an analogy with the flower in the mirror and the moon reflected in water: formal style and musical tone are the water and the mirror; inspired imagery and personal airs or spirit are [the reflections of] the moon and the flower. The water must be limpid and the mirror bright before the flower and the moon can appear clearly. How can one seek to see these two in a dimmed mirror or a murky flow? Therefore, method is what one should attend to first, and awakening cannot be forced.[40]

It is interesting to note that Hu's use of the metaphor of the mirror differs in some ways from all the other critics, both Chinese and Western, that we have discussed in chapter 2. To him, the mirror represents the outer or formal elements of poetry, while the image in the mirror represents the inner or supraformal elements, which involve both reflection of the external world (inspired imagery) and that of the poet's personal airs or spirit. To compare his use of this metaphor with those of the other critics, we may summarize the various uses as follows:

1. In Western mimetic theories:
   mirror = work or writer's mind
   image = reflection of universe
2. In Western expressive theories:
   mirror = work
   image = reflection of writer's mind or soul
3. In Chinese metaphysical theories (Yen Yü and Hsieh Chen):
   mirror = writer's mind
   image = work = reflection of cosmic Tao
4. In Hu Ying-lin's theory:
   mirror = formal elements of work
   image = supraformal elements of work = reflections of universe and of writer's mind.

It appears, then, that Hu's theory of poetry contains mimetic and expressive elements in addition to technical and metaphysical ones.

Apart from Hu Ying-lin, other archaistic critics sometimes also reveal expressive elements in their theories. For instance, Li Meng-yang himself admitted that poetry is an expression of emotion, although his attention is focused on technique. Hsieh Chen's expressive tendencies, which are more pronounced, have been discussed in chapter 2.

The revolt against archaism that took place in late Ming times has been described in chapter 3. It need only be added that the expressive critics who revolted against archaism were rejecting both the technical and the metaphysical concepts that underlay archaism: by condemning imitation and advocating spontaneity, they were attacking the technical concept, and by recommending the preservation of the naïve state of mind (which Li Chih called the "childlike heart" and Yüan Hung-tao called instinctive "gusto"), they were rejecting the metaphysical ideas of mental emptiness and the attainment of a second intuition. The triumph of expressive theories was temporary, but its effects have been felt down to the present day.

Final Interactions

The Ch'ing, or Manchu, Dynasty (1644–1911) saw the final developments of all the six kinds of traditional Chinese theories of literature before the influence of Western theories became pervasive. These different kinds of theories did not develop independently but interacted, resulting in many controversies as well as some syntheses.

The metaphysical concept of literature, having been developed in the theories of Wang Fu-chih and Wang Shih-chen (as described in chapter 2), was transformed into an aesthetic one by Yao Nai (as described also in chapter 2) and a partly aesthetic and partly technical one by Weng Fang-kang (mentioned in chapters 2 and 4), but revived at the end of the Ch'ing period by Wang Kuo-wei, whose concept of *ching-chieh* ("world" or "realm") bears some resemblance to the contemporary phenomenological one of "world" in literature.

The deterministic concept found a clear exposition in Wang Wan's theory, which has been described in chapter 3.

Expressive theories were developed by such critics as Chin Sheng-t'an, Yeh Hsieh, and Yüan Mei, as we saw in chapter 3. The inconsistency between Chin's theory and practice has been mentioned in chapter 3; Yüan's inconsistencies will be analyzed later. Yeh alone succeeded in synthesizing the expressive concept with the pragmatic and the metaphysical, and he did so by stressing, on the one hand, that poetry expresses the poet's moral character and social concern, and, on the other, that the poet should measure the "principles," "events," and "manners" of the universe with his own "talent," "daring," "judgment," and "strength."

The technical concept can be illustrated by Li Yü's theory of drama, Weng Fang-kang's of poetry, and those of Liu Ta-k'uei, Yao Nai, and Tseng Kuo-fan concerning Archaic Prose (all discussed in chapter 4), and the aesthetic concept by Juan Yüan's theory, which advocated Parallel Prose (described in chapter 5). It is somewhat ironic that advocates of Archaic Prose and Parallel Prose should have opposed each other, since both groups were concerned with aesthetic qualities of writing and the means to achieve them, even though they differed in their choice of medium. However, there was a deeper difference between the two groups also: the advocates of Archaic Prose generally showed pragmatic concerns as well as aesthetic ones, while those of Parallel Prose usually did not. That is why the T'ung-ch'eng School of Archaic Prose writers emphasized *yi-fa*, or "principles and methods," whereas Juan Yüan and his followers spoke mostly of *wen*, understood as "verbal patterns" or "embellished language."

The pragmatic concept was held by many Confucians, from the Ming loyalist and scholar Ku Yen-wu (1613–82), who lived at the beginning of the Ch'ing and who declared, "Literature must be beneficial to the world,"[41] through such orthodox writers as Shen Te-ch'ien (whose views have been given in chapter 6), down to scholars like Huang Chieh (also discussed in chapter 6), who survived the fall of the Ch'ing by more than two decades.

We may conclude our survey of the development of theories of literature during the Ch'ing period by considering a few controversies as well as self-contradictions. The controversies, though caused partly by personal animosities, can be seen as illustrations of conflicts between different conceptions of literature. The first case I shall mention involves Wang Shih-chen and Chao Chih-hsin (1662–1744), who married a niece of Wang's but turned against him. How their conceptions of poetry differed from each other may be illustrated by the following conversation among Wang, Chao, and the poet and dramatist Hung Sheng (1659–1704), as recorded by Chao:

> Hung Fang-ssu [Sheng] of Ch'ien-t'ang, who had long been a disciple of [Wang Shih-chen of] Hsin-ch'eng, made friends with me. One day, we discussed poetry together at the home of the Minister of Justice [Wang.] Fang-ssu, hating the lack of methods of composition in contemporary popular writing, said, "Poetry is like a dragon, with its head and tail, its horns and claws, its scales and bristles: if any of these is lacking, then it is not a dragon." The Minister laughed at him and said, "Poetry is like a divine dragon, of which one can see the head but not the tail; or perhaps it may reveal a claw or a scale in the clouds, and that is all. How can one get its whole body? [If one can], then it is a carved or painted one." I said, "To be sure, the divine dragon coils or stretches and changes its appearance without a fixed form, but when someone who sees it dimly points only at a scale or a claw, the dragon's head and tail will have remained intact all the time. If one is limited by what one sees and thinks that the whole dragon is here, that will give the carvers and painters some excuse.[42]

This conversation, which Chao thought so significant that he placed it at the beginning of his book of collected comments on poetry and named the book after it as *T'an-lung lu* or "Talking about Dragons," suggests that the conflict between Wang Shih-chen and Chao Chih-hsin can be viewed as one between metaphysical and technical theories: whereas Wang saw poetry as intimations of the mysteries of the universe, Chao saw it as a concrete object whose anatomy can be studied. Chao's technical conception is further evidenced by his own account of the way he came to compile his *Manual of Tone Patterns* (*Sheng-tiao p'u*): according to him, Wang had learned the secrets of tone patterns for Ancient Verse (*ku-shih,* which does not have prescribed tone patterns but which Chao believed to have its own rules regarding them) but refused to divulge them to anyone, including Chao, who then somehow managed (in his own words) to steal them and decided to make them public.[43] Whether or not the story is true, it indicates that Chao believed that the secrets of poetry could be contained in a set of prosodic rules—a belief surely based on a technical conception of poetry. Elsewhere Chao also expresses some pragmatic and expressive views, but his objection to Wang Shih-chen's metaphysical theory of poetry mainly stems from his own technical conception.

Posthumously Wang Shih-chen met opposition from another quarter, namely Yüan Mei, who, in addition to criticizing Wang's poetry for its alleged deficiencies in true emotion and personal nature and in "force of talent" (*ts'ai-li*),[44] not realizing that Wang was not primarily concerned with expressing his personal emotion and nature and that a forceful display of individual talent would be contrary to the metaphysical concept of poetry, also attacked Wang for using Ch'an as an analogy for poetry:

> Poetry originated with Emperor Shun of Yü and was first edited by Confucius. Why should we Confucian scholars not revere the teachings of these two sages but go out of our way to quote Buddhist and Taoist works? Juan-t'ing [Wang Shih-chen] was fond of comparing Ch'an enlightenment to poetry, and some people revered this as the ultimate theory. I repudiated them, saying, "Are the three hundred poems of the *Book of Poetry* not unsurpassable music? Can you tell me: At that time, where was Ch'an and where was Buddha?" These people could not reply. I therefore told them, "Poetry is one's personal nature, and it is enough to draw from one's own person. If its words move one's heart, its colors dazzle one's eye, its taste pleases one's mouth, and its sound delights one's ear, then it is good poetry. Confucius said, 'If you do not study *Poetry*, you will not be able to

> speak.' He also said, 'Poetry can be used to inspire.' These two sayings echo each other. For it is only because of the skillfulness and subtlety of its words that poetry can make people feel moved and inspired; if its words are straightforward, plain, commonplace, and hackneyed, then who can be inspired by it?"[45]

This passage is more interesting as an example of Yüan's prejudices and sophistry than as a contribution to a dialogue between metaphysical and expressive theorists of poetry. His objection to the analogy between Ch'an enlightenment and poetry, apart from its chauvinism, is not valid, for, as Ch'ien Chung-shu pointed out, the kind of intuitive enlightenment advocated by the Ch'anists could have existed long before Ch'anism itself did.[46] As for his interpretation of Confucius, it reminds one of the saying, "The Devil can cite Scripture for his purpose." Having first stated his expressive concept of poetry and supplemented this with an aesthetic one by his reference to the sensuous delights of poetry, Yüan then quotes Confucius to support both these concepts, although it is doubtful that Confucius meant what Yüan claimed he did.[47]

Yüan's sophistry and adroitness at quoting Confucius to support his own views are also evident in the two letters he wrote to Shen Te-ch'ien to attack the latter's moralistic views. At the end of the first letter, he writes,

> As for your remarks that in poetry one should value moderation and should not speak without restraint, and that poetry must be concerned with human relationships and everyday uses, these words have the grand airs of loose Court robes: in my mouth I dare not say you are wrong, but in my heart I dare not say you are right. Why? Among the sayings of Confucius, those transmitted by Tai [Sheng] in the *Canon* [the *Book of Rites*] are not reliable, only those in the *Analects* are. [In the *Analects*] the Master says, "Poetry can be used to inspire; to make you fit for company": these remarks refer to poems that speak in a restrained and oblique manner, such as . . . When he says, "It can be used to observe; to express grievances," these refer to poems that speak without restraint, such as . . . When he says, "Near at hand, it will teach you how to serve your father, and, looking further, how to serve your sovereign," this refers to poems that are concerned with human relationships; when he says, "It enables you to learn the names of many birds, beasts, plants, and trees," this refers to poems that are not. In reading poetry I have always followed the middle way of Confucius, and that is why I cannot help holding a theory somewhat different from yours.[48]

With all its "bantering" tone, which Arthur Waley noticed,[49] this passage makes two serious points: that poetry need not be restrained in expression, and that it need not be socially and morally relevant. Both points are consistent with the expressive concept of literature but at variance with the pragmatic. Yüan was brave enough to make these points but also clever enough to cite Confucius as his authority.

In the second letter Yüan criticizes Shen for excluding love poems from his anthology of Ch'ing poetry, and points out that the very first poem in the *Book of Poetry*, traditionally said to be an expression of the sage King Wen's longing for a virtuous lady to be his queen, is a love poem. He then adds facetiously: "For the sake of a 'virtuous lady,' he went so far as to 'toss and turn' without sleep: if King Wen were alive today and should meet you, sir, he would be in danger!" In a more serious vein, he continues, "The *Book of Changes* has it, 'One *yin* and one *yang*: this is called the Tao.' And again, 'There must be husband and wife before there can be father and son.' *Yin* and *yang*, or husband and wife, are the ancestors of love poetry."[50] By arguing that love is the basis of human relationships, he is attempting to prove that love poetry is not against morality and that the expressive concept of poetry is not irreconcilable with the pragmatic. However, in what follows he seems to shift his ground:

> Fu Ch'un-ku [Fu Hsüan][51] excelled in describing the love between boys and girls, but exerted moral influence at the Imperial Secretariat: he was a virtuous man. Shen Yüeh served two dynasties [instead of remaining loyal to the first] and practiced Buddhist idolatry, but repented having written "beautiful words" [i.e., love poems]: he was a petty man.[52]

The drift of this passage is that one cannot judge a poet's moral character by his poetry—an idea that contradicts Yüan's general thesis that poetry is an expression of personal nature.

Yüan's self-contradictions can be further illustrated by the following passage from his *Sui-yüan's Remarks on Poetry* (*Sui-yüan shih-hua*).

> Duke Wang [An-shih] of Ching . . . wrote, "The word 'poetry' [*shih*] consists of 'Court' [*ssu*] and 'words' [*yen*]. The Court is where the Nine Ministers dwell, where no words that are not in accordance with propriety and law may be allowed. That is why [Confucius] said, 'No evil thoughts.'" Recently a certain Academician[53] reverently held this theory and often said that poetry could be used to observe a man's moral character. In jest, I recited a couplet, "On the sad zither, [strings like] two lines of

> wild geese;/Binding her finger, a single silver band," and asked him who the author was. The Academician said contemptuously, "It can only be Tung-lang [Han Wo],[54] or Wen [T'ing-yün],[55] or Li [Shang-yin]." I laughed and said, "This is from a poem by Duke Wen [Yen-po] of Lu,[56] elder statesman under four reigns of the Sung." The Academician was greatly astonished. I then recited these lines from "To a Singing Girl" by Li Fang, [posthumously canonized as] Wen-cheng:[57] "From to-day on, you will entangle my soul and dreams;/Whenever shall I see your beauty again?" The love expressed is long-lasting and deep, and the words come from the innermost heart. Yet Wen-cheng was a famous minister at the beginning of the [Sung] dynasty. How does this damage his moral character? The commentary *Containing Divine Mist* [*Han-shen-wu*] on the *Canon of Filial Devotion* [*Hsiao-ching*] has it, "Poetry means 'hold.'" It holds one's nature and emotion so that they will not run wild.[58] This idea is somewhat better than the Duke of Ching's.[59]

Apart from the surprising and unaccountable error of mistaking *Containing Divine Mist*, a surviving chapter of the *Apocryphal Commentary on the Book of Poetry*, to be a commentary on the *Canon of Filial Devotion*, Yüan makes several different assertions about poetry in this passage. In the first place, in rejecting Wang An-shih's pseudo-etymology and making fun of the anonymous Academician, Yüan asserts that poetry cannot be used to judge a man's moral character. Then, in his reference to Li Fang, he asserts that to express love for a woman, even a courtesan, in poetry is not a blemish on a man's character, provided the love is sincere. Thus, he appears to want to eat his cake and have it by arguing, on the one hand, that you cannot tell a man's moral character from his poetry and someone who writes "immoral" love poetry may in fact be of impeccable moral character, and, on the other, that you can tell a man's sincerity in love from his poetry but there is nothing immoral about sexual love. The impossibility of having it both ways aside, the second of these assertions exhibits the "Intentional Fallacy," for obviously Yüan would be hard put to it if asked to produce independent evidence that Li Fang did feel sincere love for the girl to whom he addressed the poem.[60] Finally, in quoting the definition of poetry as "hold" and echoing Liu Hsieh's interpretation of this definition, Yüan asserts, perhaps as a conciliatory gesture to pragmatists, that poetry can restrain one's nature and emotion. It is difficult to see how a consistent theory of poetry can be derived from the different assertions contained in this passage.

Other examples of Yüan's inconsistencies have been noted by Ch'ien Chung-shu and by Kuo Mo-jo,[61] but since these for the most part do not concern basic theories of literature, they need not be discussed here. Similarly, we need not discuss the vicious attacks on Yüan made by the historian and critic Chang Hsüeh-ch'eng (1738–1801),[62] for they were mainly directed against Yüan's moral character rather than his theories, which in fact have certain things in common with Chang's own views on literature.[63] However, it should be realized that in addition to the inconsistencies mentioned above, Yüan also shows a dualistic attitude to prose and poetry: in discussing prose, he tends to adopt a pragmatic stance, while his theory of poetry, as we have seen, is mainly expressive. Kuo Shao-yü attempted to justify Yüan's dualism by referring to the historical circumstances and the influences of certain neo-Confucian philosophers on Yüan,[64] but it seems to me that these historical circumstances and influences can only explain, but not explain away, Yüan's inconsistencies.

Conclusion

This leads conveniently to a more general consideration of the place of historicism or historical relativism in practical criticism, including the criticism of criticism. For some years René Wellek has repudiated historicism and espoused what he calls perspectivism, according to which we should refer a literary work to the values of its own time and of all the periods subsequent to its own.[65] More recently, D. W. Fokkema, writing with reference to Chinese literature, pointed out that perspectivism can only be applied to a single literary tradition, and therefore advocated cultural relativism in comparative literature. While I sympathize with Fokkema's wish to rid comparative literature of either "eurocentrism" or "sinocentrism,"[66] I think that cultural relativism is still not enough. As far as interpretation is concerned, historical relativism and cultural relativism are useful and even necessary, for we cannot correctly understand a work of literature or of criticism without taking into full account the historical and cultural environments in which it is produced; but with regard to evaluation, which I believe to be the second main part of practical criticism, we cannot, nor should we try to, become ancient Athenians, or T'ang Chinese, or Elizabethan Englishmen. Having made due allowances for differences in beliefs, assumptions, prejudices, and ways of thinking, between different cultures and different ages, we must aspire to be transhistorical and transcultural, searching for literary features and qualities and critical concepts and standards that transcend historical and cultural differences. Otherwise we should no longer speak of "literature" but only of discrete "literatures," nor of "criticism" but only of "criticisms."

Notes

Chapter One

1. For the tripartite division see Wellek and Warren, chapter 4, esp. p. 39.

[N.B. In the notes, works listed by author in the bibliography are referred to by author only, and when two or more works by the same author are referred to, a roman numeral is added, as in the bibliography. Works listed by title in the bibliography are referred to by title or abbreviation.]

2. Wellek himself has used the word "criticism" in the wider sense, including literary theory, as he acknowledges (Wellek, I, p. 1). On the other hand, E. D. Hirsch, Jr., limits "criticism" to evaluation, in contradistinction to "interpretation."

3. I am indebted to my friend and colleague Professor Kung-yi Kao, whose insistence on the distinction between "theories of language" and "linguistic theories" suggested to me the desirability of drawing a similar distinction with regard to theories about literature.

4. Eliot, p. 16.

5. Tate, p. 44.

6. Etiemble, p. 101. Surely by "poétique comparée" he means "comparative poetics" and not "comparative poetry," as his translators have it.

7. Wellek, II, pp. 52–53.

8. Block, p. 47, quoted in Fokkema, II, p. 66.

9. See Ueda. Miner's study of Japanese literary theories has not yet been published.

10. Although the Chinese critical tradition has to some extent been influenced by Buddhism, which originated in India, vis-à-vis the Western tradition the Chinese one may be considered an independent tradition.

11. See bibliography under Fokkema, I, Galik, and McDougall.

12. See J. J. Y. Liu, I, pp. 91–100; idem, V, pp. 199–206.

13. This word will be discussed below and again in Chapter 3.

14. The term *shen-yün* will be discussed in chapter 2.

15. See J. J. Y. Liu, I, pp. x, 9–13; idem, V, pp. 35–37.

16. Of course the word "literature" in English also has various meanings, but in current literary criticism there is some general tacit understanding of what it refers to. For a survey of the semantic history of the word "literature" and its equivalents in French, German, and Italian, see Wellek, II, pp. 3–13.

17. For other early variant forms of *wen*, see Lo Chen-yü, I, section 1, p. 18a; II, *chüan shang*, p. 19; Chu Fang-p'u, I, section 9, p. 1a; II, p. 67; Karlgren, II, p. 131.

18. In Yin inscriptions on oracle shells and bones and on bronzes, *wen* occurs in the titles Wen-wu 文武 and Wen-wu Ti 文武帝. There appears to be general agreement that Wen-wu was the same person as Wen-wu-ting 文武丁, also known in an abbreviated form as Wen-ting. (See Wu Ch'i-ch'ang, pp. 226, 264; Ch'en Meng-chia, p. 429; Tung Tso-pin, I, pp. 102–3, where the dates of Wen-wu-ting's reign are given as 1222–1210 B.C.) But opinions differ about the identity of Wen-wu Ti. Tung Tso-pin (in BIHP, vol. 13, p. 199, reprinted in Tung Tso-pin, II, p. 823) identified Wen-wu Ti with Wen-wu-ting, and was followed by Chou Hung-hsiang, who gives the dates of this king's reign as ca. 1184–ca. 1171 B.C. (p. 11). However, Ch'en Meng-chia (p. 422) claims that Tung misread an inscription and that Wen-wu Ti should be identified with Ti Yi 帝乙. The question of identity apart, it is significant that *wen* was used in juxtaposition with *wu*, probably to signify "civil" virtues in contradistinction to "military" ones. Cf. note 26 of this chapter.

19. The theory that the graph for *wen* originally represented a tatooed body was first advanced by Wu Ch'i-ch'ang (pp. 226–27) and repeated by Chu Fang-p'u (II, pp. 67–68), though without reference to Wu. This theory is questionable on several grounds. First, although it is known that in ancient China, at sacrificial ceremonies to ancestral spirits, a relative of the chief mourner would impersonate the dead person and was called a *shih* 尸 (which also means "corpse"), there is no documentary evidence that the *shih* was tatooed. The only references to tatooing the body cited by Chu, from the *Li-chi* and the *Ku-liang chuan*, date several centuries later than the Yin inscriptions and refer to "barbarian" tribes in Southeast China. To these references we may add another from the *Tso-chuan*, Duke Ai, 7th year (487 B.C.), where the "barbarian" custom of tatooing the body is mentioned. It is hard to believe that the Northern Chinese, after having practiced tatooing for an unknown period of time, stopped doing so and began to consider the custom barbarian when they found other people practicing it. Secondly, as I have already pointed out in the main text, this theory would not fit the simpler variant forms of *wen* as found in early inscriptions. If the pattern in the middle of the graph (as found in the more elaborate variant forms) really represented a tatooed mark, it is highly unlikely that this all-important element would ever be left out, as it in fact often was. It is much more likely that such patterns were added to the simpler forms for decorative purposes (cf. Chow Tse-tsung, II). Finally, although it is true, as Wu stated, that in bronze inscriptions and ancient texts *wen* is often used to refer to the dead, it seems, judging by examples of such usage in the *Shih-ching* and the *Shu-ching*, that the word was used as a term of eulogy and not just to signify "deceased." If *wen* indeed meant no more than "deceased," then why was it not applied to all the deceased Yin kings rather than only to one or two? Anyway, to call a dead king "tatooed" because he was represented by a tatooed *shih* would seem to be an extraordinary piece of circumlocution. (For further discussion see note 26 of this chapter.)

20. Ting Fu-pao, III, p. 3983b. It is interesting that Hsü Shen actually used the word *wen* (in the sense of "pattern") itself in defining the same word.

21. *Shang-shu t'ung-chien*, p. 21, mentioned in Chow Tse-tsung, II.

22. Cheng Hsüan, II, *chüan* 6, p. 10a. Cf. Karlgren, I, p. 82 (Ode 128); Waley, II, p. 111. The date of this poem is given according to Ma Chen-li, p. 1675. For the *Book of Poetry*, see J. J. Y. Liu, VI, pp. 161–62. Other examples of *wen* used in the sense of animal markings are given in Chow Tse-tsung, II.

23. *Tso-chuan*, Duke Yin, 1st year (721 B.C.); Duke Min, 2d year (660 B.C.); Duke Chao, 1st year (540 B.C.). Cf. Legge, vol. 5, pp. 3, 129, 580. These examples are cited in Ting Fu-pao, III, p. 3983b.

24. Cheng Hsüan, III, *chüan* 8, p. 3b; idem, IV, *chüan* 11, p. 15b. Cf. Biot, vol. 1, p. 162; Legge/Chai, p. 111. Cited in Ting Fu-pao, III, p. 3983b.

25. *Chan-kuo tse, chüan* 11, p. 92. Cited in Ting Fu-pao, III, p. 3983b.

26. It is difficult to ascertain what precisely *wen* denoted when it was used as a title, as Waley (II, p. 346) long ago pointed out. The explanations given in the "shih fa" ("system of bestowing posthumous titles" or "system of canonization") chapter of the *Yi Chou-shu* (a work of dubious date) partially quoted by Chow Tse-tsung (II), seem to be later rationalizations and cannot be taken as evidence of the original meaning or meanings of *wen* when used as a title. For one thing, even if the *Yi Chou-shu* is not wholly spurious, this chapter has long been suspect: T'ang Ta-p'ei did not even include it in his edition of the book (1836), and Kuo Mo-jo (II, p. 101) considers it to be a forgery of the Warring States period (ca. 4th century B.C.). Furthermore, according to Wang Kuo-wei (I, *chüan* 18, p. 7; p. 895 in 1959 ed.), the titles of early Chou kings—for example, Wen and Wu—were not given posthumously, and Kuo Mo-jo (II, pp. 90–101) has produced further evidence to show that the system of posthumous "canonization" probably did not exist until after the middle of the Spring and Autumn period (ca. 6th century B.C.). Although it remains uncertain what *wen* signified as a title in late Shang and early Chou times (12th century B.C.), it seems reasonable to believe that it was a eulogistic term, and that it denoted nonmilitary qualities, since it was used in juxtaposition to *wu* or "military."

27. *Lun-yü*, III, 14, and IX, 5. Cf. Legge, vol. 1, pp. 16, 217; Waley, III, pp. 97, 139.

28. *Lun-yü*, VI, 16, and XII, 8. Cf. Legge, vol. 1, pp. 190, 254–55; Waley, III, pp. 119, 164.

29. *Lun-yü*, I, 6; VI, 25; XIII, 15. Cf. Legge, vol. 1, pp. 140, 193, 257; Waley, III, pp. 84, 121, 167.

30. *Meng-tzu* ,V, i, 4. Cf. Legge, vol. 2, p. 353; D. C. Lau, II, p. 142. A different interpretation of *wen* is given in Chow Tse-tsung, I, p. 156. Other examples occur in Wei Chao, pp. 38, 198. Some commentators take *wen* in *Lun-yü*, I, 6, also as "writings."

31. Lo Ken-tse, vol. 1, pp. 81–84.
32. *Ibid.*, pp. 84–86; Kuo Shao-yü, V, pp. 23–25. For further discussions, see chapter 5.
33. Lo Ken-tse, vol. 1, pp. 81–84.
34. Ibid., p. 122; Kuo Shao-yü, V, pp. 92–96.
35. Lo Ken-tse, pp. 133–34. The word *ching* is often translated as "classics," but in view of the fact that the Confucian *ching* held a position in traditional China comparable to that of the Scriptures in the West, I have translated the word as "Scriptures" or "Canon" according to the context.
36. Ibid., pp. 142–43; Kuo Shao-yü, V, pp. 55–56, VII, pp. 84–92; Liu Shih-p'ei, pp. 4–7.
37. Lo Ken-tse, vol. 1, p. 141.
38. Abrams, pp. 6–7.
39. Ibid., pp. 3–29.
40. See bibliography under Gibbs, Lynn, Pollard, and John Wang.
41. I have previously (J. J. Y. Liu, I, pp. 65–87, and III) classified Chinese views of poetry under four headings, three of which are somewhat similar to Western pragmatic, expressive, and objective theories in Abrams's classification, but the last, which I called "Intuitionalist" and now prefer to call "metaphysical," seems distinct. The point will be elaborated in chapter 2.
42. I have actually so asserted in a previous work (J. J. Y. Liu, V, p. 202). Similar assertions have been made by others, including Mikel Dufrenne, who will be discussed in chapter 2.
43. See Wellek and Warren, pp. 142–57; Ingarden, pp. 9–19, et passim.
44. Ts'ao P'i, p. 51. Cf. Vincent Shih, p. xxvi. For the explanations of *ch'ing* and *cho* as "light" and "heavy" respectively, see Hsü Fu-kuan, II, p. 302.
45. Ts'ao P'i, pp. 48, and 49, n. 6.
46. For various meanings of *ch'i*, see Kuo Shao-yü, III; Hsü Fu-kuan, II, 297–349; and also chapters 3 and 7 below.

CHAPTER TWO

1. For various meanings of Tao in Chinese philosophy, see Fung/Bodde, and Chan Wing-tsit, II; for the etymology of Tao and its relation to *wen*, see Chow Tse-tsung, II; for meanings of Tao in literary criticism, see Kuo Shao-yü, VI, and also Lu K'an-ju and Mou Shih-chin.
2. Cf. Creel, in Chow Tse-tsung, I, pp. 257–68, esp. 260–64.
3. The authors of the *Commentaries* on the *Yi-ching* may have borrowed ideas from the *Lao Tzu*. See Fung/Bodde, vol. 1, pp. 384–85.
4. Cf. Wilhelm/Baynes, pp. xxxviii–xxxix. Wilhelm accepted the traditional attributions except the first one. For more recent opinions see Fung/Bodde, vol. 1, pp. 379–82; Chan Wing-tsit, II, p. 262.
5. For the prevailing view, see Ch'en Meng-chia's postscript to Kuo

Mo-jo, I, pp. 74–77; Fung Yu-lan, vol. 1, pp. 476–77; Kao Heng, II, p. 7. For other views see Kuo Mo-jo, I; Hsü Shih-ta.

6. Sun Hsing-yen, p. 200. Cf. Legge/Sung, p. 100; Wilhelm/Baynes, vol. 2, p. 135.

7. According to the commentators Yü Fan and Kan Pao, cited in Sun Hsing-yen, p. 202.

8. Ibid., pp. 412–13. Cf. Legge/Sung, p. 210; Wilhelm/Baynes, vol. 2, p. 289.

9. Sun Hsing-yen, p. 547. Cf. Legge/Sung, p. 278; Wilhelm/Baynes, vol. 1, p. 315. In translating *chun* as "co-equal," *mi* as "encompass," and *lun* as "enwrap," I follow, respectively, Yü Fan, Ching Fang, and Wang Su, all cited in Sun Hsing-yen.

10. Sun Hsing-yen, pp. 620–22. Cf. Legge/Sung, p. 309; Wilhelm/Baynes, vol. 1, p. 353.

11. Lo Ken-tse, vol. 1, p. 53.

12. The *Li-chi* as we have it was edited by Tai Sheng (1st century B.C.). See Fung Yu-lan, vol. 2, p. 33. For the date of the chapter on music, see Hsü Fu-kuan, I, pp. 9–12.

13. Cheng Hsüan, IV, *chüan* 11, pp. 10a–b. Cf. Legge/Chai, pp. 99–100.

14. Cheng Hsüan, p. 12a. Cf. Legge/Chai, p. 104. Several sentences in this passage echo the "Appended Words" to the *Yi-ching.*

15. *Shih-wei, Han-shen-wu,* p. 1a.

16. This sentence is derived from the *Yi-ching, t'uan-chuan* under the 30th hexagram, Li. See Sun Hsing-yen, pp. 259–60; Legge/Sung, p. 131; Wilhelm/Baynes, vol. 2, p. 179.

17. Juan Yü, in YWLC, *chüan* 22, p. 411; *Ch'üan Hou-Han wen, chüan* 93, p. 974, in Yen K'e-chün.

18. This sentence is derived from the same source as that mentioned in note 16 above.

19. Ying Yang, in YWLC, *chüan* 22, pp. 411–12; *Ch'üan Hou-Han wen, chüan* 42, p. 701, in Yen K'e-chün.

20. Liu Hsieh, in the last chapter of the *Wen-hsin tiao-lung,* referred to Ying Yang's "Discourse on Literature" (*Wen-lun*) and criticized it as "florid but careless and sketchy." Modern scholars have taken this as a reference to Ying's essay on *wen* and *chih* (*Wen-chih lun*). For example, Fan Wen-lan, in his edition of the *Wen-hsin tiao-lung* (p. 755), quotes Ying's essay while noting that it is not concerned with literature; Liu Ta-chieh (*shang,* p. 236) mentions it as a work on literature and dismisses it as of no importance; Lo Ken-tse (vol. 1, p. 211) remarks that Ying's essay is "political and cultural," not literary, and conjectures that this was the reason why Liu Hsieh thought it "careless and sketchy"; Jao Tsung-yi (p. 4) thinks that the reason why Liu condemned Ying was that the latter overemphasized the importance of *wen* in the sense of "embellishment." It does not seem to have occurred to anyone that perhaps Liu was not referring

to Ying's essay on *wen* and *chih* but another essay on *wen* as literature, now lost to us.

21. See note 28 to chapter 1.

22. Chih Yü, in YWLC, *chüan* 56, p. 1018; *Ch'üan Chin wen, chüan* 77, p. 1905. Also see Lo Ken-tse, vol. 1, p. 155; Jao Tsung-yi, pp. 13–14.

23. Lu Chi, in WCNP, p. 274. Cf. Ch'en Shih-hsiang, III, in Birch, I, p. 214; Achilles Fang, pp. 545–46 (reprinted in Bishop, pp. 21–22).

24. The title *Wen-hsin tiao-lung* requires some explanation. The first half is relatively simple: *wen* means "literature" and *hsin* means "mind" or "heart." Liu Hsieh himself, in the last chapter of his book, explained the compound *wen-hsin* this way: "*Literary Mind* refers to the use of the mind in creating literature" (Wang Li-ch'i, p. 127; Fan Wen-lan, p. 725; cf. Vincent Shih, p. 3). The second half, *tiao-lung*, literally "carving dragons," is a metaphor for elaborate writings. The term was first used with reference to Tsou Shih, a sophist of the third century B.C., but Liu Hsieh made it clear that he was not merely alluding to Tsou Shih: "Since antiquity, literary compositions [*wen-chang*] have been formed like carvings or polychrome silk, so how can I be taking this expression from Tsou Shih's dragon-carving-like multitude of words?" (Wang Li-ch'i, p. 127; Fan Wen-lan, p. 725. Cf. Vincent Shih, p. 3, and Hightower's review of Shih.) How to render *Wen-hsin tiao-lung* into an acceptable English title has been, and remains, a problem. In 1951 the late Ch'en Shih-hsiang in an article (Ch'en Shih-hsiang, I, p. 57) suggested *Anatomy of Literature*, which is an admirable title but involves a change of metaphor from the original. Vincent Shih, in his translation of the book (1959), rendered the title as *The Literary Mind and the Carving of Dragons*, which is not accurate, as pointed out by Hightower in his review (1959). Quoting Liu Hsieh's own explanation (which is given above in wording different from Hightower's), Hightower concluded that the title really meant "an elegant treatise on literature." This is correct, but it is a paraphrase rather than a translation. Besides, the word "elegant" smacks more of self-congratulation than the original does. Ch'en Shou-yi, in his *Chinese Literature* (1961, p. 227), translated the title as *The Carved Dragon of the Literary Mind* and added that it might be loosely translated as *Secrets to Literary Success*. Neither translation is satisfactory. In 1962, Yang Hsien-yi and Gladys Yang (Yang and Yang, I, p. 58), in their translation of excerpts from the book, gave the title as *Carving a Dragon at the Core of Literature*, which is at variance with Liu Hsieh's own explanation. In the same year, the present writer (J. J. Y. Liu, I, p. 71) referred to the book as *Dragon-carvings of a Literary Mind*, which is also inaccurate. A more accurate wording would be *Dragon-carvings on the Literary Mind*, which, however, would not be immediately comprehensible. Most recently, Donald Gibbs (1970, p. 84) suggested *The Genesis and Artistry of Literature*, a translation that contradicts not only Liu Hsieh's own explanation but also common usage in Classical Chinese. It is abundantly clear that *wen-hsin* refers to the subject of the book while *tiao-lung* refers to its nature; the

two phrases cannot be taken as the two main subjects of the work. Syntactically, titles of traditional Chinese works generally assume the form of "verb plus object" (e.g., *Lun-wen*, "discussing literature") or of "noun plus noun," where the first noun states the subject and the second describes the nature of the work (e.g., *Wen-fu*, "an Exposition on literature"). In default of a perfect translation of the title, I am using for the time being *The Literary Mind: Elaborations*, in the hope that the word "elaborations," taken in a double sense, may suggest something of what is intended by the metaphor "dragon-carving." However, for the sake of brevity I shall refer to the work simply as *The Literary Mind*, following the example of Liu Hsieh himself, who referred to the book as *Wen-hsin*. It does not seem necessary to worry, as Hightower apparently does, that the expression "the literary mind" may be ambiguous; it has actually been used as the title of a book, by Max Eastman, though naturally with different connotations.

25. My previous opinion of Liu Hsieh (J. J. Y. Liu, I, p. 71) needs modification. The point will be discussed in chapter 7.

26. For the meaning of "yüan tao," see Huang K'an, pp. 3–4; Fan Wen-lan, pp. 3–4; Liu Yung-chi, p. 4; Jao Tsung-yi, p. 37; Kuo Shao-yü, VI; Yang Ming-chao, II (in WHTL, pp. 49–50).

27. The idea that heaven was dark and earth brown (*huang*, which is usually translated as "yellow," though in fact it often corresponds to "brown"—e.g., *huang-niu* is not a yellow cow but a brown cow) is derived from the *Yi-ching*, as commentators pointed out. See Fan Wen-lan, p. 6. I have accepted the interpretation of Lu K'an-ju and Mou Shih-chin (in Chou K'ang-hsieh, p. 3) that this sentence refers to conditions before heaven and earth were separated (according to Chinese mythology), and have therefore used the past tense.

28. This is derived from the same source as that mentioned in note 16 above. The word *li* here means "adhere to," not "beauty." Neither Shih's nor Gibbs's translation has rendered it correctly.

29. The "Two Forms" may refer either to heaven and earth (Fan Wen-lan, p. 7; Jao Tsung-yi, p. 13) or to *yang* and *yin* (Shih, p. 9). Since heaven was supposed to be *yang* and earth *yin*, the two interpretations really come to the same thing.

30. Fan Wen-lan, p. 1; Wang Li-ch'i, p. 1. Cf. Shih, pp. 8–9; Gibbs, pp. 42–44.

31. See quotation from the *Yi-ching* above at note 8.

32. Perhaps the words "compositions" (*chang*) and "patterns" (*wen*) should be transposed, as suggested by Kuo Chin-hsi (p. 4).

33. Fan Wen-lan, p. 1; Wang Li-ch'i, p. 1. Cf. Shih, p. 9; Gibbs, pp. 44–45.

34. My translation of *yu tsan* (a phrase derived from the *Shuo-kua* commentary on the *Yi-ching*) as "profoundly manifesting" instead of "mysteriously assisting" (Shih, p. 9) or "lending aid in mysterious ways to" (Gibbs, p. 45) is based on Han K'ang-po's annotation, as quoted by Fan Wen-lan, p. 7.

35. Fan Wen-lan, p. 2; Wang Li-ch'i, p. 1. Cf. Shih, pp. 9–10; Gibbs, pp. 45–46.

36. See Sun Hsing-yen, pp. 13–14.

37. The expression "man is the mind of heaven and earth" is derived from the *Li-chi*, as pointed out by Fan Wen-lan (p. 7), but in applying this expression to poetry Liu Hsieh seems to have been influenced by the *Shih-wei*. See note 15 above. That he was familiar with the work is evidenced by his quoting another remark from it (which will be discussed in chapter 7).

38. "Distant sages" is my translation of *hsüan-sheng* 玄聖 which can also mean "dark sage(s)." Many commentators prefer the latter meaning and identify the "dark sage" with Confucius because of the legend that his mother dreamt of a dark god when she conceived him. See Jao Tsung-yi, p. 45. However, Chi Yün (in Huang Shu-lin, *chüan* 1, p. 2b) pointed out that this would make the reference to Confucius in the next sentence redundant. He therefore took it as a reference to the earlier sages Fu-hsi and others, and he was followed by Kuo Chin-hsi (p. 11). It is also possible to take *hsüan-sheng* as a reference to Fu-hsi only (Lu K'an-ju and Mou Shih-chin in Chou K'ang-hsieh, p. 7; Shih, p. 12).

39. According to one legend, a dragon emerged from the Yellow River carrying a chart, on which Fu-hsi based the Eight Trigrams. (This legend about the origin of the Eight Trigrams differs from that given in the *Yi-ching* quoted above.) Another legend has it that after King Yü had controlled the deluge, a divine tortoise appeared from the river Lo, carrying inscriptions on its back. See Fan Wen-lan, p. 8; Yang Ming-chao, I, pp. 2–3; Jao Tsung-yi, pp. 41, 64; Shih, p. 10.

40. See note 6 above.

41. The words *ching wei* 經緯 ("warp and woof") are here used as verbs. Shih's translation "legislate for the universe" (p. 12) seems unwarranted; how Gibbs arrived at the meaning "control their destiny" (p. 50) is beyond my imagination.

42. See note 9 above.

43. The word *ch'ui* 垂 can mean "bestow" (by someone superior to someone inferior) or "hand down to posterity." Cf. Shih, p. 12; Gibbs, p. 52.

44. Sun Hsing-yen, p. 610. Cf. Legge/Sung, p. 340; Wilhelm/Baynes, vol. 1, p. 348. In the original passage, the word *tz'u* 辭 refers to the *hsiao-tz'u* 爻辭 or words explaining the lines of the hexagrams, but Liu Hsieh is playing on its literal meaning, "words."

45. Fan Wen-lan, p. 2; Wang Li-ch'i, pp. 2–3.

46. I have kept the word order of the original sentence because of its importance, in spite of the resulting awkward English.

47. Fan Wen-lan, p. 2; Wang Li-ch'i, p. 2; Jao Tsung-yi, p. 44, note.

48. Hsiao T'ung, I, preface; or WCNP, p. 563.

49. "Kingly Rule" (*wang cheng* 王政) implies rule by moral influence and not by force.

50. Hsiao Kang, in *Ch'üan Liang wen, chüan* 12, p. 3016, in Yen K'e-chün; or in Hsiao T'ung, II. Quoted in Lo Ken-tse, vol. 1, p. 127.

51. Li Pai-yao, *chüan* 45, p. 2255. Partially quoted in Lo Ken-tse, vol. 2, p. 135. Lo's quotation contains two variant readings. I have followed the K'ai-ming text, as it makes better sense.

52. *Tso-chuan,* Duke Hsiang, 25th year (547 B.C.). Cf. Legge, vol. 5, p. 517.

53. See Lo Ken-tse, vol. 1, p. 491.

54. Wei Cheng, *chüan* 76, p. 2522. Quoted in Lo Ken-tse, vol. 2, p. 134.

55. See chapter 6.

56. Wang Po, in Tung Kao, *chüan* 182, pp. 15b–16a. Quoted in Lo Ken-tse, vol. 2, p. 118.

57. Lu Chi, in WCNP, p. 260. Cf. Ch'en Shih-hsiang, III, in Birch, I, p. 208; Achilles Fang, in Bishop, p. 12.

58. See Lo Ken-tse, vol. 1, p. 96.

59. Po Chü-yi, *chih* 7, *chüan* 45, p. 18. Cf. Waley, IV, p. 108.

60. For examples, see Lo Ken-tse, vol. 3, pp. 21–22. Lo unaccountably refers to these as "new evidence" of the didactic theory.

61. Han Yü, *chüan* 11, p. 1.

62. For the rise of neo-Confucianism, see Fung/Bodde, vol. 2, chap. 10.

63. See Fung Yu-lan, vol. 2, p. 249; Chan Wing-tsit, I, pp. 35–53; D. C. Lau, I, pp. 8–12.

64. Fung Yu-lan, vol. 1, pp. 250–56; Chan Wing-tsit, I, pp. 71–74; D. C. Lau, I, pp. 163–74.

65. See Fung Yu-lan, vol. 1, pp. 363–68; Kuan Feng, pp. 1–2; Watson, pp. 1–3.

66. Fung Yu-lan, vol. 1, p. 364; D. C. Lau, I, pp. 149–55.

67. Waley, I; Watson, p. 3.

68. *Lao Tzu,* X (Kao Heng, p. 24).

69. D. C. Lau, I, p. 66.

70. *Lao Tzu,* XVI (Kao Heng, pp. 38–39). Cf. D. C. Lau, I, p. 72.

71. *Chuang Tzu yin-te,* 28/11/54; Ch'ien Mu, I, p. 85. Cf. Watson, pp. 122–23.

72. *Chuang Tzu yin-te,* 30/12/45; Ch'ien Mu, I, p. 95. Cf. Watson, p. 133.

73. *Chuang Tzu yin-te,* 18/6/68; Ch'ien Mu, I, p. 56. Cf. Watson, p. 87.

74. *Chuang Tzu yin-te,* 7/2/96; Ch'ien Mu, I, p. 23. Cf. Watson, p. 49.

75. *Chuang Tzu yin-te,* 9/4/26; Ch'ien Mu, I, p. 30. Cf. Watson, pp. 57–58.

76. Watson, pp. 57–58.

77. Kuo Shao-yü, IV, p. 124; Hsü Fu-kuan, I, pp. 70–75.

78. *Chuang Tzu yin-te,* 7/3/2; Ch'ien Mu, I, pp. 24–25. Cf. Watson, pp. 50–51.

79. *Chuang Tzu yin-te*, 50/19/54; Ch'ien Mu, I, pp. 150–51. Cf. Watson, pp. 205–6.

80. *Meng Tzu*, II, A, 6 (*Meng Tzu yin-te*, p. 13). Cf. D. C. Lau, II, pp. 82–83; see also pp. 16–18.

81. *Meng Tzu*, II, A, 2 (*Meng Tzu yin-te*, p. 11). Cf. D. C. Lau, II, p. 78.

82. Lu Chi, in WCNP, pp. 254–57. Cf. Ch'en Shih-hsiang, III, in Birch, I, pp. 205–207; Achilles Fang, pp. 532–33 (reprinted in Bishop, pp. 8–9).

83. *Chuang Tzu yin-te*, 79/28/56; Ch'ien Mu, I, p. 238. Cf. Watson, p. 317.

84. Fan Wen-lan, p. 493; Wang Li-ch'i, p. 80. Cf. Vincent Shih, pp. 154–55.

85. *Chuang Tzu yin-te*, 58/22/29; Ch'ien Mu, I, p. 175. Cf. Watson, p. 238.

86. Liu Yung-chi, p. 11, Kuo Chin-hsi, p. 68, Lu and Mou, p. 95, all adopt the former interpretation; Vincent Shih, p. 154, chooses the latter.

87. Cassirer, pp. 8, 9, 24, 28, 58.

88. The word *p'in* 品 usually means "class," "rank," or "quality," and was used in the sense of "Class" by Chung Hung (see note 51 to chapter 3), but Ssu-k'ung T'u used it in a different sense, to refer to different moods or worlds in poetry. Yang and Yang (II) translated the word as "modes," which does not seem appropriate here.

89. Kuo Shao-yü, II, p. 19; Tsu Pao-ch'üan, p. 40.

90. Kuo Shao-yü, II, p. 23; Tsu, p. 44.

91. Kuo Shao-yü, II, p. 36; Tsu, p. 59, where a different interpretation is given.

92. *Lao Tzu*, IV (Kao Heng, p. 12), recurring in LVI (Kao Heng, p. 119). Translated as "all dust smoothed" by Waley (I, pp. 146, 210), "mix with all that is humble as dust" by Chu Ta-kao (p. 71), "submerge its turmoil" by Lin Yutang (I, p. 257), "let your wheels move along old ruts" by D. C. Lau (I, pp. 60, 117), and "becomes one with the dusty world" by Chan Wing-tsit (I, pp. 105, 199).

93. Su Shih, *Tung-p'o chi, chüan* 10, pp. 4b–5a. Quoted in Hsü Fu-kuan, I, p. 134.

94. Su Shih, *Tung-p'o chi, chüan* 16, p. 10a. Quoted in Kuo Shao-yü, V, p. 182; Hsü Fu-kuan, I, p. 362.

95. *Chuang Tzu yin-te*, 3/21/1; Ch'ien Mu, I, p. 8; Cf. Watson, p. 36.

96. For Huang T'ing-chien's theory of imitation, see J. J. Y. Liu, I, p. 78, and idem, II.

97. For Ch'an or Zen, see Fung/Bodde, vol. 2, pp. 386–406; Chan Wing-tsit, II, pp. 425–30.

98. The *Ts'ang-lang shih-hua* has been translated into German by Günther Debon (*q.v.* in bibliography). For Yen's sources see Kuo Shao-yü, I, and idem, V, pp. 235–38; Chang Chien, pp. 34 –36.

99. Kuo Shao-yü, I, p. 6. My previous translation of this passage (Liu, I, p. 81) is slightly different.

100. *Tu-shih yin-te*, 1/1/73. Cf. William Hung, p. 56. Strictly speaking, "volumes" should be "scrolls" and "pen" should be "brush," but I have used the former two words for easier comprehension. For further discussion of *ju-shen*, see Ch'ien Chung-shu, pp. 48–53.

101. J. J. Y. Liu, I, p. 82.

102. Chang Chien, p. 32; Lynn, pp. 42–43.

103. Sun Hsing-yen, p. 636. Cf. Legge/Sung, p. 317; Wilhelm/Baynes, vol. 1, p. 363; Chan Wing-tsit, II, pp. 42, 268.

104. Fan Wen-lan, p. 21; Wang Li-ch'i, p. 6. Cf. Vincent Shih, p. 18.

105. Wang Po-min, p. 17.

106. See text above, at note 91.

107. See note 104.

108. Kuo Shao-yü, I, p. 10. For the expressions *tang-hang* 當行 ("ply one's proper trade") and *pen-se* 本色 ("show one's true colors") see ibid., p. 103. My previous translation of this passage (Liu, I, p. 85) is somewhat different.

109. See Kuo Shao-yü, I, pp. 15–23, 38–40.

110. This is derived from two Ch'an masters' sayings. See ibid., p. 25.

111. My translation of the phrase *pu-k'o ts'ou-po* 不可湊泊 as "cannot be pieced together" differs from previous translators': "cannot be condensed or diluted" (Ch'en Shih-hsiang, II, p. 138); "*unfassbar*" (Günther Debon, p. 61); "free from blocking" (Richard Lynn, p. 54), "unblurred and unblocked" (Wai-lim Yip, p. 191), and "unable to be converged" (Tu Ching-I, I, p. 6). I think that the disyllable *ts'ou-po* should be taken as one word meaning "piece together," not two words, and that the second syllable is not to be taken in the literal sense of "mooring," for some later critics such as Yüan Mei (I, p. 3) wrote the second syllable with a different character, *p'o* 拍, which suggests that *ts'ou-po* or *ts'ou-p'o* has nothing to do with "mooring" or "blocking." Cf. Kuo Shao-yü, I, p. 25.

112. Kuo Shao-yü, I, p. 25.

113. This is derived from the *Yüeh-chi* chapter of the *Li-chi* (Cheng Hsüan, IV, *chüan* 11, p. 8b). My previous translation of this sentence (Liu, I, p. 82) is inaccurate.

114. Kuo Shao-yü, I, p. 24.

115. *Chuang Tzu yin-te*, 75/26/48; Ch'ien Mu, I, p. 227. Cf. Watson, p. 115. It is interesting to note that Wittgenstein (p. 151) reached a similar conclusion.

116. Wai-lim Yip, pp. 191–97. Another interpretation is that these images represent aesthetic experiences (Chang Chien, p. 281).

117. See also J. J. Y. Liu, I, pp. 79–80; Lynn, pp. 91–94.

118. Hsieh Chen, *chüan* 3, p. 2b. This passage and the next one quoted in the main text have been partially translated by Richard Lynn (p. 97) and by Wong Siu-kit (I, p. 240). My translation differs from both in places.

In particular, the ambiguous sentences *kuan tse t'ung yü wai, kan tse yi yü nei* 觀則同於外感則異於內, which I translate as "what is observed without is the same, but the feelings aroused within may be different," are rendered by Lynn as "One looks and [his impression] is the same as that which is external to him. He experiences emotion and [the scene] is different from that which is inside him," and by Wong as "that, objectively, viewing a scene is the same from person to person (because what is viewed is the same scene), and that, subjectively, feeling is always different from person to person." Both Lynn's and Wong's intrepretations are possible, but I think what Hsieh means is that the same scene may arouse different emotions, not necessarily from different persons, but also from the same person at different times. I have therefore left this point ambiguous in my translation.

119. See note 48 to chapter 3.

120. According to the *Li-chi* (quoted in Fan Wen-lan, p. 69), the seven emotions are joy, anger, sadness, fear, love, hate, and desire.

121. Hsieh Chen, p. 3b. Wong Siu-kit in his partial translation of this passage (*loc. cit.*) left out the core of the first sentence, *ho yü teng t'iao* 合於登眺 ("fuse with one another as one climbs high and looks afar"), and was left with the subjects "ten thousand scenes" and "seven emotions" with nothing to follow. He therefore added "there may be" and "there can only be" to these two subjects respectively. This misses the point of the original completely.

The expression "climbs high" may also allude to the remark from a commentary on the *Book of Poetry*: "If a man can compose or recite [*fu*] poetry when climbing high, he may be made an official," which Liu Hsieh quoted to support his theory of the origin of the *fu* (Fan Wen-lan, pp. 134–37).

122. Wang Fu-chih, in Ting Fu-pao, II, p. 11. My previous translation of this passage (Liu, I, p. 83) is somewhat different.

123. Wang Fu-chih, p. 10.

124. Kuo Mao-ch'ien, *chüan* 38, p. 1b.

125. Wang Fu-chih, p. 14.

126. Ibid., pp. 6, 14.

127. Ibid., pp. 19, 20.

128. This is a brief reply to the objection of Wong Siu-kit (II).

129. For more detailed discussions of Wang Shih-chen's views on poetry, see Kuo Shao-yü, V, pp. 457–72; Aoki/Ch'en, pp. 47–54; and Lynn.

130. Wang Shih-chen, I, *chüan* 3, p. 6b.

131. Ibid., p. 1b.

132. Ibid., pp. 1b–2a.

133. Ibid., p. 1b. "Mileage-recording drum" refers to the ancient practice of beating a drum to mark the mileage covered by a carriage. See also *Ts'an-wei hsü-wen, chüan* 3, p. 6a, in Wang Shih-chen, II.

134. See Hsü Fu-kuan, I, pp. 169–78.

135. Wang Shih-chen, I, p. 4b. Cf. J. J. Y. Liu, I, p. 83.

136. Yao Nai, I, p. 71; quoted in Kuo Shao-yü, V, pp. 565–66. For further information about the T'ung-ch'eng School, see Pollard, pp. 140–57.

137. Hazlitt, vol. 4, p. 78; reprinted in Bate, p. 302.

138. For brief discussions of the *Jen-chien tz'u-hua*, see J. J. Y. Liu, I, pp. 84, 97, 99. For further discussions and translation, see Tu Ching-I, I and II. There are also several unpublished dissertations on Wang Kuo-wei.

139. Plato, *Republic*, Book X, 596–97, in Jowett, vol. 2, pp. 469–70; quoted in Wimsatt and Brooks, pp. 11–12.

140. Aristotle, *Poetics*, Books I and II; quoted in Wimsatt and Brooks, p. 27; Abrams, p. 9; McKeon in Crane, p. 162.

141. Abrams, p. 30.

142. Ibid., pp. 42–45.

143. *Chuang Tzu yin-te*, 59/22/45; Ch'ien Mu, I, p. 177. Cf. Watson, pp. 18, 241.

144. See above text, at note 30.

145. Sydney, in Gregory Smith, vol. 1, p. 182.

146. Although Liu Hsieh studied Buddhism in his youth and became a monk towards the end of his life, the conceptions of man and of the world that he shows in the *Wen-hsin tiao-lung* are Confucian. Such Buddhist influence as is perceptible in this work seems to pertain to methodology only. Cf. Fan Wen-lan, p. 728; Wang Li-ch'i, pp. xv–xvii. For a different view see Jao Tsung-yi, pp. 17–19.

147. See Wimsatt and Brooks, p. 71.

148. Plato, *Ion* (in Jowett, vol. 1, p. 226); quoted in Bays, p. 4; also see Wimsatt and Brooks, p. 9.

149. See McKeon in Crane, pp. 149–59; Abrams, p. 8.

150. Abrams, pp. 52–53, 58–59, 235–244.

151. Ibid., p. 347.

152. Ibid., pp. 30, 32–35, 42, 50, 57, 59, 127, 130.

153. *Lao Tzu*, LXXXI (in Kao Heng, p. 152). Cf. Chan Wing-tsit, I, p. 240; D. C. Lau, I, p. 143.

154. Fan Wen-lan, p. 537; Wang Li-ch'i, p. 88. Cf. Vincent Shih, p. 175.

155. See text above, at note 115.

156. Marlowe, *Tamburlaine* I, 5. 2. 102–10.

157. Goethe, tr. Steinhauer, p. 3. Cf. Abrams, p. 44.

158. Cicero, *De Oratore* 3. 59. 221.

159. Hazlitt, vol. 5, p. 3; quoted in Abrams, p. 52.

160. *Chuang Tzu yin-te*, 21/7/32, 33/13/4, 93/33/57; Ch'ien Mu, I, pp. 66, 103, 276. Cf. Watson, pp. 97, 142, 372; Chan Wing-tsit, II, pp. 207, 208. For further discussions of the metaphor of the mirror in Taoist and Buddhist texts and some Western parallels, see Demiéville.

161. See text above, at note 69.

162. See Wimsatt and Brooks, p. 148.

163. A typical example is La Primaudaye. For modern studies, see Hardin Crag and E. W. M. Tillyard.

164. See Wimsatt and Brooks, p. 590; Bays, pp. 24, 124.

165. Baudelaire, p. 768.

166. See text above, at note 32.

167. See Michaud (English tr.), p. 66.

168. Raymond (English tr.), pp. 12–14.

169. Ibid.; also Wimsatt and Brooks, p. 591.

170. Mallarmé, II, vol. 1, p. 242. English translation as in Michaud (English tr.), p. 55.

171. Mallarmé, I, p. 663; quoted in Michaud (English tr.), p. 64.

172. Michaud (English tr.), p. 107; Cf. slightly different translation in Wimsatt and Brooks, p. 593.

173. Mallarmé, II, vol. 1, p. 216. Michaud (n.e. p. 68, English tr. p. 58) appears to be mistaken in quoting this as from a letter to Catulle Mendès instead of Cazalis.

174. Ibid., p. 220; Michaud (English tr.), p. 54.

175. Ibid., p. 243. My translation.

176. See text above, at note 45.

177. Mallarmé, I, p. 70.

178. Michaud (English tr.), p. 164. I do not know when Mallarmé made this remark, but it must have been after 1891, since he first met Mauclair that year. See Barbier, vol. 3, p. 201.

179. *Chuang Tzu yin-te*, 7/3/1; Ch'ien Mu, I, p. 24. Cf. Watson, p. 50. For the interpretation of *tai* as "exhausting" rather than "dangerous," see Kuan Feng, p. 148.

180. Mallarmé, I, pp. 35–36.

181. See Bays. I am indebted to Professor R. G. Cohn for calling my attention to this work.

182. Rimbaud, pp. 302, 306.

183. Ch'ien Chung-shu, pp. 321–48.

184. Dufrenne, I, pp. 79–80; III, pp. 199, 676.

185. Dufrenne, I, p. 6; II, p. 80; III, p. 675.

186. Kockelmans, pp. 67–68.

187. Dufrenne, I, p. 6. My translation.

188. Dufrenne, III, pp. 661–62. Page numbers given in text, below, following other Dufrenne quotes are also from Dufrenne, III.

189. *Chuang Tzu yin-te*, 5/2/52; Ch'ien Mu, I, p. 17. Cf. Watson, p. 43. Graham (p. 138) suggests that Chuang Tzu may be quoting someone else's remark, but this would not affect the fact that traditional Chinese critics took the saying as Chuang Tzu's.

190. Heidegger (English tr.), p. 62; reprinted in Kockelmans, p. 311. Cf. Fung/Bodde, vol. 1, pp. 178–79, for Tao as Being and Non-being.

191. Dufrenne, III, p. 674.

192. Dufrenne, II, p. 97.

193. *Chuang Tzu yin-te*, 7/2/94; Ch'ien Mu, I, p. 23. Cf. Watson, p. 49; Graham, p. 159.
194. Husserl (English tr.), pp. 107–10; reprinted in Kockelmans, pp. 74–77. Cf. Schmitt, in ibid., pp. 59–60.
195. Husserl, pp. 110–11; reprinted in Kockelmans, pp. 77–78.
196. Kockelmans, p. 31.
197. Husserl (English tr.), pp. 193–211; reprinted in Kockelmans, pp. 105–17.
198. Merleau-Ponty, p. x; English tr. reprinted in Kockelmans, p. 367.
199. Ibid.
200. Ibid.
201. Dufrenne, II, pp. 97, 101.
202. *Chuang Tzu*, 7/2/94.
203. Dufrenne, III, p. 677. My translation.

CHAPTER THREE

1. *Tso-chuan*, Duke Hsiang, 29th year (543 B.C.). Cf. Legge, vol. 5, pp. 549–50.
2. Cheng Hsüan, IV, *chüan* 11, pp. 7a–b; quoted in Lo Ken-tse, vol. 1, p. 76.
3. See Lo Ken-tse, vol. 1, p. 74.
4. See Lu K'an-ju and Feng Yüan-chün, pp. 13–22.
5. Cheng Hsüan, I, p. 12b; quoted in Lo Ken-tse, vol. 1, p. 75; Chu Tzu-ch'ing, p. 145.
6. Cheng Hsüan, I, pp. 1–5; quoted in Lo Ken-tse, vol. 1, pp. 79–80; Chu Tzu-ch'ing, pp. 144–45.
7. Pan Ku, *chüan* 27, p. 0408; quoted in Chu Tzu-ch'ing, pp. 154–56.
8. *Julius Caesar* 1. 3. 10–18; *Hamlet* 1. 1. 113–20. See also *Macbeth* 2. 4. 5–20.
9. *Lun-yü*, XVII, 8. Cheng's interpretation quoted in Ho Yen, et al., *chüan* 17, p. 4b.
10. Chu Tzu-ch'ing, pp. 163–85.
11. Wang Wan, pp. 19–20; quoted in Chu Tzu-ch'ing, p. 160.
12. Kuo Shao-yü, VII, pp. 17, 47.
13. Cf. Abrams, pp. 82–84.
14. "Archaic Chinese" refers to the pronunciation of Chinese of the Chou period (ca. 1100–ca. 250 B.C.). For the reconstructed pronunciations of words mentioned in the text, see Karlgren, II, pp. 253–54. I have omitted the asterisk in the orthography.
15. See Chow Tse-tsung, I, pp. 153–54.
16. Ting Fu-pao, III, pp. 968 a–b. Cf. Chow Tse-tsung, I, p. 160.
17. Cf. Ch'en Shih-hsiang, IV, p. 905; Chow Tse-tsung, I, pp. 163–66, 196–207.
18. See J. J. Y. Liu, I, p. 5.
19. Ch'en Shih-hsiang, I, pp. 50–52.

20. Chow Tse-tsung, I, pp. 191–93, 207–08.
21. Yang Shu-ta, pp. 25–26; quoted in Chow Tse-tsung, I, p. 164.
22. Wen Yi-to, vol. I, p. 185; quoted in Chow Tse-tsung, I, p. 164.
23. Chu Tzu-ch'ing, p. 11; quoted in Chow Tse-tsung, I, p. 166.
24. *Mao-shih yin-te*, p. 47. Cf. Karlgren, I, p. 149 (Ode 199). Some scholars follow Chu Hsi (I, *chüan* 12, p. 17a) in interpreting *fan-ts'e* as "inconstancy," but I prefer the interpretation "restless" (i.e., "toss and turn," as in the first poem in the *Book of Poetry*). These lines have been quoted in Aoki/Wang, p. 15, and Lo Ken-tse, vol. 1, p. 35.
25. *Mao-shih yin-te*, p. 49. Cf. Karlgren, I, p. 156 (Ode 204); Waley, II, p. 139. Quoted in Aoki/Wang, p. 15; Lo Ken-tse, vol. 1, p. 35.
26. Wen Yi-to, vol. 1, p. 181; Ch'en Shih-hsiang, IV, p. 901.
27. *Mao-shih yin-te*, p. 65. Cf. Karlgren, I, pp. 209–10 (Ode 252); Waley, II, p. 183.
28. *Shang-shu t'ung-chien*, p. 2. Cf. Chow Tse-tsung, I, p. 152.
29. Chu Tzu-ch'ing, p. 13; Lo Ken-tse, vol. 1, p. 36.
30. Lo Ken-tse, vol. 1, p. 36; Ch'en Shih-hsiang, I, p. 53; Chow Tse-tsung, I, pp. 155–57.
31. See note 3 above.
32. Cheng Hsüan, I, pp. 5 a–b. The translation given here differs somewhat from my previous one (Liu, I, p. 70). Among other English versions, see Chow Tse-tsung, I, p. 157.
33. Cheng Hsüan, IV, *chüan* 11, pp. 16, 26. See also Lo Ken-tse, vol. 1, p. 75; Chow Tse-tsung, I, p. 158.
34. See note 44 to chapter 1.
35. See note 81 to chapter 2.
36. *Meng-tzu*, II, A, 2 (*Meng-tzu yin-te*, p. 11). Cf. D. C. Lau, II, pp. 77–78.
37. Chao Yung-hsien, *shang*, p. 59. Cf. Fung Yu-lan, vol. 1, p. 293; D. C. Lau, II, pp. 24–25.
38. Chao Yung-hsien, *hsia*, p. 40. Cf. Fung Yu-lan, vol. 1, p. 295. I have followed Fung's interpretation of *tao* as *t'ung* and translated it as "flows freely."
39. Liu Wen-tien, *chüan* 3, pp. 1 a–b. Cf. Fung Yu-lan, vol. 1, p. 149; Chan Wing-tsit, II, p. 307; D. C. Lau, II, p. 24.
40. Liu Wen-tien, *chüan* 7, pp. 3 a–b.
41. Renaissance writers who dealt with these concepts include Sir Thomas Elyot, Lemnius, Thomas Phair, and Thomas Walkington.
42. Chao Yi, "Fei-ts'ao-shu," in *Ch'üan Hou-Han wen*, *chüan* 82, p. 916, in Yen K'e-chün. Quoted in Wang Yao, p. 95.
43. *Chuang Tzu yin-te*, 36/13/17; Ch'ien Mu, I, p. 111. Cf. Watson, pp. 152–53.
44. See Wang Yao, p. 95.
45. Lu Chi, in WCNP, p. 254. Cf. Ch'en Shih-hsiang, III, in Birch, I, p. 205; Achilles Fang, p. 531 (in Bishop, p. 7).
46. See note 57 to chapter 2.

47. Ch'en Shih-hsiang, I, pp. 56–57.

48. Lu Chi, in WCNP, p. 259. Cf. Ch'en Shih-hsiang, III, in Birch, I, p. 207; Achilles Fang, p. 534 (in Bishop, p. 10).

49. See Abrams, pp. 272–85, and Chang Heng for detailed analysis of Lu Chi's ideas about the creative process.

50. The "six emotions" are joy, anger, sadness, pleasure, love, and aversion. Cf. the "seven emotions" mentioned in note 120 to chapter 2.

51. My translation of this line follows the note in WCNP, p. 274, and differs radically from those of Ch'en Shih-hsiang, III, in Birch, I, p. 213, and of Achilles Fang, p. 544 (in Bishop, p. 20).

52. Lu Chi, in WCNP, p. 273.

53. Fan Wen-lan, p. 505; Wang Li-ch'i, p. 81. Cf. Vincent Shih, p. 158.

54. Fan Wen-lan, p. 538; Wang Li-ch'i, p. 88. Cf. Vincent Shih, p. 176.

55. Fan Wen-lan, p. 538 (and note on p. 541); Wang Li-ch'i, p. 89. Cf. Vincent Shih, p. 177.

56. Fan Wen-lan, p. 65; Wang Li-ch'i, p. 16. Cf. Vincent Shih, p. 32; J. J. Y. Liu, I, p. 71.

57. Fan Wen-lan, p. 136; Wang Li-ch'i, p. 24. Cf. Vincent Shih, p. 48; Liu Shou-sung, in WHTL, p. 21.

58. Fan Wen-lan, p. 693; Wang Li-ch'i, p. 120. Cf. Vincent Shih, p. 246.

59. See note 84 to chapter 2.

60. Fan Wen-lan, p. 505; Wang Li-ch'i, p. 81. Cf. Vincent Shih, pp. 158–59.

61. Fan Wen-lan, p. 506; Wang Li-ch'i, p. 82. Cf. Vincent Shih, p. 160.

62. See note 136 to chapter 2.

63. The word *p'in* is here translated as "classes" because Chung Hung actually classified poets according to his opinions of their merits. For a different use of the word, see note 88 to chapter 2. For the date of this work, see Kuo Shao-yü, III, p. 52. For a general introduction, see Hellmut Wilhelm.

64. Chung Hung, p. 1a. Cf. Hellmut Wilhelm, in Chow Tse-tsung, I, p. 118.

65. Yao Ssu-lien, II, *chüan* 34, p. 1892.

66. See text above, at note 30, and Wang Li-ch'i, pp. 1, 5, 9, 88, 127. For other early uses of the term *hsing-ling*, see Kuo Shao-yü, V, p. 47; Ku Yüan-hsiang, pp. 35–44. However, Ku's interpretations are not always convincing.

67. Yao Ssu-lien, I, *chüan* 49, p. 1834.

68. Shao Yung, p. 2; quoted in Kuo Shao-yü, V, p. 154.

69. Shao Yung, p. 2. Cf. Lo Ken-tse, vol. 3, p. 71.

70. Cf. John Wang, pp. 15–16.

71. Li Chih, pp. 97–99; quoted in part in Kuo Shao-yü, V, p. 350.

72. *Meng-tzu*, IV, B, 12 (*Meng-tzu yin-te*, p. 31). Cf. D. C. Lau, II, p. 130.
73. *Lao Tzu*, X (Kao Heng, p. 23). Cf. Chan Wing-tsit, I, p. 116; D. C. Lau, I, p. 24.
74. Li Chih, pp. 96–97; quoted in Kuo Shao-yü, V, p. 351.
75. *Lun-yü*, XV, 41. Cf. Legge, vol. 1, p. 305; Waley, III, p. 201 (given as No. 40).
76. Yüan Tsung-tao, p. 253; quoted partially in Kuo Shao-yü, V, p. 364. Cf. John Wang, p .19; André Levy, p. 262.
77. Yüan Tsung-tao, p. 254; quoted in Kuo Shao-yü, III, p. 365. Cf. André Levy, pp. 264–66; Pollard, pp. 161–62.
78. Yüan Hung-tao, p. 5; quoted in Kuo Shao-yü, V, p. 374. Cf. John Wang, p. 19.
79. Yüan Hung-tao, p. 6. Cf. John Wang, p. 20.
80. Yüan Hung-tao, p. 5; quoted in Kuo Shao-yü, V, p. 376. Cf. Lin Yutang, II, p. 112; Pollard, pp. 79–80.
81. Yüan Chung-tao, "Hua-hsüeh-fu yin," in Shen Ch'i-wu, p. 43; quoted in Kuo Shao-yü, V, p. 367.
82. For detailed discussions of Chin's views, see John Wang, esp. chapter 3. For the major works of Chinese fiction and drama, see J. J. Y. Liu, VI, pp. 167–70.
83. Chin Sheng-t'an, p. 546. Cf. J. J. Y. Liu, I, pp. 73–74.
84. The authenticity of this preface has been questioned on stylistic grounds, but the ideas expressed in it are similar to those in Chin's letters, and there is no reason why he should not have adopted a different style. See Chin Sheng-t'an, pp. 544–45; John Wang, pp. 41–42.
85. See note 30 to chapter 2.
86. Chin Sheng-t'an, p. 1.
87. Ibid., p. 2.
88. These allude to two poems in the *Book of Poetry*. See *Mao-shih yin-te*, pp. 21, 31; Karlgren, I, pp. 66 (Ode 102), 96 (Ode 154); Waley, II, pp. 49, 164.
89. Yeh Hsieh, p. 572.
90. Ibid., p. 596.
91. Ibid., p. 597.
92. Ibid., p. 576. See also pp. 574–75.
93. See Fung/Bodde, vol. 2, pp. 500–14.
94. See note 37 above. Kuo Shao-yü (V, pp. 441–42) interpreted *ch'i* as a general term for the four inner qualities, which is not plausible, since Yeh states that *ch'i* is what controls the three principles of external things.
95. Yeh Hsieh, p. 579. The punctuation is wrong in the new edition with Kuo's introduction, as in Ting's original edition of the *Ch'ing shih-hua*.
96. Ibid., p. 593.
97. This interpretation of Yüan Mei's concept of *hsing-ling* agrees basically with Ku Yüan-hsiang's (pp. 50–51), although I do not agree that

"feeling belongs to the intellect." For other interpretations, see Kuo Shao-yü, V, pp. 494–96; Aoki/Ch'en, p. 110.

98. Cf. J. J. Y. Liu, I, p. 74.

99. Yüan Mei, II, *wen-chi, chüan* 28, p. 1a; quoted in Ku Yüan-hsiang, p. 50.

100. Ku Yüan-hsiang, p. 91. Yüan Mei, I, pp. 3, 35, 73, 74, 87, 90, 183, 196, 216, 565; III, p. 167.

101. Yang Hung-lieh, Ku Yüan-hsiang.

102. For discussions of Yüan's sources, see Ku Yüan-hsiang, pp. 52–65; Aoki/Ch'en, pp. 328–29. For a discussion of Yüan's general views on literature, see Waley, V, pp. 166–75.

103. Coleridge, vol. 1, p. 202; quoted in Wimsatt and Brooks, p. 389; Abrams, p. 168.

104. Wordsworth, pp. 160–61; quoted in Wimsatt and Brooks, p. 405.

105. Coleridge, vol. 1, p. 202. Cf. note 19 to chapter 4.

106. Wordsworth, pp. 15, 34; quoted in Wimsatt and Brooks, p. 407.

107. Croce, chapter 1. See Wimsatt and Brooks, pp. 502–3.

108. Joyce Cary, pp. 6, 41, 42.

CHAPTER FOUR

1. The four tones of Classical Chinese are not identical with those of modern Pekinese. On verse forms involving tone patterns, see J. J. Y. Liu, I, pp. 26–33.

2. Shen Yüeh, *chüan* 67, p. 1595; quoted in Lo Ken-tse, vol. 1, p. 170. For technical terms, see Chan Ying, pp. 185–92.

3. For the interpretation of *shu* as "principles" rather than "skill," see Liu Yung-chi, p. 61.

4. Fan Wen-lan, p. 656; Wang Li-ch'i, p. 115. Cf. Vincent Shih, p. 231.

5. Kao Ch'i, *chüan* 2, p. 12a; quoted in Kuo Shao-yü, V, p. 287.

6. Li Tung-yang, I, *wen hou-kao, chüan* 4, p. 16b; quoted in Kuo Shao-yü, V, p.290.

7. Li Tung-yang, I, *wen kao, chüan* 5, p. 17b; quoted in Kuo Shao-yü, V, p. 291.

8. Li Tung-yang, II, p. 1a; quoted in Kuo Shao-yü, V, p. 293, Cf. J. J. Y. Liu, I, p. 79.

9. Li Tung-yang, I, *wen hou-kao, chüan* 3, p. 14a; quoted in Kuo Shao-yü, V, p. 291.

10. Li Meng-yang, *chüan* 62, pp. 7a–b; quoted in Kuo Shao-yü, V, p. 301 (where the *chüan* number is given as 61).

11. T'ang Shun-chih, *pu-yi* (supplement), *chüan* 5, pp. 8a–b; quoted in Kuo Shao-yü, V, p. 311 (where the *chüan* number is given as 10).

12. For a brief introduction to traditional Chinese drama, see J. J. Y. Liu, IV, pp. 141–49.

13. Li Yü, p. 2.

14. Ibid., p. 4.

15. See Abrams, pp. 272–85.

16. Li Yü, p. 10; quoted in Kuo Shao-yü, V, p. 421.
17. See chapter 2 and Weng Fang-kang, *chüan* 8, pp. 2a, 4a, 5b.
18. Weng Fang-kang, *chüan* 8, p. 5b; quoted in Kuo Shao-yü, V, p. 516.
19. *Tu-shih yin-te*, 476/44/11.
20. Ibid., 280/13/4.
21. Weng Fang-kang, *chüan* 8, pp. 1a–b; quoted in Kuo Shao-yü, V, p. 519.
22. Liu Ta-k'uei, p. 3. Also in Wang Huan-piao, p. 166. Quoted in Kuo Shao-yü, V, p. 557.
23. Ibid., p. 4; quoted in Kuo Shao-yü, V, pp. 557, 559.
24. Ibid., p. 6; Wang Huan-piao, p. 166.
25. Ibid., p. 3; quoted in Kuo Shao-yü, V, p. 557.
26. Yao Nai, II, pp. 16 a–b.
27. Tseng Kuo-fan, vol. 3, p. 53; quoted in Kuo Shao-yü, V, p. 560.
28. Ibid., vol. 4, p. 17; quoted in Kuo Shao-yü, V, pp. 560–61. Kuo gave the date of this letter as "14th year of Hsien-feng," but the Hsien-feng reign lasted only 11 years. The correct year is 11th year of Hsien-feng (1861).
29. Collingwood, pp. 15–41.

CHAPTER FIVE

1. *Tso-chuan*, Duke Hsiang, 25th year (547 B.C.). Cf. Legge, vol. 5, p. 517.
2. See Lo Ken-tse, vol. 1, p. 491.
3. See Sun Hsing-yen, pp. 13–14.
4. Sun Hsing-yen, p. 654. Cf. Lo Ken-tse, vol. 1, p. 54.
5. Lo Ken-tse, vol. 1, pp. 81–84.
6. Chu Fang-p'u, II, p. 20. Cf. Jung Keng, p. 118; Karlgren, II, p. 191.
7. Ting Fu-pao, III, pp. 1107–08.
8. Karlgren, II, p. 191.
9. *Mao-shih yin-te*, 39/177/4, 47/203/6, 53/214/2, 56/225/1, 60/238/4–5, 64/249/2, 65/252/33, 67/256/47, 71/261/2, 76/283/1.
10. See Fung Yu-lan, vol. 2, p. 33; Lo Ken-tse, vol. 1, p. 86.
11. Cheng Hsüan, III, *chüan* 8, p. 3b. Cf. Biot, vol. 1, p. 162; and note 24 to chapter 1.
12. *Hsi-ching tsa-chi, chüan shang*, p. 11b; quoted in Lo Ken-tse, vol. 1, p. 94.
13. See Lao Kan, pp. 19–34.
14. According to Pi Yüan, preface, pp. 1–2.
15. Liu Hsi, *chüan* 4, p. 97 (in Pi Yüan). Cf. Lo Ken-tse, vol. 1, p. 84, where a slightly different version is quoted.
16. Lu Chi, in WCNP, p. 262. Cf. Achilles Fang, p. 536 (in Bishop, p. 12), and Ch'en Shih-hsiang, III, in Birch, I, p. 209.
17. The word here translated as "mobile," *hsü* 虛, literally means "empty," but sometimes means "moving" or "functional." For instance,

hsü-tzu, or "emtpy words," really means "functional words." Vincent Shih (p. 174) translated the word as "plastic."

18. This is derived from the *Lun-yü*, XII, 8. Cf. Legge, vol. 1, p. 255; Waley, III, p. 165.

19. This is derived from the *Tso-chuan*, Duke Hsüan, 2d year. Cf. Legge, vol. 5, pp. 289–90.

20. Fan Wen-lan, p. 537; Wang Li-ch'i, p. 88.

21. The five temperaments are explained as "humanity, rightness, propriety, wisdom, and faith," or as "quietness, impetuosity, strength, firmness, and wisdom." See Lu and Mou in Chou K'ang-hsieh, p. 151; Kuo Chin-hsi, p. 134.

22. Shao and Hsia were supposed to be the music of the legendary sages Shun and Yü respectively.

23. Fan Wen-lan, p. 537; Wang Li-ch'i, p. 88.

24. Hsiao T'ung, I, preface, p. 2a; WCNP, p. 567.

25. Ssu-k'ung T'u, in Kuo Shao-yü, II, p. 47.

26. Ou-yang Hsiu, *wen-chi, chüan* 2, p. 4b; quoted in Kuo Shao-yü, V, p. 180 (where the *chüan* number is given as 1).

27. Lo Ken-tse, vol. 1, p. 122; Kuo Sho-yü, V, pp. 55–56, VII, pp. 84–92; Liu Shih-p'ei, pp. 4–7.

28. *Tso-chuan*, Duke Hsiang, 25th year (547 B.C.). Cf. Legge, vol. 5, p. 517.

29. Juan Yüan, *san-chi, chüan* 2, p. 567; quoted in Fan Wen-lan, p. 13 (where the *chüan* number is given as 3).

30. Ibid., *chüan* 2, pp. 569–70; quoted in Fan Wen-lan, p. 14.

31. Liu Shih-p'ei, p. 1.

32. Puttenham, pp. 159–60.

33. Pound, pp. 25–28. The resemblance between Liu Hsieh and Pound has been noted by Ch'ien Chung-shu (p. 51). Whether Pound derived his ideas from Puttenham I do not know.

CHAPTER SIX

1. See Ch'ü Wan-li, p. 82.

2. *Mao-shih yin-te*, p. 29. Cf. Karlgren, I, p. 89 (Ode 141); Waley, II, p. 65; Chu Tzu-ch'ing, p. 5.

3. Ch'ü Wan-li, p. 118.

4. *Mao-shih yin-te*, p. 43. Cf. Karlgren, I, pp. 133–34 (Ode 191). Missing in Waley, II.

5. *Mao-shih yin-te*, p. 65. Cf. Karlgren, I, p. 212 (Ode 253). Missing in Waley, II.

6. *Mao-shih yin-te*, p. 70. Cf. Karlgren, I, p. 228 (Ode 259); Waley, II, p. 135; Ch'ü Wan-li, p. 183; Chow Tse-tsung, I, p. 154.

7. *Mao-shih yin-te*, p. 71. Cf. Karlgren, I, p. 230 (Ode 260); Waley, II, p. 143.

8. Abrams, p. 9.

9. E.g., Ma Yau-woon, Donald Holzman.

10. Lo Ken-tse, vol. 1, p. 49.

11. The tradition that Confucius selected 300 poems out of 3,000 is not supported by evidence.

12. *Lun-yü*, II, 2. Cf. J. J. Y. Liu, I, p. 65. It is well known that Confucius is quoting the phrase out of context and giving it a new meaning.

13. *Lun-yü*, VIII, 8. Cf. J. J. Y. Liu, I, p. 66.

14. Holzman, following Pao Hsien (6 B.C.–A.D. 65) and Huang K'an (488–545). See Ho Yen et. al., *chüan* 8, pp. 4a–b.

15. Ma Yau-woon, p. 20.

16. *Lun-yü*, XIII, 5. Cf. J. J. Y. Liu, I, p. 66.

17. *Lun-yü*, XVI, 13. Cf. Liu, p. 66.

18. Hsü Fu-kuan, I, p. 33.

19. *Lun-yü*, XVII, 8. Cf. Liu, p. 66.

20. Cheng Hsüan, I, pp. 5a–b.

21. See Ch'en Shih-hsiang, V; Hu Nien-yi.

22. E.g., Lo Ken-tse, vol. 1, p. 39; Waley, III, p. 212 ("incite people's emotions"); J. J. Y. Liu, I, p. 66 ("inspire emotion").

23. E.g., Chu Hsi, II, *chüan* 9, p. 788, followed by Chu Tzu-ch'ing, p. 75; Kuo Shao-yü, V, p. 17; Hsü Fu-kuan, I, p. 34; Legge, vol. 1, p. 323 ("stimulate the mind").

24. Holzman, following the pseudo-K'ung An-kuo commentary quoted by later commentators, e.g., Liu Pao-nan. Ch'ien Mu (II, p. 600) appears to combine all previous interpretations.

25. Cheng Hsüan's commentary quoted by later commentators, e.g., Ho Yen et al., *chüan* 8, p. 5a; Liu Pao-nan, p. 374.

26. Chu Hsi's commentary followed by Kuo Shao-yü and Hsü Fu-kuan (see above, note 23).

27. Legge, vol. 1, p. 323.

28. Waley, III, p. 212.

29. Ch'ien Mu, II, p. 600.

30. Holzman, with reference to *Tso-chuan*, Duke Hsiang, 27th year.

31. Pseudo-K'ung An-kuo commentary, quoted by later commentators, e.g., Liu Pao-nan, p. 374.

32. Ibid.

33. Cheng Hsüan, I, pp. 5 a–b. Cf. J. J. Y. Liu, I. p. 66.

34. Ibid.

35. Wang Ch'ung, *chüan* 20, p. 220; quoted in Kuo Shan-yü, VI, p. 32; Lo Ken-tse, vol. 1, p. 111.

36. Cheng Hsüan, I, pp. 1–5; quoted in Lo Ken-tse, vol. 1, pp. 79–80.

37. Ts'ao P'i, in WCNP, p. 52.

38. Lu Chi, in WCNP, p. 274. Cf. Achilles Fang, p. 546 (in Bishop, p. 22); Ch'en Shih-hsiang, III, in Birch, I, p. 214.

39. These refer to rites concerning auspicious events (sacrifices), inauspicious events (e.g., funerals), guests (court audiences), military affairs,

and celebrations (e.g., coming of age, wedding). See Cheng Hsüan, III, *chüan* 18, pp. 1a–5b; IV, *chüan* 14, p. 6a.

40. These refer to general administration, education, rites, military affairs, punishment, and public works. See Cheng Hsüan, III, *chüan* 2, pp. 1a–b.

41. Fan Wen-lan, p. 726; Wang Li-ch'i, p. 128. Cf. Vincent Shih, p. 4.

42. Chou Tun-yi, *chüan* 6, p. 117; quoted in Kuo Shao-yü, V, p. 156; Lo Ken-tse, vol. 3, p. 73.

43. See Kuo Shao-yü, V, pp. 157–58; Lo Ken-tse, vol. 3, pp. 74–75.

44. Shen Te-ch'ien, I, p. 1a.

45. Shen Te-ch'ien, II, preface.

46. Shen Te-ch'ien, III, preface.

47. Huang Chieh, II, p. 1a.

48. Huang Chieh, I, preface.

CHAPTER SEVEN

1. Lo Ken-tse, vol. 1, pp. 81–84.

2. *Lun-yü*, XV, 41. Cf. Legge, vol. 1, p. 305; Waley, III, p. 201 (given as No. 40). *Tso-chuan*, Duke Hsiang, 25th year (547 B.C.). Cf. Legge, vol. 5, p. 517.

3. Lo Ken-tse, vol. 1, pp. 84–86; Kuo Shao-yü, V, pp. 23–25. For further discussions, see chapter 5.

4. In Hsiao T'ung, I, *chüan* 8.

5. Quoted in Kuo Shao-yü, V, p. 28. Cf. Lo Ken-tse, vol. 1, pp. 96–97, where Yang Hsiung is said to be reconciling the two views.

6. Cheng Hsüan, I, p. 12b; quoted in Lo Ken-tse, vol. 1, pp. 79–80; Chu Tzu-ch'ing, pp. 144–45.

7. Ts'ao P'i, in WCNP, p. 52.

8. *Tso-chuan*, Duke Hsiang, 24th year (548 B.C.). Cf. Legge, vol. 5, p. 507.

9. Fan Wen-lan, p. 1; Wang Li-ch'i, p. 1. Cf. Shih, p. 9; Gibbs, pp. 44–45.

10. Donald Gibbs, passim.

11. Fan Wen-lan, p. 494; Wang Li-ch'i, p. 80. Cf. Vincent Shih, p. 156. Kuo Chin-hsi's suggested emendation (p. 66) that *hsin*, or "mind," and *shu*, or "artistry," should be transposed seems unnecessary.

12. The disyllable *hsün-chih* 馴致 originated from the *Yi-ching* and can be taken as a single compound meaning "tame," but I have adopted the interpretation of Lu and Mou (p. 96, reprinted in Chou K'ang-hsieh, p. 110) that *chih* means *ch'ing-chih* 情致 or "feelings." Cf. Shih, p. 155; Hsü Fu-kuan, II, p. 64.

13. The "cook" alludes to Chuang Tzu's parable (see note 78 to Chapter 2), and is a metaphor for the writer's intuition.

14. The phrase *ting-mo* ("fix ink"), as pointed out by Kuo Chin-hsi (p. 67), originated from the *Li-chi*, where it refers to divination, but here it simply means writing.

15. *Chuang Tzu yin-te*, 50/19/54; Ch'ien Mu, I, pp. 150–51. Cf. Watson, pp. 205–6.

16. Fan Wen-lan, p. 493; Wang Li-ch'i, p. 80.

17. I take *kuei-chü* 規矩 ("compasses and square") as verbs and *hsü-wei* 虛位 ("empty place") as their object, parallel in syntax to *tiao-lou wu-hsing* 雕鏤無形 ("carve and engrave the formless"). This agrees with the interpretations of Lu and Mou (p. 96), Kuo Chin-hsi (p. 67), and Chang Heng (pp. 15, 27). Shih's translation (p. 155) seems untenable.

18. Fan Wen-lan, p. 494; Wang Li-ch'i, p. 80.

19. Wang Yüan-hua, pp. 221–223; see also Huang Hai-chang, reprinted in CKWH, p. 75.

20. Shih translated *shen-ssu* as "Spiritual Thought or Imagination" (p. 154), and Gibbs approved of the latter (pp. 72–73). Among those writing in Chinese, Liao Wei-ch'ing (pp. 236–39), Liu Shou-sung (in WHTL, pp. 33–36), and Kuo Chin-hsi (pp. 64 ff.) all identified *shen-ssu* with *hsiang-hsiang*, or "imagination." Hsü Fu-kuan (II, p. 42) and Chang Heng (pp. 15–16) recognized some differences.

21. Coleridge, vol. 1, p. 202; quoted in Wimsatt and Brooks, p. 405.

22. J. J. Y. Liu, I, pp. 70–72.

23. Fan Wen-lan, p. 65; Wang Li-ch'i, p. 16. Cf. Vincent Shih, p. 32. My previous translation of the last sentence (*ut supra*) is wrong.

24. Fan Wen-lan, p. 538; Wang Li-ch'i, p. 88.

25. J. J. Y. Liu, I, p. 66. I refer only to their basic conceptions of literature. With regard to how to write, they have more original views. For an interesting, though debatable, interpretation of Tu Fu's views on poetry, see Yoshikawa.

26. Feng Hao, *chüan* 8, p. 4a. Feng identified the recipient of the letter as Ts'ui Kuei-ts'ung and dated the letter ca. 837.

27. Lo Ken-tse, vol. 2, p. 170. Lo quoted the letter from the *Ch'üan T'ang wen*, which contains a variant reading.

28. Feng Hao, *chüan* 3, pp. 30b–31a. Feng identified the recipient as Wei Tsung and dated the letter 847.

29. Kuo Shao-yü, V, pp. 160–65, refers to this group as "statesmen" (*cheng-chih-chia*), and Lo Ken-tse, vol. 3, pp. 80–97, as "School of Scriptural Scholarship and Statecraft" (*ching-shu-p'ai*).

30. For the distinctions between "verse" (*shih*) and "lyrics" (*tz'u*), see J. J. Y. Liu, VII; for Ou-yang's lyrics, see Liu, VIII, chapter 1.

31. See Lo Ken-tse, vol. 3, pp. 62–63.

32. See his preface to a group of lyrics in *Ch'üan Sung tz'u*, p. 121.

33. Ou-yang Hsiu, *chüan* 47, pp. 5a–b; quoted in Kuo Shao-yü, III, p. 151; Lo Ken-tse, vol. 3, p. 55.

34. Ou-yang Hsiu, *chüan* 128, p. 7b; quoted in Lo, vol. 3, p. 59.

35. Ou-yang Hsiu, 42, p. 7a; quoted in Lo, vol. 3, pp. 57–58.

36. Lo Ken-tse, vol. 2, pp. 153–54.

37. Su Shih, *hou-chi, chüan* 14, p. 10a; quoted in Kuo Shao-yü, V, p. 170; Lo Ken-tse, vol. 3, p. 108.

38. Su Ch'e, *chüan* 22, pp. 1a–b; quoted in Kuo Shao-yü, V, pp. 174–75; Lo Ken-tse, vol. 3, pp. 114–15.

39. Some of them may have been influenced by neo-Confucianism in their conception of spiritual self-cultivation.

40. Hu Ying-lin, p. 100; quoted in Kuo Shao-yü, V, p. 333.

41. Ku Yen-wu, *chüan* 19, p. 445; quoted in Kuo, V, p. 404.

42. Chao Chih-hsin, in Ting Fu-pao, II, p. 310.

43. Ibid., and p. 309.

44. See Kuo Shao-yü, V, p. 494; J. J. Y. Liu, I, pp. 75, 84.

45. Yuan Mei, I, p. 565.

46. Ch'ien Chung-shu, pp. 234–35.

47. *Lun-yü*, XVI, 13; XVII, 8. Cf. Liu, p. 66.

48. Yüan Mei, II, *chüan* 17, pp. 6a–b.

49. Waley, V, p. 171.

50. Yüan Mei, II, *chüan* 17, p. 6b.

51. Fu Hsüan (217–78) was a poet and official of the Chin dynasty. The phrase "exerted moral influence at the Imperial Secretariat" (*t'ai-ke sheng feng*) is taken from his official biography in the *Chin-shu* (p. 1210).

52. Yüan Mei, II, chüan 17, p. 6b.

53. The term "Academician" (*t'ai-shih*) literally means "grand historiographer" but was used in Ch'ing times to refer to a member of the Academy of Letters (Han-lin Yüan).

54. Han Wo (fl. 885–905) is a late T'ang poet noted for his poems about women.

55. Wen T'ing-yün (812–70?) is another late T'ang poet noted for his poems about love and women.

56. Wen Yen-po (1006–97) was a famous Sung minister and general who was enfeoffed as Duke of Lu.

57. Li Fang (925–96) was another famous Sung official, who was posthumously "canonized" as Wen-cheng.

58. Yüan seems to be echoing Mencius in contrasting "run wild" (*pao-ch'ü*) 暴去 with "hold" (*ch'ih*) 持. Perhaps in the relevant passage in the *Mencius* the word *pao* should also be taken to mean "run wild" or "get out of control" rather than "do violence to" (Legge, vol. 2, p. 189) or "abuse" (D. C. Lau, II, p. 78).

59. Yüan Mei, I, p. 35.

60. The locus classicus of the "Intentional Fallacy" is Wimsatt and Beardsley, pp. 3–18. Also see Victor Erlich for a discussion of the relation between an author's life and works.

61. Ch'ien Chung-shu, pp. 253–55; Kuo Mo-jo, III, pp. 12–14, 69–70.

62. See Nivison, pp. 263–67.

63. Ibid., pp. 203, 264n. See also Ch'ien Chung-shu, pp. 260, 313–15; Kuo Shao-yü, V, pp. 479, 524.

64. Kuo Shao-yü, V, pp. 482–88.

65. Wellek and Warren, p. 43; Wellek, I, pp. 1–20.

66. Fokkema, II, pp. 59–69.

Abbreviations

BIHP *Bulletin of the Institute of History and Philology*. Academia Sinica, Taipei 中央研究院歷史語言研究所集刊

BSS Basic Sinological Series (*Kuo-hsüeh chi-pen ts'ung-shu*) 國學基本叢書

CHWS *Chung-hua wen-shih lun-ts'ung* 中華文史論叢

CKWH *Chung-kuo wen-hsüeh-p'i-p'ing yen-chiu lun-wen chi, Wen-hsin tiao-lung yen-chiu chuan-hao* 中國文學批評研究論文集文心雕龍研究專號. Hong Kong, 1969.

CL *Chinese Literature*. Peking

ESWS *Erh-shih-wu-shih* 二十五史.(Kaiming ed.). Shanghai, 1934

HJAS *Harvard Journal of Asiatic Studies*

JAOS *Journal of the American Oriental Society*

SPPY *Ssu-pu pei-yao* 四部備要

SPTK *Ssu-pu ts'ung-k'an* 四部叢刊

TR *Tamkang Review*. Taipei

TSCC *Ts'ung-shu chi-ch'eng* (1st series)叢書集成初編

WCNP *Wei Chin Nan-pei-ch'ao wen-hsüeh-shih ts'an-k'ao tzu-liao* 魏晉南北朝文學史參考資料.Peking, 1961.

WHTL *Wen-hsin tiao-lung yen-chiu lun-wen chi* (1st series)文心雕龍研究論文集初編. Hong Kong, n.d.

WHYC *Wen-hsüeh yen chiu* 文學研究. Peking. (Also known as *Wen-hsüeh p'ing-lun* 文學評論.)

YWLC *Yi-wen lei chü* 藝文類聚 Shanghai, 1965 ed.

Bibliography

This bibliography consists only of works cited or mentioned in the present book and is not intended to be a complete bibliography of Chinese literary criticism, for to list everything that has been written on the subject, good, bad, or indifferent, would be both impractical and pointless. Nor does this bibliography include common reference books like dictionaries.

The bibliography is in three sections. Section A consists of primary sources in Chinese, including modern editions of traditional works, which are *listed under the editors' names* and cross-listed under the original authors or titles. Section B lists secondary sources and references, namely, studies of traditional Chinese works by modern scholars, as well as translations of such works into Western languages. Section C lists Western works that are not concerned with Chinese studies but that have been cited or mentioned for comparative purposes. In all sections, except for anonymous works, the Confucian Canon, and other early Chinese philosophical works, all works are listed by author, and when two or more works by the same author are listed, a roman numeral is given after the author's name.

A. Primary Sources in Chinese

Chan-kuo ts'e 戰國策. TSCC.

Chao Chih-hsin 趙執信 (1662–1744). *T'an-lung lu* 談龍錄. In Ting Fu-pao, II.

Chao Yi 趙壹 (2d cent. A.D.). "Fei ts'ao-shu" 非草書. In *Ch'üan Hou-Han wen* 全後漢文, in Yen K'e-chün.

Chao Yung-hsien 趙用賢, ed. *Kuan-tzu chi-chieh* 管子集解 1582; rpt. Shanghai, 1936.

Ch'en shu. See Yao Ssu-lien, II.

Cheng Hsüan 鄭玄 (127–200), I, ed. *Mao-shih chu-shu* 毛詩注疏. With sub-commentary by K'ung Ying-ta 孔穎達. Nanch'ang, 1815; rpt. of Sung ed., in *Shih-san Ching Chu-shu* 十三經注疏

———, II, ed. *Mao-shih Cheng chu* 毛詩鄭注 SPPY.

———, III, ed. *Chou-li Cheng chu* 周禮鄭注 SPPY.

———, IV, ed. *Li-chi Cheng chu* 禮記鄭注. SPPY.

Ch'ien Mu, 錢穆, I, ed. *Chuang-tzu tsuan-chien* 莊子纂箋 Hong Kong, 1963.

———, II, ed. *Lun-yü hsin-chieh*, 論語新解. Hong Kong, 1963.

Chih Yü 摯虞 (d. ca. 312). *Wen-chang liu-pieh chih-lun* 文章流別志論 In YWLC, and in *Ch'üan Chin wen* 全晉文 in Yen K'e-chün.

Chin Sheng-t'an 金聖嘆 (1610?–61), ed. *T'ang ts'ai-tzu shih* 唐才子詩. 1660; rtp. with his letters, Taipei, 1963.

Chin shu. See Fang Ch'iao.

Ch'ing shih-hua. See Ting Fu-pao, II.

Chou K'ang-hsieh周康燮, ed. *Wen-hsin tiao-lung hsüan-chu*文心雕龍選注. Hong Kong, 1970.
Chou li. See Cheng Hsüan, III. For translation, see Biot.
Chou shu. See Ling-hu Te-fen.
Chou Tun-yi 周敦頤(1017–73). *Chou Lien-hsi chi*周濂溪集. TSCC.
*Chou Yi yin-te*周易引得 Peiping, 1935; rpt. Taipei, 1966.
Chu Hsi 朱熹 (1130–1200), I, ed. *Shih chi-chuan*詩集傳; rpt. Shanghai, 1955.
———, II, ed. *Lun-yü chi-chu* 論語集注 rpt. Taipei, 1958.
Ch'ü Wan-li屈萬里, ed. *Shih-ching hsüan-chu*詩經選注. Taipei, 1955; 2d ed., 1959.
Ch'üan Sung tz'u. See T'ang Kuei-chang.
Ch'üan T'ang wen. See Tung Kao.
*Chuang Tzu yin-te*莊子引得 Peiping, 1947. For other editions, see Ch'ien Mu, I; Kuan Feng. For translations, see Graham, Watson.
Chung Hung 鍾嶸 (fl. 483–513). *Shih-p'in* 詩品. In Ho Wen-huan.
Fan Wen-lan 范文瀾 ed. *Wen-hsin tiao-lung chu*文心雕龍注 Peking, 1962.
Fang Ch'iao 房喬 (Fang Hsüan-ling 房玄齡 578–648), et al. *Chin shu* 晉書. In ESWS.
Feng Hao 馮浩 (1719–1801), ed. *Fan-nan wen-chi hsiang-chu* 樊南文集詳註. 1765; rpt. in SPPY.
Han shu. See Pan Ku.
Han Yü 韓愈 (768–824). *Ch'ang-li hsien-sheng chi* 昌黎先生集 SPPY.
Ho Wen-huan 何文煥 ed. *Li-tai shih-hua*歷代詩話 1740; rpt. Taipei, n.d.
Ho Yen 何晏 (d. 249) et al., eds. *Lun-yü chi-chieh* 論語集解. SPPY.
*Hsi-ching tsa-chi*西京雜記. In Lu Wen-ch'ao.
Hsiao Kang 蕭綱 (503–51). "Chao-ming T'ai-tzu chi hsü"昭明太子集序 In *Ch'üan Liang wen* 全梁文 in Yen K'e-chün; also in Hsiao T'ung, II.
Hsiao T'ung 蕭統 (501–31), I, ed. *Wen-hsüan* 文選. SPPY.
———, II. *Chao-ming T'ai-tzu chi* 昭明太子集 SPPY.
Hsieh Chen 謝榛 (1495–1575). *Ssu-ming shih-hua* 四溟詩話. In Ting Fu-pao, I.
Hsieh Ho 謝赫 (fl. 479–532). See Wang Po-min.
Hsü Shen 許慎 (1st cent. A.D.). See Ting Fu-pao, III.
Hu Ying-lin 胡應麟 (1551–1602). *Shih-sou* 詩藪; rpt. Peking, 1958.
Huai-nan tzu. See Liu Wen-tien.
Huang Chieh 黃節 (1874–1935), I, ed. *Juan Pu-ping yung-huai-shih chu*阮步兵詠懷詩注. Peking, 1926; rpt. Hong Kong, 1961.
———, II. *Shih hsüeh*詩學; rpt. Hong Kong, 1964.
Huang Shu-lin 黃叔琳, ed. *Wen-hsin tiao-lung*文心雕龍. 1738; rpt. with commentary by Chi Yün 紀昀 (1724–1805), Shanghai, n.d.
I Ching. See *Yi-ching*.
Juan Chi 阮籍 (210–63). See Huang Chieh, I.
Juan Yü 阮瑀 (d. 212). "Wen chih lun"文質論. In YWLC; also in *Ch'üan Hou-Han wen* in Yen K'e-chün.
Juan Yüan 阮元 (1764–1949). *Yen-ching-shih chi*揅經室集. TSCC.

Kao Ch'i 高啟 (1336–74). *Fu-tsao chi* 鳧藻集. Printed with *Kao Ch'ing-ch'iu shih chu* 高青丘詩集注 SPPY.
Kao Heng 高亨, I, ed. *Lao Tzu cheng-ku* 老子正詁 Rev. ed. Peking, 1956.
Ku Yen-wu 顧炎武 (1613–82). *Jih-chih lu* 日知錄. With notes by Huang Ju-ch'eng 黃汝成. 1834; rpt. Taipei, 1968.
Kuan Tzu. See Chao Yung-hsien.
Kuo Chin-hsi 郭晉稀 ed. *Wen-hsin tiao-lung yi-chu shih-pa-p'ien* 文心雕龍譯注十八篇. Hong Kong, 1964.
Kuo Mao-ch'ien 郭茂倩 (fl. 1264–69), ed. *Yüeh-fu shih-chi* 樂府詩集 SPPY.
Kuo-yü. See Wei Chao.
Kuo Shao-yü 郭紹虞, I, ed. *Ts'ang-lang shih-hua chiao-shih* 滄浪詩話校釋. *Peking*, 1962.
———, II, ed. *Shih-p'in chi-chieh* 詩品集解. Printed together with Yüan Mei, III; preface dated 1962; rpt. Hong Kong, 1965.
Lao Tzu. See Kao Heng, I. For translations, see Chan Wing-tsit, I; Chu Ta-kao; D. C. Lau, I; Lin Yutang, I; Waley, I.
Li-chi. See Cheng Hsüan, IV. For translation, see Legge/Chai.
Li Chih 李贄 (1527–1602). *Fen-shu* 焚書 Peking, 1961.
Li Meng-yang 李夢陽 (1472–1528). *K'ung-t'ung-tzu chi* 空同子集 1602.
Li Pai-yao 李百藥 (565–648). *Pei-Ch'i shu* 北齊書, in ESWS.
Li Shang-yin 李商隱 (813?–58). See Feng Hao.
Li-tai shih-hua. See Ho Wen-huan.
Li Tung-yang 李東陽 (1447–1516), I. *Huai-lu-t'ang chi* 懷麓堂集 1681.
———, II. *Huai-lu-t'ang shih-hua*. In Ting Fu-pao, I.
Li Yü 李漁 (1611–80?). *Li Li-weng ch'ü-hua* 李笠翁曲話. Peking, 1959.
Liang shu. See Yao Ssu-lien, I.
Ling-hu Te-fen 令狐德棻 (583–666) et al. *Chou shu* 周書, in ESWS.
Liu Hsi 劉熙 (3d cent.). See Pi Yüan.
Liu Hsieh 劉勰 (d. ca. 523). For editions, see Chou K'ang-hsieh, Fan Wen-lan, Huang Shu-lin, Kuo Chin-hsi, Wang Li-ch'i, Yang Ming-chao. For translation, see Vincent Shih.
Liu Pao-nan 劉寶楠 (1791–1855), ed. *Lun-yü cheng-yi* 論語正義 rpt. Peking, 1957.
Liu Ta-k'uei 劉大櫆 (1698–1780). *Lun-wen ou-chi* 論文偶記 Peking, 1959.
Liu Wen-tien 劉文典, ed. *Huai-nan Hung-lieh chi-chieh* 淮南鴻烈集解. Peking, 1923; 3d ed., 1926.
Lu Chi 陸機 (261–303). *Wen-fu* 文賦, in WCNP. For translations, see Achilles Fang; Ch'en Shih-hsiang, III.
Lu Wen-ch'ao 盧文弨 (1717–95), ed. *Pao-ching-t'ang ts'ung-shu* 抱經堂叢書. 1786; rpt. in *Pai-pu ts'ung-shu chi-ch'eng* 百部叢書集成. Taipei, n.d.
Lun-yü yin-te 論語引得. Peiping, 1940. For other editions, see Ch'ien Mu, II; Chu Hsi, II; Ho Yen; Liu Pao-nan. For translations, see Legge; Waley, III.
Ma Kuo-han 馬國翰 ed. *Yü-han-shan-fang chi yi-shu* 玉函山房佚書 1844.
Mao-shih yin-te 毛詩引得. Peiping, 1934. For other editions, see Cheng

Hsüan, I and II; Chu Hsi, I; Ch'ü Wan-li. For translations, see Karlgren, I; Waley, II.

*Meng Tzu yin-te*孟子引得Peiping, 1941. For translations, see Legge; D. C. Lau, II.

Ou-yang Hsiu 歐陽修 (1007–72). *Ou-yang Wen-chung chi*歐陽文忠集 SPPY.

Pan Ku 班固 (A.D. 32–92). *Han shu* 漢書. In ESWS.

Pei-Ch'i shu. See Li Pai-yao.

Pi Yüan 畢沅 (1730–97), ed. *Shih-ming shu-cheng* 釋名疏証. 1789; rpt. in TSCC.

Po Chü-yi 白居易 (772–846). *Po-shih Ch'ang-ch'ing chi* 白氏長慶集.Rpt. Peking, 1955.

*Shang-shu t'ung-chien*尚書通檢. Peiping, 1936.

Shao Yung 邵雍 (1011–77). *Yi-ch'uan chi-jang chi*伊川擊壤集. SPTK.

Shen Ch'i-wu沈啟无, ed. *Chin-tai san-wen ch'ao*近代散文抄. Peiping, 1931; rpt. Hong Kong, 1957.

Shen Te-ch'ien沈德潛 (1673–1769), I. *Shuo-shih tsui-yu*說詩晬語. SPPY.

———, II, ed. *Ch'ung-ting T'ang-shih pieh-ts'ai*重訂唐詩別裁 1763; rpt. in BSS.

———, III, ed. *Ch'ing-shih pieh-ts'ai*清詩別裁. BBS.

Shen Yüeh沈約 (441–513). *Sung shu* 宋書. In ESWS.

Shih-ching. See *Mao-shih yin-te*.

*Shih-wei*詩緯. In Ma Kuo-han.

Shu-ching. See *Shang-shu t'ung-chien*.

Ssu-k'ung T'u 司空圖 (837–908). For editions, see Kuo Shao-yü, II; Tsu Pao-ch'üan. For translation, see Yang Hsien-yi and Gladys Yang, II.

Su Ch'e 蘇轍 (1039–1112). *Luan-ch'eng chi*欒城集. SPPY.

Su Shih 蘇軾 (1037–1101). *Tung-p'o ch'i-chi*東坡七集. SPPY.

Sui shu. See Wei Cheng.

Sun Hsing-yen 孫星衍 (1753–1818), ed. *Chou-yi chi-chieh* 周易集解. TSCC.

Sung shu. See Shen Yüeh.

T'ang Kuei-chang 唐圭璋, ed. *Ch'üan Sung tz'u*全宋詞. New ed. Shanghai, 1965.

T'ang Shun-chih 唐順之 (1507–60). *Ching-ch'uan hsien-sheng chi* 荆川先生集. 1549.

T'ang Ta-p'ei 唐大沛, ed. *Yi Chou shu fen-pien chu-shih*逸周書分編注釋. 1836; rpt. Taipei, 1969.

Ting Fu-pao丁福保 (1874–1952), I, ed. *Li-tai shih-hua hsü-pien* 歷代詩話續編. 1915; rpt. Taipei, n.d.

———, II, ed. *Ch'ing shih-hua*清詩話. 1916; rpt., with introduction by Kuo Shao-yü, Shanghai, 1963.

———, III, ed. *Shuo-wen chieh-tzu ku-lin*說文解字詁林Shanghai, 1930.

Ts'ao P'i 曹丕 (187–226). *Lun-wen* 論文. In WCNP.

Tseng Kuo-fan 曾國藩 (1811–72). *Tseng Wen-cheng kung ch'üan-chi* 曾文正公全集. Shanghai, 1936.

Tso-chuan 左傳. With commentary by Tu Yü 杜預 (222–84). Peking, 1955. For translation, see Legge.

Tsu Pao-ch'üan 祖保泉, ed. *Ssu-k'ung T'u Shih-p'in chu-shih chi yi-wen* 司空圖詩品注釋及譯文 Hong Kong, 1966.

Tu Fu 杜甫 (712–70). *Tu-shih yin-te* 杜詩引得. Peiping, 1940; rpt. Taipei, 1966.

Tung Kao 董誥 et al., eds. *Ch'üan T'ang wen* 全唐文. 1814; rpt. Taipei, n.d.

Wang Ch'ung 王充 (27–ca. 101). *Lun-heng* 論衡. TSCC.

Wang Fu-chih 王夫之 (1619–92). *Hsi-t'ang yung-jih hsü-lun* 夕堂永日緒論 and *Shih-yi* 詩繹. In *Ch'uan-shan yi-shu* 船山遺書. Shanghai, 1933; printed together as *Chiang-chai shih-hua* 薑齋詩話 in Ting Fu-pao, II.

Wang Huan-piao 王煥鑣, ed. *Chung-kuo wen-hsüeh-p'i-p'ing lun-wen chi* 中國文學批評論文集, 1936; rpt. Taipei, 1953.

Wang Li-ch'i 王利器, ed. *Wen-hsin tiao-lung hsin-shu* 文心雕龍新書. With concordance (*t'ung-chien* 通檢). Peking, 1952; rpt. Hong Kong, 1967 (text only); rpt. Taipei, 1968 (with concordance but without introduction).

Wang Po 王勃 (648–75). "P'ing-t'ai mi-lüeh lun" 平臺秘略論 In Tung Kao.

Wang Po-min 王伯敏 ed. *Ku-hua p'in-lu* 古畫品錄. Peking, 1962.

Wang Shih-chen 王士禛 (1634–1711), I. *Tai-ching-t'ang shih-hua* 帶經堂詩話. 1760; rpt. Shanghai, n.d.

———, II. *Tai-ching-t'ang ch'üan-chi* 帶經堂全集 Shanghai, 1921.

Wang Wan 汪琬 (1624–90). *Wang Yao-feng wen* 汪堯峰文. Shanghai, 1936; 3d ed., 1941.

Wei Chao 韋昭 (3d cent. A.D.), ed. *Kuo-yü* 國語. TSCC.

Wei Cheng 魏徵 (580–643). *Sui shu* 隋書. In ESWS.

Weng Fang-kang 翁方綱 (1733–1818). *Fu-ch'u-chai wen-chi* 復初齋文集. 1877.

Yang Ming-chao 楊明照 I, ed. *Wen-hsien tiao-lung chiao-chu* 文心雕龍校注. Shanghai, 1958.

Yao Nai 姚鼐 (1731–1815), I. *Hsi-pao-hsüan ch'üan-chi* 惜抱軒全集 Shanghai, 1936.

———, II, ed. *Ku-wen-tz'u lei-tsuan* 古文辭類纂 SPPY.

Yao Ssu-lien 姚思廉 (ob. 637), I. *Liang shu* 梁書. In ESWS.

———, II. *Ch'en shu* 陳書. In ESWS.

Yeh Hsieh 葉燮 (1627–1703). *Yüan-shih* 原詩. In Ting Fu-pao, II.

Yen K'e-chün 嚴可均 (1762–1843), ed. *Ch'üan shang-ku San-tai Ch'in Han San-kuo Liu-ch'ao wen* 全上古三代秦漢三國六朝文. Peking, 1958.

Yen Yü 嚴羽 (fl. 1180–1235). For edition, see Kuo Shao-yü, I. For translation, see Debon.

Yi-ching. For editions, see *Chou-yi yin-te*; Sun Hsing-yen. For translations, see Legge /Sung; Wilhelm/Baynes.

Yi Chou shu. See T'ang Ta-p'ei.

Ying Yang 應瑒 (d. 217). "Wen chih lun" 文質論. In YWLC; also in *Ch'üan Hou-Han wen* in Yen K'e-chün.

Yüan Hung-tao 袁宏道 (1568–1610). *Yüan Chung-lang ch'üan-chi* 袁中郎全集. Shanghai, 1935.
Yüan Mei 袁枚 (1716–98), I. *Sui-yüan shih-hua* 隨園詩話 Peking, 1960.
———, II. *Hsiao-ts'ang-shan-fang wen chi* 小倉山房文集. SPPY.
———, III. *Hsü shih-p'in* 續詩品. Printed with Kuo Shao-yü, II.
Yüan Tsung-tao 袁宗道 (1560–1600). *Po-su-chai lei-kao* 白蘇齋類稿. Shanghai, 1935.

B. SECONDARY SOURCES IN CHINESE AND WESTERN LANGUAGES

Aoki/Ch'en.
Aoki Masaru 青木正兒 Trans. by Ch'en Shu-nü 陳淑女. *Ch'ing-tai wen-hsüeh-p'ing-lun shih* 清代文學評論史 Taipei, 1969.
Aoki/Wang.
Aoki Masaru. Trans. by Wang Fu-ch'üan 汪馥泉 *Chung-kuo wen-hsüeh-ssu-hsiang shih kang* 中國文學思想史綱. Shanghai, 1936.
Biot, Edouard, trans. *Le Tcheou-Li*, Paris, 1851; rpt. Taipei, 1969.
Birch, Cyril, I, ed. *Anthology of Chinese Literature*. New York, 1965.
———, II, ed. *Studies in Chinese Literary Genres*. Berkeley, 1974.
Bishop, J. L., ed. *Studies in Chinese Literature*. Cambridge, Mass., 1965.
Chan Wing-tsit, I, trans. *The Way of Lao Tzu*. Indianapolis and New York, 1963.
———, II, ed. and trans. *A Source Book in Chinese Philosophy*. Princeton, 1963.
Chan Ying 詹鍈. "Ssu-sheng wu-yin chi ch'i tsai Han Wei Liu-ch'ao wen-hsüeh chung chih ying-yung" 四聲五音及其在漢魏六朝文學中之應用. In CHWS. 3d series, 1963.
Chang Chien 張健. *Ts'ang-lang shih-hua yen-chiu* 滄浪詩話研究 Taipei, 1966.
Chang Heng 張亨. "Lu Chi lun wen-hsüeh te ch'uang-tso kuo-ch'eng" 陸機論文學的創作過程 In *Chung-wai wen-hsüeh* 中外文學 vol. 1, no. 8. Taipei, 1973.
Ch'en Meng-chia 陳夢家. *Yin-hsü pu-tz'u tsung-shu* 殷虛卜辭綜述 Peking, 1956.
Ch'en Shih-hsiang 陳世驤 I. "In Search of the Beginning of Chinese Literary Criticism." In *Semitic and Oriental Studies*. University of California Publications in Semitic Philology, vol. 11, 1951.
———, II. "Chinese Poetics and Zenism." In *Oriens*, vol. 10, no. 1, Leiden, 1957.
———, III, trans. Lu Chi's *Essay on Literature*. In Birch, I.
———, IV. "Chung-kuo *shih* tzu chih yüan-shih kuan-nien shih-lun" 中國詩字之原始觀念試論. BIHP, extra volume no. 4, 1961.
———, V. "The *Shih-ching*: Its Generic Significance in Chinese Literary History and Poetics." In Birch, II.
Ch'ien Chung-shu 錢鍾書. *T'an-yi lu* 談藝錄. Shanghai, 1948; rpt. Hong Kong, 1965 (where the original date of publication is wrongly given as 1931).

Chou Hung-hsiang周鴻翔. *Shang-Yin ti-wang pen-chi* 商殷帝王本紀 Hong Kong (privately printed), 1958.

Chow Tse-tsung, I, ed. *Wen-lin: Studies in the Chinese Humanities*. Madison, 1968. (Contains an article on the word *shih* by Chow himself.)

———, II. "Ancient Chinese Views on Literature, the Tao, and their Relationship." Unpublished paper.

Chu Fang-p'u朱芳圃, I. *Chia-ku-hsüeh wen-tzu pien*甲骨學文字編Shanghai, 1933.

———, II. *Yin Chou wen-tzu shih-ts'ung*殷周文字釋叢Peking, 1962.

Chu Ta-kao, trans. *Tao Te Ching*. London, 1937; 5th ed., 1959.

Chu Tzu-ch'ing朱自清. *Shih-yen-chih pien* 詩言志辨. Shanghai, 1945; rpt. Hong Kong, 1960.

Creel, H. G. "The Great Clod: A Taoist Conception of the Universe." In Chow Tse-tsung, I; rpt. in *What is Taoism?* Chicago, 1970.

Debon, Günther, trans. *Ts'ang-lang's Gesprüche über die Dichtung*. Wiesbaden, 1962.

Demiéville, Paul. "Le miroir spirituel." *Sinologica*, vol. 1. Basel, 1948.

Fang, Achilles, trans. "Rhymeprose on Literature." HJAS, vol. 14 (1951); rpt. in Bishop.

Feng Yu-lan. See Fung Yu-lan.

Fokkema, D. W., I. *Literary Doctrine in China and Soviet Influence, 1956–1960*. The Hague, 1965.

———, II. "Cultural Relativism and Comparative Literature." TR, vol. 3, no. 2 (1972).

Fung/Bodde.
Fung Yu-lan. Trans. by Derk Bodde. *A History of Chinese Philosophy*. Vol. 1, 1952; vol. 2, 1953. Princeton.

Fung Yu-lan馮友蘭. *Chung-kuo che-hsüeh shih hsin-pien*中國哲學史新編. Peking, 1964.

Gálik, Marián. *Mao Tun and Modern Chinese Literary Criticism*. Wiesbaden, 1969.

Gibbs, Donald. "Literary Theory in the *Wen-hsin Tiao-lung*." Ph.D. dissertation, University of Washington, Seattle, 1970.

Graham, A. C. "Chuang Tzu's Essay on Seeing Things as Equal." *History of Religions*, vol. 9, nos. 2–3 (1969/70).

Hightower, J. R. Review of Vincent Shih's translation of the *Wen-hsin tiao-lung*, HJAS, vol. 22 (1959).

Holzman, Donald. "Confucius and Ancient Chinese Literary Criticism." Unpublished paper.

Hsü Fu-kuan 徐復觀 , I. *Chung-kuo yi-shu ching-shen*中國藝術精神. Taichung, 1966.

———, II. *Chung-kuo wen-hsüeh lun chi*中國文學論集Taichung, 1966.

Hsü Shih-ta徐世大. *Chou-yi shan-wei*周易闡微. Shanghai, 1947.

Hu Nien-yi胡念貽. "*Shih-ching* chung te fu pi hsing"詩經中的賦比興*Wen-hsüeh yi-ch'an tseng-k'an* 文學遺產增刊. 1st series, 1955.

Huang Hai-chang 黃海章. "Liu Hsieh te ch'uang-tso-lun ho p'i-p'ing-lun" 劉勰的創作論和批評 *Chung-shan Ta-hsüeh hsüeh-pao* 中山大學學報. 1958; rpt. in CKWH.

Huang K'an 黃侃 (1886–1935). *Wen-hsin tiao-lung tsa-chi* 文心雕龍札記. Shanghai, 1962.

Hung, William. *Tu Fu: China's Greatest Poet*. Cambridge, Mass., 1952.

Jao Tsung-yi 饒宗頤, ed. *Wen-hsin tiao-lung yen-chiu chuan-hao* 文心雕龍研究專號. Hong Kong, 1962.

Jung Keng 容庚. *Chin wen pien* 金文編. Peking, 1959.

Kao Heng, II. *Chou-yi ku-ching t'ung-shuo* 周易古經通說 Peking, 1958.

Karlgren, Bernhard, I, trans. *The Book of Odes*. Stockholm, 1950.

———, II. *Grammata Serica Recensa*. Stockholm, 1957.

Ku Yüan-hsiang 顧遠薌. *Sui yüan shih-shuo te yen-chiu* 隨園詩話的研究. Shanghai, 1936.

Kuan Feng 關鋒. *Chuang Tzu nei-p'ien yi-chu ho p'i-p'an* 莊子內篇譯注和批判. Peking, 1961.

Kuo Mo-jo 郭沫若, I. *Chou-yi te kou-ch'eng shih-tai* 周易的構成時代. Shanghai, 1940.

———, II. *Chin-wen ts'ung-k'ao* 金文叢考 Rev. ed., Peking, 1952.

———, III. *Tu Sui-yüan shih-hua tsa-chi* 讀隨園詩話札記. Peking, 1962.

Kuo Shao-yü, III. "Chung-kuo wen-hsüeh-p'i-p'ing shih shang chih shen-ch'i shuo" 中國文學批評史上之神氣說. *Hsiao-shuo yüeh-pao* 小說月報. 1927.

———, IV. "Hsing-ling shuo" 性靈說, *Yenching Hsüeh-pao* 燕京學報, no. 23 (1938).

———, V. *Chung-kuo wen-hsüeh-p'i-p'ing shih* 中國文學批評史 Rev. ed., Shanghai, 1956.

———, VI. "Chung-kuo wen-hsüeh li-lun p'i-p'ing chung *tao* te wen-t'i" 中國文學理論批評中道的問題. WHYC, no. 2 (1957).

———, VII. *Chung-kuo ku-tien wen-hsüeh li-lun p'i-p'ing shih* 中國古典文學理論批評史. Peking, 1959.

Lao Kan 勞榦. "Lun *Hsi-ching tsa-chi* chih tso-che chi ch'eng-shu shih-tai" 論西京雜記之作者及成書時代. BIHP, vol. 33 (1962).

Lau, D. C., I, trans. *Lao Tzu*. Baltimore, 1963; rpt. 1969.

———, II, trans. *Mencius*. Baltimore, 1970.

Legge, James (1815–97), trans. *The Chinese Classics*. Rpt. Hong Kong, 1960.

Legge/Chai.

James Legge, trans. *The Book of Rites*. Ed. by Ch'u Chai and Winberg Chai. New York, 1967.

Legge/Sung.

James Legge, trans. *Yi King* (*Yi-ching*). In Z D. Sung, *The Text of the Yi King*. Shanghai, 1935.

Levy, André. "Un document sur la querelle des anciens et des modernes *more Sinico*." *T'oung Pao*, vol. 54, nos. 4–5 (Leiden, 1968).

Liao Wei-ch'ing 廖蔚卿 "Liu Hsieh te ch'uang-tso lun 劉勰的創作論 *Wen-shih-che hsüeh-pao* 文史哲學報, no. 6 (Taipei, 1954).

Lin Yutang, I, trans. *The Wisdom of Laotse*. New York, 1948.

———, II, trans. and ed. *The Importance of Understanding*. New York, 1960.

Liu, James J. Y. (Liu Jo-yü劉若愚), I. *The Art of Chinese Poetry*. London and Chicago, 1962.

———, II. Rejoinder to Günther Debon's review of *The Art of Chinese Poetry*, JAOS, vol. 84, no. 2 (1964).

———, III. "Ch'ing-tai shih-shuo lun-yao"清代詩說論要. *Symposium on Chinese Studies Commemorating the Golden Jubilee of the University of Hong Kong*. 1964.

———, IV. *The Chinese Knight Errant*. London and Chicago, 1967.

———, V. *The Poetry of Li Shang-yin*. Chicago, 1969.

———, VI. "Worlds and Language: The Chinese Literary Tradition." In Arnold Toynbee, ed., *Half the World: The History and Culture of China and Japan*. London, 1973.

———, VII. "Some Literary Qualities of the Lyric." In Birch, II.

———, VIII. *Major Lyricists of the Northern Sung*. Princeton, 1974.

Liu Shih-p'ei 劉師培 (1884–1919). *Chung-kuo chung-ku wen-hsüeh shih* 中國中古文學史. Rpt. Hong Kong, 1958.

Liu Shou-sung 劉綬松 . "*Wen-hsin tiao-lung* ch'u-t'an"文心雕龍初探. WHYC, no. 2 (1957). Rpt. in WHTL.

Liu Ta-chieh劉大杰. *Chung-kuo wen-hsüeh fa-chan shih*中國文學發展史. Shanghai, 1957.

Liu Yung-chi劉永濟*Wen-hsin tiao-lung chiao-shih*文心雕龍校釋1948; rpt. Taipei, 1961.

Lo Chen-yü 羅振玉 (1866–1940), I. *Yin-hsü shu-ch'i ch'ien-pien*殷虛書契前編. 1912.

———, II. *Yin-hsü shu-ch'i hou-pien*後編. 1916.

Lo Ken-tse羅根澤. *Chung-kuo wen-hsüeh-p'i-p'ing shih*中國文學批評史. Vol. 1, 1958; vol. 2, 1958; vol. 3, 1962. Shanghai.

Lu K'an-ju陸侃如and Feng Yüan-chün馮沅君. *Chung-kuo shih shih* 中國詩史. Peking, 1956.

Lu K'an-ju and Mou Shih-chin牟世金. *Liu Hsieh lun ch'uang-tso* 劉勰論創作. 1962; rpt. Hong Kong n.d.

Lynn, R. J. "Tradition and Synthesis: Wang Shih-chen as Poet and Critic." Ph.D. dissertation, Stanford University, 1971.

Ma Chen-li馬振理. *Shih-ching pen-shih*詩經本事 Shanghai, 1936.

Ma Yau-woon, "Confucius as a Literary Critic." *Essays in Chinese Studies Dedicated to Jao Tsung-I*. Hong Kong, 1970.

McDougall, Bonnie S. *The Introduction of Western Literary Theories into Modern China, 1919–1925*. Tokyo, 1971.

Nivison, David S. *The Life and Thought of Chang Hsüeh-ch'eng*. Stanford, 1966.

Pollard, David E. *A Chinese Look at Literature: The Literary Values of Chou Tso-jen in Relation to the Tradition*. Berkeley, 1973.

Shih, Vincent Yuchung, trans. *The Literary Mind and the Carving of Dragons*. New York, 1959.

Tu, Ching-I, I, trans. *Poetic Remarks in the Human World*. Taipei, 1970.

———, II. "Some Aspects of the *Jen-chien Tz'u-hua*." JAOS, vol. 93, no. 3 (1973).

Tung Tso-pin 董作賓, I. *Chung-kuo nien-li tsung-p'u* 中國年曆總譜 Hong Kong, 1960.

———, II. *Tung Tso-pin hsüeh-shu lun-chu* 董作賓學術論著. Taipei, 1962.

Waley, Arthur, I, trans. *The Way and Its Power*. London, 1934; rpt. New York, 1958.

———, II, trans. *The Book of Songs*. London, 1937; rev. ed., 1954; rpt. New York, 1960.

———, III, trans. *The Analects of Confucius*. London, 1938; rpt. New York, 1960.

———, IV. *The Life and Times of Po Chü-i*. London, 1949.

———, V. *Yüan Mei*. London, 1956; rpt. Stanford, 1970.

Wang, John C. *Chin Sheng-t'an*. New York, 1972.

Wang Kuo-wei 王國維 (1877–1927), I. *Kuan-t'ang chi-lin* 觀堂集林. In *Hai-ning Wang Ching-an hsien-sheng yi-shu* 海寧王靜安先生遺書. Changsha, 1940; rpt. separately, Peking, 1959.

———, II. *Jen-chien tz'u-hua* 人間詞話. In *Hai-ning Wang Ching-an hsien-sheng yi-shu* (see above entry); also with notes by Hsü T'iao-fu 徐調孚. Shanghai, 1955. For translation see Tu Ching-I, I.

Wang Yao 王瑤. *Chung-ku wen-hsüeh ssü-hsiang* 中古文學思想. Peking, 1948; rpt. Hong Kong, 1957.

Wang Yüan-hua 王元化. "*Shen-ssu* p'ien hsü-ching shuo chien-shih." 神思篇虛靜說柬釋. CHWS, 3d series, 1963.

Watson, Burton, trans. *The Complete Works of Chuang Tzu*. New York, 1968.

Wen Yi-to 聞一多 (1899–1946). *Wen Yi-to ch'üan-chi* 聞一多全集 Shanghai, 1948.

Wilhelm, Hellmut. "A Note on Chung Hung and His *Shih-p'in*." In Chow Tse-tsung, I.

Wilhelm/Baynes.
Richard Wilhelm, trans. *The I Ching or Book of Changes*. Rendered into English from German by Cary F. Baynes, New York, 1950; 2d ed., 1961.

Wong Siu-kit, I. "A Reading of the *Ssu-ming shih-hua*." TR, vol. 2, no. 2, and vol. 3, no. 1 (1971/72).

———, II. "*Ch'ing* and *ching* in the Critical Writings of Wang Fu-chih." Unpublished paper.

Wu Ch'i-ch'ang 吳其昌. *Yin hsü shu-ch'i chieh-ku* 殷虛書契解詁 *Wu-han Ta-hsüeh wen-che chi-k'an* 武漢大學文哲季刊 1934; rpt. Taipei in book form, 1960.

Yang Hsien-yi and Gladys Yang, I, trans. "Carving the Dragon at the Core of Literature." CL, August, 1962.

———, II, trans. "The Twenty-four Modes of Poetry." CL, July, 1963.

Yang Hung-lieh 楊鴻烈 *Ta ssu-hsiang-chia Yüan Mei p'ing-chuan* 大思想家袁枚評傳. Shanghai, 1927.

Yang Ming-chao, II. "Ts'ung *Wen-hsin tiao-lung yüan-tao hsü-chih* liang p'ien k'an Liu Hsieh te ssu-hsiang" 從文心雕龍原道序志兩篇看劉勰的思想 WHTL.

Yang Shu-ta 楊樹達. *Chi-wei-chü hsiao-hsüeh chin-shih lun-ts'ung* 積微居小學金石論叢. Rev. ed. Peking, 1955.

Yip, Wai-lim. "Yen Yü and the Poetic Theories in the Sung Dynasty." TR, vol. 1, no. 2 (1970).

Yoshikawa, Kōjirō. "Tu Fu's Poetics and Poetry." *Acta Asiatica*, no. 16 (Tokyo, 1969).

C. Other Western Works

Abrams, M. H. *The Mirror and the Lamp*. Oxford, 1953; rpt. New York, 1958.

Aristotle. *The Poetics of Aristotle*. Trans. by S. H. Butcher. 4th ed. London, 1936.

Barbier, Carl Paul, ed. *Documents Stéphane Mallarmé*. Vol. 3. Paris, 1971.

Bate, Walter Jackson, ed. *Criticism: the Major Texts*. New York, 1951.

Baudelaire, Charles. *Oeuvres Complètes*. Ed. by Yves Florenne, Paris, 1966.

Bays, Gwendolen. *The Orphic Vision*. Lincoln, Neb. 1964.

Block, Haskell M. *Nouvelles tendences en littérature comparée*. Paris, 1970.

Cary, Joyce. *Art and Reality*. New York, 1958; rpt. 1961.

Cassirer, Ernst. *Language and Myth*. Trans. by Susanne K. Langer. New York, 1946.

Cicero. *De Oratore*. Loeb Classical Library. Cambridge, Mass., 1942.

Coleridge, Samuel Taylor. *Biographia Literaria*. Ed. by J. Shawcross. Oxford, 1907.

Collingwood, R. G. *The Principles of Art*. Oxford, 1938; rpt. 1950.

Craig, Hardin. *The Enchanted Glass*. Oxford, 1950.

Crane, R. S., ed. *Critics and Criticism*. Chicago, 1952.

Croce, Benedetto. *Aesthetic as Science of Expression and General Linguistics*. Trans. by Douglas Ainslie. 2d ed. London, 1922.

Dufrenne, Mikel, I. *Le Poétique*. Paris, 1963.

———, II. *Language and Philosophy*. Trans. by Henry B. Veatch. Bloomington, 1963.

———, III. *Phénoménologie de l'expérience esthétique*. 2d ed. Paris, 1967. English trans. by Edward Casey et al. Evanston, Ill., 1974.

Eliot, T. S. *The Use of Poetry and the Use of Criticism*. London, 1933; rpt. 1948.

Elyot, Sir Thomas. *The Castell of Health*. London, 1595.

Erlich, Victor. "Limits of the Biographical Approach." *Comparative Literature*, vol. 6 (1954).

Etiemble, René. *Comparaison n'est pas raison*. Paris, 1963. English trans.

by H. Weisinger and G. Joyaux, *The Crisis in Comparative Literature*. East Lansing, Mich., 1966.

Goethe, J. W. von. *The Sufferings of Young Werther*. Trans. by Harry Steinhauer. New York, 1970.

Hazlitt, William. *Complete Works*. Ed. by P.P. Howe. London, 1930.

Heidegger, Martin. *Being and Time*. Trans. by John Macquarrie and Edward Robinson, London, 1962.

Hirsch, E. D. Jr. *Validity in Interpretation*. New Haven, 1967.

Husserl, Edmund. *Ideas: General Introduction to Phenomenology*. Trans. by W. R. Boyce Gibson. London, 1931.

Ingarden, Roman. *The Literary Work of Art*. Trans. by George G. Grabowicz. Evanston, Ill., 1973.

Kockelmans, Joseph J., ed. *Phenomenology*. New York, 1967.

La Primaudaye, Pierre de. *The French Academy* (English trans.). London, 1618.

Lemnius, Levine. *The Touchstone of Complexions*. Trans. by Thomas Newton. London, 1581.

Mallarmé, Stéphane, I. *Oeuvres Complètes*. Ed. by Henri Mondor and G. Jean-Aubry. Paris, 1945.

———, II. *Correspondances, 1862–1871*. Ed. by Henri Mondor. Paris, 1959.

Marlowe, Christopher. *Tamburlaine the Great*. Ed. by U. M. Ellis-Fermor. London, 1930.

McKeon, Richard. "The Concept of Imitation in Antiquity." In Crane.

Merleau-Ponty, Maurice. *Phénoménologie de la Perception*. Paris, 1945. English trans. by Colin Smith. London, 1962; introduction rpt. in Kockelmans.

Michaud, Guy. *Mallarmé*. Paris 1953; new ed., 1971. English trans. by Marie Collins and Bertha Humez. New York, 1965.

Phair, Thomas. *The Regiment of Life*. London, 1546.

Plato. *The Dialogues of Plato*. Trans. by Benjamin Jowett. Rev. ed. Oxford, 1953.

Pound, Ezra. *How to Read*. London, 1931.

Puttenham, George (or Richard?). *The Arte of English Poesie*. Ed. by G. Willcock and A. Walker. Cambridge, 1936.

Raymond, Marcel. *De Baudelaire à Surréalisme*. Paris, 1933. English trans. London, 1950; rpt. 1970.

Rimbaud, Arthur. *Complete Works*. With translation, introduction, and notes by Wallace Fowlie. Chicago, 1966.

Schmidtt, Richard. "Husserl's Transcendental-Phenomenolgical Reduction." In Kockelmans.

Shakespeare, William. *The Complete Works of William Shakespeare*. London, 1923.

Sidney, Sir Philip. *An Apologie for Poetrie*. In Gregory Smith.

Smith, G. Gregory, ed. *Elizabethan Critical Essays*. Oxford, 1904.

Tate, Allen. *Essays of Four Decades*. Chicago, 1968.

Tillyard, E. M. W. *The Elizabethan World Picture*. London, 1943.
Ueda, Makoto. *Literary and Art Theories in Japan*. Cleveland, 1967.
Walkington, Thomas. *The Optick Glasse of Humours*. London, 1607.
Wellek, René, I. *Concepts of Criticism*. New Haven, 1963.
———, II. *Discriminations*. New Haven, 1970.
Wellek and Warren.
Réne Wellek and Austin Warren. *Theory of Literature*. New York, 1942; 3d ed., 1962.
Wimsatt and Beardsley.
W. K. Wimsatt, with Monroe C. Beardsley. *The Verbal Icon*. Lexington, 1954; rpt. 1967.
Wimsatt and Brooks.
W. K. Wimsatt and Cleanth Brooks. *Literary Criticism: A Short History*. New York, 1965.
Wittgenstein, Ludwig. *Tractatus Logico-Philosophicus*. With English trans. by D. F. Pears and B. F. McGinness. London, 1961.
Wordsworth, William. *Wordsworth's Literary Criticism*. Ed. by Nowell C. Smith. London, 1925.

Glossary-Index